Good News About Aging

Charles H. Russell, Ph.D.

in association with

Anthony P. Russell, Ph.D.
and
Inger Megaard, R.N.

WILEY

JOHN WILEY & SONS

New York • Chichester • Brisbane • Toronto • Singapore

Library of Congress Cataloging-in-Publication Data

Russell, Charles H.
  Good news about aging.

  Bibliography: p.
    1. Old age—United States—Public opinion.— 2. Aging—
United States—Public opinion. 3. Aged—United States—
Social conditions—Public opinion. 4. Public opinion—
United States. 5. Aged—United States—Attitudes.
6. General Social Survey (U.S.).   I. Russell, Anthony P.
II. Megaard, Inger.   III. Title.
HQ1064.U5R87   1989   305.2'6'0973   89-5659

ISBN 0-471-61686-9

Printed in the United States of America

10 9 8 7 6 5 4 3 2 1

For Helen and Chad Hoover,
who were superb models of aging

Foreword

T he twentieth century offers Americans a much longer life than was enjoyed in the past. How can we appreciate and savor the extra time this affords us? This book describes our prospects for living longer and the options that we can exercise as individuals in taking advantage of an optimistic future. Improved standards of living, better public health, and better scientific knowledge about longevity and health have dramatically increased life expectancy, from about age 47 years in 1900 to the current age of 75, and life expectancy continues to grow. By the end of this century, we may even regard anyone who dies before the age of 80 as having died prematurely.

Despite these radical changes in longevity, we continue to hold attitudes about old age that describe the living conditions of an earlier, more harsh industrial society, when workers had only a few hours of leisure in which to recuperate from oppressive job demands. Now, relieved of the consequences of infectious disease, most of us can consider a long life. Perhaps the average person will spend more time outside of the labor force than within it. Alan Pifer, one of the authors of the Carnegie Foundation project report on the aging society, speaks of the ages 50 to 75 as being a very active third quarter of life. If ages 50 to 75 are the third quarter of life, then there must be a fourth quarter from ages 75 to 100 years and beyond.

Given the negative attitudes that we carry with us from the past, it is not surprising that many older adults find life in old age better than they had expected. Indeed, many find it better than young people believe them to be experiencing. Most people into the second and third quarters of life find unanticipated challenges and opportunities for growth. This book may suggest to us that a new population of older people might be called "the experimental aged." These persons have discovered that—in Yogi Berra's words—"[It] ain't over till it's over."

This book seems to point a finger at each of us, as it asks, "How do you want to spend the second half of life?" Certainly, it is longer than most of us expected it to be, and it would seem to be full of more opportunities. A 102-year-old woman visited the Gerontology Center that I directed for many years. When I was introduced to her, I asked her why she came to the university's center. She said that she was curious about what a gerontology center did. I then asked her how she came to the university. She said that she took a bus. Then I asked her with whom did she come and she said that she came alone. Does this fit your concept? Curiosity motivated a 102-year-old person to take a bus across Los Angeles to see what a university was doing in gerontology.

Curiosity should expose us to the facts about human aging as they are presented in this book. Curiosity should also lead us to consider both the implications for our own lives and the ways in which we can maximize the opportunities that are available to us.

This book will open our curiosity about old age. It will also serve as a much-needed corrective for the bad press aging has encountered and as a source of useful information about this active period of life. Dr. Russell is to be congratulated for dispelling many of the gloomy myths about aging and for demonstrating that the second half of life can be positive, productive, and rewarding.

JAMES E. BIRREN, PH.D.

Professor and Brookdale Distinguished Scholar
Institute for Advanced Study in Gerontology and Geriatrics
Ethel Percy Andrus Gerontology Center
University of Southern California

Preface

As the French writer Simone de Beauvoir observed in her book *La Vieillesse*, the young dismiss age with an indifferent shrug. She might have added that the old themselves often fail to get the best from their later years simply because they make too little effort to understand this period in their lives.

Whether or not we've learned from the experience, most of us have been aware of later life through associations with parents and other members of the older generation. Further, we probably have at least some inkling that some day we too will become old—assuming that we are among the fortunate majority who live to old age. Yet few of us have ever given the slightest thought as to what it is like to be old.

Ignorance about old age abounds in epic proportions in America, where youth is the hero. Instead of seeking knowledge about our advanced years, we shun it. We flounder amid dark legends and swamps of superstition and prejudice. Most of us do not realize that we will spend at least one third, and perhaps as much as one half, of our lives in the unique state of being old. In fact, most of us do not like to think of ourselves as old—even those of us already advanced in years.

The book you are now reading turns all this around. It not only informs you about old age in general, but also makes you more fully appreciate whatever stage of life you're in, whether young or old. When you read this book, you will gain insight into life at all levels of maturity, though its main concern is with late adulthood. You will arrive at a more sophisticated understanding that will give you the power (young or old, male or female) both to live a well-filled life now and to make your advanced years the capstone of your lifetime.

To accomplish this, the book presents the most interesting and important findings from the field of social gerontology—the scientific study of aging. It does not deal with the physical processes, but rather with the experience of increasing age—the attitudes, feelings, convictions, pleasures, and pains of older Americans. The major sources of this information are national opinion polls, some of which have been conducted annually for more than 15 years. From them comes a true picture of what older Americans really think and feel about the important issues affecting their lives.

This book is worthwhile to the young and the old, but it is especially so to those between ages 35 and 70, all of whom need to begin serious thinking and planning for advanced maturity. Even those of us who have reached 70, 80, 90, or beyond should read this. We never grow too old to learn, and greater insight into our own age enriches our present lives.

Though this book is written especially for both the present older generation and the aging Baby Boom population, anyone who has older parents, grandparents, or other relatives, or who simply wants to reflect on her or his own later years, will find this book helpful.

Further, precisely because it is written for a wide audience of readers, this book has something to say to professionals as well. Physicians, nurses, and social workers who are not primarily specialists in aging will find it a useful guide to the ways in which their clients experience later life. Also, clergy, businesspersons, legislators, and others who offer services to the elderly will profit from reading this book. In addition, this book will appeal to economists because it surveys some of the emerging ideas about the contributions of the growing older population to our economic well-being.

The content of this book is as truthful as it is interesting and entertaining. It hides nothing. It deals frankly with the realities of aging—the difficulties as well as the delights. Many subjects are treated candidly and forthrightly, such as retirement; triumph over death; the role of age in poetry, philosophy, and literature;

later-life experiences of health, family relations, sex, and leisure; economics and other challenges of later life; and the role of personality in later life.

Note that the book makes no use of honeyed clichés such as "golden ager," "senior citizen," and "85 years young." The principal author loathes the patronizing and candied approach to aging implied by these terms. Those who wish to be sympathetic or supportive toward older people often err by portraying them in cloyingly sweet and sentimental ways that destroy their individuality. The facts presented in this book show that older persons are hardy and spirited, and that they wouldn't have reached an advanced stage of life without those qualities. The search for these distinctive characteristics of older persons inspired this book. My associates and I found the search challenging, frequently surprising, and fully rewarding, and we hope that you share our enthusiasm.

Special acknowledgments of our sources of information appear at the end of this book. There we cite the main sources from the field of gerontology (the study of aging) used in composing this volume. Here, we especially wish to express thanks for the valuable contribution of Russell Bourne, himself an author, who suggested the title of the book and took time to offer editorial advice on the early chapters, even as he pressed hard to complete one of his own manuscripts.

We also acknowledge the authors of the General Social Survey, Professors Tom Smith of the University of Chicago and Jim Davis of Harvard University, and the staff who so faithfully have conducted the annual polls since 1972 for that remarkable research. The General Social Survey ranges widely over American opinion, attitudes, and experience, and it has supplied essential information—released here for the first time to the general public—on the way that people experience age.

Let your journey of discovery begin.

CHARLES H. RUSSELL

Bethlehem, Connecticut
August 1989

Contents

America's Stake in Successful Aging

HOW CAN SCIENTIFIC INFORMATION HELP AMERICANS TO AGE SUCCESSFULLY?

Good news about aging is at hand. We're on the threshold of the "Aging Boom," when the millions of Americans born during the Baby Boom will live to advanced maturity. Already more than 60 million of us have reached age 50 or beyond. During the next century, when the children of the Baby Boom reach their 50s, more than 100 million older Americans will populate our nation. Americans live longer today than ever before. This is good news because it gives us more time to enjoy life.

This remarkable increase in lifespan will stimulate us to embrace maturity as an extension of our traditional devotion to youth and young adulthood. But we haven't reached that happy time yet because we don't appreciate old age. We have yet to discover that older persons can lead enjoyable, successful lives. We still have misunderstandings, doubts, and even fears of aging. We identify old age with nursing homes and decrepitude. To better understand older age, we need to clear away the misinformation, the suspicion, and the fog that cloud our vision of aging. We must sweep out the pall of ignorance and overcome the superstitious fears conjured by the vision of wrinkles and gray hair.

Once we see older age more clearly, we can begin to plan for a successful later life, and we can learn how to enjoy it. Most of us know the goals for enjoying a successful young adulthood—a good education, a good job, and a good family situation. Though we sometimes fail to achieve these aims, we know what to do, and we plan accordingly. A successful later life requires the same kind of foresight and planning. When we understand older age, we can design it well, just as a trained architect understands how to plan a sturdy, useful, and pleasant building. But it's impossible to design a rewarding old age as long as we mistakenly think of it as a time of decline rather than of opportunity.

The aim of this book is to help you to lead a successful later life. The book does not offer advice on how to age gracefully, because older people generally have a pretty clear idea of what they are doing. They don't need counseling. They need solid facts. Prescriptions may work well for some people, but they fail miserably for others. Instead of telling you how to live, this book gives you the information you require to choose how to live your later years according to your own best design.

Once you have the essential facts about older age, only you can plan your later years. Consequently this book doesn't furnish biographical accounts of the successful aging experienced by some celebrities. Nor does it relate entertaining anecdotes of the sort that make all older people seem charming and likable. Instead, this book provides you with the information you need to map out your own old age. Given this information, you will understand how to develop your own potential to the fullest throughout your later years.

This book presents scientifically researched, well-documented facts on the most important questions about aging. How long can we expect to live? How many years are we likely to live once we reach an advanced age? What is the likelihood of being happy and having fun in later life? When we are older, will we enjoy sex, and are we likely to be sexually active? What are our chances of becoming ill in later life, and what sorts of diseases and costs may result? Do most of us suffer mental decline or end up in nursing homes? What have other persons thought about aging in the past? What do they think about it now? Answers to these and many others questions can help each of us to look ahead. It's like knowing the weather forecast—not only are we better informed but also we can plan better what to do.

The information in this book draws on studies in the field of gerontology (the *g* is soft like a *j*)—the scientific study of aging. The major studies included are national public opinion polls and census information that highlight the experience, feelings, and attitudes of older Americans. The main study used is the General Social Survey, which supplies information that has never before been published in its present form. This information was extracted specifically for the present volume.

The data in the General Social Survey is a digest of interviews with over 22,000 Americans, a statistically representative group that includes more than 7500 persons over age 50. The survey (familiarly know to social scientists as the GSS) was designed by Professors James Davis of Harvard University and Tom Smith of the University of Chicago. It has been conducted nearly every year since 1972 by the National Opinion Research Center at the University of Chicago. The Roper Center (named after the famous Roper Poll) at the University of Connecticut serves as the computerized national archive for the survey results.

A second source of public opinion used for this book is the pair of surveys made by Louis Harris and Associates for the National Council on Aging. These two polls, taken in 1974 and in 1981, posed questions directly related to aging and produced information useful to anyone interested in the subject. Besides the GSS and the Harris polls, the book draws on the research of several federal government agencies, including the National Institute on Aging, the National Center for Health Statistics, and the National Institute of Mental Health. Reports commissioned by the American Association of Retired Persons (AARP) are included. In addition, where general poll data is not available, the thousands of studies carried out in gerontology over the last 50 years become the source of information.

While the book draws on statistics and research, it does not lead the reader into a maze of complicated scientific studies or into the labyrinth of debates that twist through gerontology. Quite the contrary, the book is designed to open the science of aging to the general public and to make it available to anyone, young or old, who wants to lead a successful later life. The book answers the questions of greatest general interest and presents up-to-date findings and conclusions.

The book particularly emphasizes psychological and social topics such as attitudes, opinions, and experience. The psychological and social information is most crucially needed to correct our misunderstandings about older age so that we can manage our lives well.

Nonetheless, someone could ask, "What good will knowing about all this research do? Looking back over the thousands of years of human history, isn't it true that people have lived to be very old since the origins of humankind?" Yes, they have. Even when survival beyond youth was rare, a few individuals attained such remarkably advanced ages that they inspired legends like those of Noah (950 years) and Methuselah (969 years). Few persons today believe these fabulous reports of longevity, but the reports do tell us that some individuals will reach great age without reading this book or relying on anyone's help.

The remaining question is, "Will they live those long years well?" Age is the one period of life that can be lived with foresight. During earlier periods, change propels us onward with few choices. We are driven by our biological and social destinies. We can no more avoid the biological facts of puberty, sexual maturity, and menopause than we can prevent the tides of the ocean. We cannot easily resist the social demand to earn a living, marry, or retire, any more than we can choose the language we speak or our national identities. But older age is different. Behind it lies a vast store of experience that gives us a foundation upon which to build. To become wise architects of our later lives, we need to rid ourselves of the oppressive ignorance and superstition that surrounds aging. This book aims to provide the knowledge that can enable you to firmly grasp your own life and make your advanced years your best years.

HOW MUCH LONGER ARE WE LIVING TODAY?

The first question to consider is whether people really do live longer now than in the past. After all, anyone who's walked through an old cemetery has seen tombstones that read something like this: "JOSIAH MITCHELL 1799–1880," "ABIGAIL MITCHELL 1800–1889." Josiah and Abby certainly lived to a ripe old age. No one would argue otherwise. Reasonably enough, the tombstone reader might conclude that people in the past lived as long as or longer than they do today.

Given these noteworthy examples, why would we claim that we're just entering the epoch of the Aging Boom, during which long life on a mass scale is new in human history? The answer is that never before have *so many* lived as long as we do today. Researchers have used several methods to determine the normal length of life in the past, one of which is to study burial grounds. In ancient Rome, for instance, the estimated average life expectancy was only 25 years. Death came early through ravaging diseases and infections that we can prevent or treat today. The high death toll particularly cut down children and youths; the catacombs in Rome show that one third of the graves were those of children. Life then was brutally short by our standards.

In the past, advanced age was a rarity; but over the centuries, the average length of life has climbed. By the time the Pilgrims sailed for America, life expectancy was somewhere around 40 years. No great increase occurred in the next 300 years, and in 1900, the U.S. Census Bureau recorded accurately that life expectancy was about 47 years. But when Social Security became law in 1935, life expectancy had jumped to 60 years. Today, the average newborn can expect to live to age 75 years, and many will survive long beyond.

Some might argue that using the average length of life is misleading because it takes in everyone—those who die in infancy as well as those who die over 100. They might reason that relying on life expectancy doesn't take in the extreme old ages reached in the past. However, despite the rare exceptions, no one could reasonably expect to live a long life in the past. Further, the proportion of people who die in any particular year of life has fallen dramatically. For example, even in 1960, the death rate at age 65 was 25 deaths for every 1000 persons. Today, fewer than 20 people in 1000 die in their 65th year—a 20% drop just since 1960. More people today are living to advanced ages than ever before.

A primary consequence of the falling death rate is that we're now in the midst of a population explosion among the aged. The numbers of Americans age 65 or more has increased from 3 million in 1900 to over 27 million, a 900% growth in the 65+ generation. As a proportion of the American public, they have more than doubled, rising from 5% in 1900 to more than 12% now.

Further, persons over age 85, sometimes called the "oldest-old," are now the fastest-growing segment of the U.S. population. The number of people in this age bracket has doubled since 1960, and it will double again by the year 2000. So fast is the growth of the over-85 population and so little is known about them that the National Institute on Aging has called for special studies of this generation. Long life for the millions is now an expected privilege of modern times.

WILL THE AGING BOOM PERSIST?

The present population explosion among the aged is only the beginning. America experienced a Baby Boom after World War II, from 1946 to 1964. Of course, the Baby Boomers have matured like every one else, and the first wave, born in the mid 1940s, has already reached age 40 or more. Because all members of the Baby Boom generation have been born, we can predict quite accurately, barring some great disaster or epidemic, how many older Baby Boomers there will be in the future. Using calculations based on the present average life expectancy, we can forecast that by the year 2000, nearly 35 million persons age 65 and over will make up 13% of the population. By 2030, when most of the Baby Boomers have reached the upper age brackets, 64.5 million Americans age 65 and over will represent 21.2% of the population. In the 40 years between 1990 and 2030, the proportion of the population over 65 will grow 75%—a huge increase.

If this account of the population explosion of aged Americans seems overwhelming, it becomes even more so when you consider populations in other countries. America isn't the only nation experiencing an Aging Boom. The boom is worldwide. Nearly every nation in the world today already shows signs of a population explosion among its aged or will do so in the next few years.

For example, the United Nations classifies countries on the basis of the percentage of persons in their populations who are age 65 or older. At present, a country with 7% of its population in this age group is classified as "aged." The U.S. fits the category and is classified as "aged," along with all the European nations and Japan. Most of the developing nations of the world—Africa, China, India, and so on—are catching up. Within the next 30 to 40 years, nearly all nations of the world will have reached the 7% standard. The UN has predicted that over 1.21 billion people will have reached age 60 by 2025.

Can anyone doubt that people are living longer these days when the world is witnessing such an explosive growth of older segments of the population? Had this book been published in 1900, when life expectancy was 47, there would have been far fewer 50-year-olds to read it than there are today. Each day, more than 1600 Americans reach age 65. Today, Americans live an average of almost 30 years longer than they did in 1900, and we've gained 3 additional years of life expectancy in the last 20 years. It's clear that people live much longer now than they ever have in the past. The Aging Boom is upon us, and the world has never witnessed anything like it.

CAN WE EVER EXPECT TO LIVE FOREVER?

Because living to older ages has become a worldwide phenomenon, it seems reasonable to ask about the prospect of living forever. Leaving aside moral and spiritual issues, what are the chances that scientific advance will find a way to extend life indefinitely? Can we anticipate that death will vanish during our lifetimes? What about future generations—can they hope to live to time everlasting?

At present, we tend to dismiss the question of everlasting biological survival as a delusion, but a number of persons have invested heavily in such an eventuality. These investors hope to achieve everlasting bodily existence, and they have paid large sums to have their bodies frozen at death by means of *cryogenics*, which is used to freeze beef and vegetables, as well as humans. Unhappily, those who cherish dreams of being defrosted and living forever sometime hence are probably cherishing an implausible dream because freezing destroys human body cells. Further, even if we can overcome this and other problems, no scientific evidence suggests that we can expect to eliminate death now or in the future because all things break down over time. Perhaps more importantly, research has shown that older persons who cannot accept death frequently suffer general psychological discomfort also.

What, then, about the reports of persons living to spectacularly old ages? Are they true? Do these hold out hope of a "cure" for aging? One such report was about Mezhid Agayev, once thought to be the oldest living resident of Azerbaijan in the U.S.S.R. He was reported by the Soviet press to be 139 when he died. With 150 living descendants, he was reported to have retired from active farming at 136 to accept the lighter job of herding cows.

Mezhid's age was well publicized, but he didn't hold the record for longevity because a Russian woman, Ashura Omarova, was said to have reached age 195, and another man was thought to have reached 165. As if to make these reports more believable, the press release on Mezhid averred that a Bolivian woman was 205 years old when she died. Counting backwards from 1970, when this information was released, the Bolivian woman would have been born before the American revolution!

Some Soviet gerontologists still believe the accounts of prodigious old age, but U.S. scientists consider them exaggerated, to say the least. This skepticism grows out of careful studies that have discredited the reports of fabulous old age. The evidence against the accounts is attributed to errors of several kinds, such as forgetfulness, deliberate falsification, and even efforts to lend prestige by magnifying a person's age.

Many of the reports have come from remote regions where official records were poor or had been destroyed by fire. But, even where records do appear to uphold the claims of prodigious age, close study has shown that they were faulty. For example, in Russia, the tradition in parts of the country used to be to identify a person by a general age category rather than by a specific year. Anyone from 70 on, for instance, might be called an "older person."

After the Revolution in 1917, exact ages were recorded for the first time, and officials initiated a major campaign to register older persons. The campaign reached a peak in the 1930s, leading pressured officials simply to estimate the ages of some individuals. This guesswork occasionally involved awarding additional years to some people to give them greater prestige.

By the end of the 1970s, all the individuals of prodigious age had died, and none have appeared since. Further refutation of the Soviet data has recently come from a Yale University study of official records of census and mortality statistics. According to the Yale researchers, the two sets of records were incompatible. The records seriously understated death rates and overstated the number of existing *centenarians* (persons over 100 years of age), though clearly there'll be many more in the future.

Other reports of extraordinary old age have come mainly from Ecuador. Scholars have found that these reports sometimes mixed up the names of individuals or misidentified them. The researchers also compared reported ages with actual records and then interviewed people about dates in the lives of the very old. They found that the Ecuadorian accounts of extraordinary old age consistently exaggerated all ages beyond 70. For example, a stated age of 80 had been exaggerated by 3 years, 100 by 16 years, and 135 by 40 years.

Reports of extreme longevity also have appeared in the United States. *Life* magazine once claimed that records had been found to confirm the age of Charlie Smith, who was said to have come to this country as a slave at age 12 before the Civil War. Charlie Smith died in 1979, reputedly at the age of 137.

However, we should not treat the legends of extraordinary old age too unkindly. They are part of the folklore of humankind. They don't seem to have any more serious consequence than to provide copy for the ballyhoo press and to support convivial barroom or cocktail conversation. A few persons may have gone on a wild goose chase to find the Shangri-las of the world or responded to advertisements asserting that eating yogurt or cottage cheese will prolong life. But these folk tales have probably not hurt anyone. They may, quite coincidentally, have had the good effect of promoting the idea that a healthy lifestyle more likely produces longevity than an unhealthy one.

In spite of the negative picture for extraordinary old age and unlimited life, there is good news about the average length of life for humans. For one thing, we seem to enjoy a longer lifespan than other biological species. The term *lifespan* refers to the biological limit of life, whereas *life expectancy* applies to the actual average length of time people can be expected to live. The first is a potential, a maximum possibility, and the second an average length of life. With a lifespan of 115 to 120 years, humans outlive just about every known animal with a spine—mammal, bird, reptile, amphibian, or fish. Our only competitor seems to be the Galapagos tortoise, which has recorded lifetimes of over 100 years.

A sampling of lifespans of other vertebrates is as entertaining as it is instructive. Domestic cats can reach 28 years, the horse 48 years, and the Indian elephant 70 years—which is longer than most humans lived in previous centuries. Among birds, the eagle owl, which can reach 68 years, is one of the record holders. The vampire bat, a flying mammal, makes it to unlucky 13. Among amphibians, the common garden toad (scientific name, *Bufo bufo*) makes it to a wrinkled 36. Its more exotic cousin, the African clawed toad, only gets to 15. The house mouse, we should be glad to know, has a lifespan of just 3 years.

Besides having a superior lifespan, humans can look forward to an increasing life expectancy as lifestyles and health care improve. "Curve rectangularization" describes this trend for life expectancy to grow ever closer to lifespan. The term comes from drawing a graph of the average life expectancy in relation to lifespan, as illustrated in Figure 1.1. The present life expectancy curve looks rounded and falls away like a hillside. In the future, the curve will look more like a rectangle, squaring off on the right side. When life expectancy approaches lifespan, the majority of people will live to age 110 or more.

None of the evidence supports the idea of Methuselan lifespans in any form now or in the foreseeable future. Nor is there any likely prospect that science will overcome death. But most of us do not see an indefinite length of life, and the idea of stretching the lifespan out for an extended period is probably unrealistic to most minds. What we can look forward to is an already remarkably long life and a gradual increase in life expectancy toward the limit of the human lifespan.

% surviving

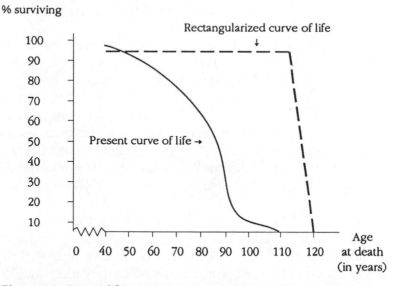

Figure 1.1. Present life expectancy curve and projected rectangularized curve of life expectancy. (Data from *Monthly Vital Statistics Report: Advance Report of Final Mortality Statistics, 1984.* The National Center for Health Statistics, *35,* 6, Supplement 2, September 26, 1986.)

HOW LONG CAN I EXPECT TO LIVE?

The issue of length of life becomes much more personal when it concerns our own individual prospects for survival. We may know that we are likely to outlive our parents or grandparents, but can we say how many years we have left to us at any particular age?

This question is important for social planning, as well as for personal interest. It's socially important because we're now at the brink of the Aging Boom and not fully prepared to manage long life on a grand scale. The social systems required to take care of millions of older persons differ from those required for smaller numbers. We have many ways of providing for the youngest generation (schooling is the main one), but we're just developing the systems required for the increasing Aging Boom population. This means that our present older individuals are pioneers. They're on the frontier taking care of themselves as individualists while society catches up. The question of how many years of life are likely to remain to them is important to the frontier enterprise of the elderly today.

The question "How long can I expect to live?" yields an answer that seems strange at first. The answer is that the longer you live, the longer life expectancy you can expect to have.

This statement is no clever paradox. The simple truth is that those who reach a later year of life can expect greater longevity. Continued life expectancy in the later years has also been given a name—"later life expectancy," or "remaining life expectancy." (See Table 1.1). When we know the average number of years we can reasonably expect to live, we can plan our lives more effectively.

Let's clarify the meanings of average life expectancy and remaining life expectancy. The average life expectancy of a baby born now is about 75 years. However, that doesn't mean that all recently born children will promptly die when they reach age 75 some time around A.D. 2065. Clearly, some will die sooner, and some will die later. The average life expectancy is determined by adding the actual total years of life of all persons who die in a given year, then dividing the total by the number of persons who died that year. About half of those persons died before the

Table 1.1.   Average Remaining Life Expectancy

Age	Remaining years of life expectancy	Total life expectancy for age
50	33.1	83.1
60	24.2	84.2
70	16	86
80	9.5	89.5
90	5	95
99	2.8	101.8

average life expectancy, and about half of them died after the average life expectancy. In 1925, the average life expectancy (based on the persons who died in that year) was 59 years. Yet many persons born in that year are alive now, when the current life expectancy is 16 years greater.

Further, your life expectancy seems to increase with each year that you live, because all persons who have died no longer enter the life expectancy calculations. Later life expectancy takes into account only those who are still alive in later life, and many of these person still have many years to live. For example, Table 1.1 shows that a 50-year-old can reasonably expect to live an average of another 33.1 years, to an age of 83.1 years. A 90-year-old can expect reasonably to live an average of only another 5 years, but the 90-year-old's average total life expectancy is now 95 years. Though the 50-year-old probably has more years left to live than a 90-year-old, she or he is less assured of living to be 95 than is the 90-year-old.

It's useful to know your life expectancy, and it may be longer than you might have thought. Insurance companies use later-life expectancy tables to calculate their premiums. Pension plans do likewise for determining annual payouts for pensions. It's known, for example, that 65-year-olds have an average remaining life expectancy close to 20 years, though women and men differ (see Chapter 8). Once you know your life expectancy at age 65, you can use it to plan for your present and your future, such as your annual withdrawals for IRAs and Keogh savings.

It's interesting to observe that the federal government uses this information in various ways, one of them in connection with a payout schedule for annuities published by the Internal Revenue Service (IRS) and updated periodically. With these figures, the IRS specifies the number of years of potential life expectancy, and we can be sure that reliable old Uncle Sam isn't going to make a serious mistake. Besides, few will argue that they have a lower life expectancy than the one the IRS forecasts.

Because these figures represent averages for both men and women, women can add about 3 years to them, and men can subtract about 3—but if you've taken good care of your health, you can probably add to them, no matter what your gender. What about people over 100? The same rule applies: The longer you live, the longer your life expectancy. (Perhaps the IRS could reward persons over 120 years by not requiring them to calculate annuity payout figures.)

How long can we expect to live? No one can say for sure. But the good news is that most of us are "average," which means that it's an even bet that our lives will match the tables for remaining life expectancy. By looking at this table, we can see that we have considerable expected longevity remaining at every age, and a newborn today can reasonably expect to live 75 years.

ARE THERE GOING TO BE TOO MANY OLD PEOPLE FOR SOCIETY TO SUPPORT?

Some might consider this question to be an insult to the older generation, and they'd dismiss it with contempt. Certainly it's fair to say that the older generation has amply paid its dues through a lifetime of work and responsibility. The question is inescapable, though, simply because it has haunted us since the early 1980s. The answer to it lies in finding out whether we can adequately support a growing older population.

Three lines of evidence help to answer this question. All three suggest that the only thing to worry about is that some people are worried. The first line of evidence concerns the national political debates over the two major federal government programs for the elderly—Social Security and Medicare. In the early 1980s, critics of Social Security tried to pit the younger generation against the older by charging that the young would pay into the nation pension system now, but they would not be able to draw out money from it later. Later in the 1980s, the effort to extend Medicare to cover catastrophic illness raised the specter of bankruptcy for federal health insurance.

It's unnecessary here to rehash all the issues involved, because the debates have been resolved through negotiated solutions and compromises. No one will be affluent if he or she retires on Social Security alone, but this system provides a good foundation for a total pension plan. Medicare doesn't take care of every exigency, but it takes care of the major costs of the most expensive illnesses. The issues concern *how much* coverage to provide, not *whether* to provide funds for the elderly. In addition, state and local governments are increasing their services for the elderly, and national public opinion polls continue to favor publicly sponsored programs for later life.

A second way to approach the question of "too many old people" is by looking at the *dependency ratio*. This term was coined to identify the proportion of the people in a nation who are not working and require support mainly from public funds. Two groups primarily require this kind of support: persons under 18 years (abbreviated here as "18-") and those over 65 (called "65+" hereafter). To determine the dependency ratio, you have to add the school-age population to the retired population. In recent years, these two groups have made up about 38% of the total population in the United States. Public schools and the retirement system (Social Security/Medicare) are the main social institutions for these two groups, and both rely heavily on public financial support. Funds for schools for young persons come primarily from local property taxes, and Social Security/Medicare for retirees come from payroll taxes.

The crucial question asked in discussions of the dependency ratio is this: Will there be enough people of working age to provide the needed public funds for the dependent population? Today, about 60% of the population is employed, and this is the principal group that supplies the payroll and local property taxes.

Those who worry about the dependency ratio are concerned because the 65+ generation will increase from its present level of about 12% to about 21% in the next century. They worry that this sort of growth will overtax the working population.

Unfortunately, this debate has concentrated only on the growth of the older population, so it has overlooked several other factors. One factor is the lifetime contributions of the elderly to public and private pensions. Another is that the overall size of the dependency ratio has actually shrunk when you consider both the 18- and the 65+ populations. The total percentage of school-age persons and retirees is smaller today than it was some years ago. It has reached its peak, is now declining, and will not reach its former peak again in the foreseeable future.

To be specific, in 1970, 43% of the U.S. population was either 18- or 65+. Between the present year and the year 2000, these two groups combined will account for only 38% of the population—a 5% drop since the peak year of 1970. Looking even further ahead, we can predict that the combined 18- and 65+ population will reach 41% at the height of the Aging Boom in 2030. The total dependency ratio in 2030 will still be lower than it was in 1970! All of these changes reflect the growth of the Baby Boom generation from childhood to adulthood and then to maturity.

Some may argue that it will cost more to support older people than it does younger ones because health care, which older people require more than the young, is more expensive than schooling. This argument ignores the savings and insurance paid by older persons. These cover nearly one third of their health expenses (government pays about 67%), whereas children can contribute little directly toward their educational expenses. Without getting into further subtleties of this argument, a general observation seems inescapable: America cared for its children during the Baby Boom, and it will provide for this same generation when it enters the Aging Boom. The sources of support will come from the savings and pensions of the older generation and from family members of older persons, as well as from public funds.

A third way to address the question of whether there'll be

too many old people is to look at the experience of nations that have larger proportions of older persons in their populations than the U.S. The U.S. actually ranks at least eighth on the list of countries with relatively high percentages of older people. According to world figures, 12 European countries (including Sweden, Norway, the United Kingdom, France, and Italy) have higher percentages of older persons in their populations than does the U.S. The U.S. percentage is also close to that of Japan and the U.S.S.R. These other nations are getting along successfully with comparatively more older people than the U.S. If they can manage, then it's reasonable to suppose that the U.S. can too.

No one can afford to sit back complacently and say that we can ignore the question of how to support a larger proportion of older persons in our population any more than we could disregard the vast increase in numbers of school-age children during the Baby Boom. What can be said is that people are conscious of changes going on in the makeup of our population and of their own aging. We won't let the situation get away from us. There won't be too many older people in the future.

HOW DO INDIVIDUALS GET THE MOST FROM A LONGER LIFE?

On the most simple level, the statistics on modern aging tell us that we can expect to live one third of our lives after age 50. It's as if there are three stages to life, each roughly equal in length. The first, from birth to age 25, is youth. The second, from 25 to 50 years, is adulthood. The third, from age 50 on, is maturity.

What are we doing to get the most out of the last third of our lives? We're looking forward more now than we have in the past, and we're beginning to plan positively for our maturity. We have plenty of lifetime ahead, so we're taking time to look down the road.

Evidence for improved planning for later life comes to light through the growth of preretirement programs run by many major corporations. These programs are frequently offered in cooperation with the American Association of Retired Persons

(AARP), which offers a wide variety of services to nearly 30 million members and other older persons. The aim of preretirement programs is to make the transition to retirement a felicitous preparation for a successful old age. Organizations such as Age-Wave of Emeryville, California, under the dynamic leadership of Ken Dychtwald, and Edith Tucker's "United Retirement Bulletin," published under the auspices of United Business Services of Boston, are pioneering a new more positive approach to aging.

Besides spawning preretirement education programs, concern for the practical consequences of long life has motivated study of what older persons consider important in planning for later life. The 1974 Harris Associates survey was one of the early efforts to question those over 65 about their preparation for retirement. Over half of the persons interviewed rated the following as "very important": planning for medical care, building up savings, learning about pensions and Social Security benefits, making a will, buying a home, developing hobbies and leisure activities, and deciding whether to move or to stay in their present homes.

An alternative question concerns the age when persons actually begin planning for later life. There's not a great deal of information on this subject, but there are some clues. For one, the Harris poll asked interviewees if they had done anything about the things they considered most important to preparing for retirement. Over 60% said they had. Medical care headed the list, with 88% saying that they'd made plans for it, and pensions followed with 87%.

In a sense, one who contributes to Social Security or other retirement plans looks ahead to a time for receiving Social Security or other retirement benefit. This may not be voluntary or deliberate planning, but it does start the minute that most individuals draw an official paycheck. Because earnings often begin in the teen years, even teenagers may be considered to have planned for later life.

Another way to think about planning for later life is to consider when it *might* begin. Certain public employee pension systems suggest a way to determine this. Quite often, these plans build up benefits at a rate of 1.5–2% for every year of service until they reach a specified maximum. Suppose that the maximum specified is 50% of the final salary earned in the last few years of employment. At a buildup of 2% a year, it takes 25 years to reach the 50% maximum—just multiply 2% times 25. At 1.5% per year, it takes 30 years to reach the maximum.

To reach the 50% maximum by age 65 requires starting at age 35 or 40. Do people start to plan for their maturity at age 35 or 40? They seldom do. But, can anyone encourage people to start thinking about later life at age 35 or 40? No one knows because the subject hasn't been studied in depth. Still, it's evident that some people find it useful to exercise foresight. The assumption of this book is that viewing the scientific facts encourages even keener perception. There's plenty of life ahead for the members of the Aging Boom, and they will enjoy a successful old age if they know what's ahead and plan for it.

2

Surprising News About Being Old

The American public holds a bleak view of aging, as was clearly shown by the original Harris poll in 1974. But the Harris poll was not the first time such views were chronicled, because previous studies of smaller groups had produced similar results. The significance of the Harris poll was that it documented public views on a national scale by means of a scientifically selected sample of all Americans, young and old. When the 1981 poll revealed the same pessimistic outlook, it confirmed the results of the first survey.

Just what did the Harris poll prove we thought about aging? Not that we're unsympathetic—quite the contrary. We simply feel that later life is diminished and deprived. Most of us think that life is a serious problem for older persons. We believe that they don't have enough money to live on. We sense that they're lonely and don't feel needed. They seem to be in poor health and to fear crime. Almost half of us think the elderly don't get enough medical care. Some of us believe they lack job opportunities. Over a third of us state that they don't have enough to do to keep busy. A third of us also hold the view that their housing is poor. Can there be any doubt about how we feel about aging?

A more realistic picture of the experience of aging appeared in the responses made by persons over age 65 to the Harris interview questions. The great majority of these persons did *not* think the problems cited by the general public were serious for older people. The only problem that was considered very serious by any sizable number was the fear of crime, but only one quarter of the older people considered crime a serious problem for their generation.

Because of the difference in perspective between the generations, we have to ask what older persons actually think about their lives. Do they really feel they're deprived and that their existence is diminished? To answer these questions, we look at public opinion poll results and other sources that directly address the experience of being old. When do people become old? Do they experience happiness, boredom, or loneliness? What do they think of their incomes? What about their physical and mental health, their social activity, and their attitudes toward others? These are most crucial to understanding how people feel about their circumstances. Let's start with the age at which we think the word "old" should apply to a person.

WHEN DO WE BECOME OLD?

Many persons deny that they're "old" at any age, and one of the worst social blunders or insults in America is to identify someone past their 20s as older than they really are. Also, many persons never admit their age, and others lie about it if they state an age. The joke about being perpetually 39 was ancient long before the great stand-up comedian Jack Benny made it part of his routine.

Gerontologists have speculated about the reason for our hang-ups about the idea of being old. One of the explanations is that we have a youth-oriented culture. Another is that modern technology changes so fast that the words *old* and *obsolete* have become almost synonymous. Also, surveys have shown that people associate unpleasant meanings with the word. To many, *old* implies worn out, secondhand, fading, unattractive, and worthless.

In spite of these negative associations with *old*, a majority of the public agrees when it comes to choosing an age for labeling someone as "old," according to some studies. During the 1960s, Bernice Neugarten, a professor at Northwestern University just outside Chicago, made a survey of middle-class, middle-aged people, which showed that 75% of the men and 57% of the women thought 65–75 was a suitable age to call men "old."

Over 80% of both men and women thought that women become old earlier than men do—at age 60–65—leading gerontologists to ponder the reasons for the difference. The biological fact of menopause is one explanation, but a more subtle one has been that we value different qualities in men and women. In women, we value youthful beauty; in men, social power. Social power reaches its peak at a time in life when the blush of youth is fading for both men and women. Consequently, later in life, men possess the characteristic most admired in them. Therefore, they can still seem attractive late in life because of their influential positions; but we rarely acknowledge mature beauty in women no matter how great.

In both the 1974 and the 1981 surveys, the Harris Associates inquired about the appropriate age of which to describe someone as "old." A small proportion of the people interviewed (15%) rated some ages below 59 as "old," but the majority of those choosing any age at all picked 60 and up. A scattering said "never" (2%) or "80 or more" (1%). A difference between the ages for labeling men and women as "old" did appear in the Harris poll, but it was negligible when compared to the Neugarten survey.

The Harris poll revealed an interesting fact: Nearly half of those interviewed refused to name any specific age at which a person becomes old. Instead, they said either that "it depends," or that a specific change, such as retirement or the failure of health, signals the start of old age. A given year in life ("chronological age") can be used to mark the age for becoming old, but a growing trend among gerontologists is to say that chronological age doesn't make a good marker. They observe that determinations of chronological old age, typically 65 years, have resulted from compulsory retirement policies and eligibility for full benefits under Social Security, but that these official definitions have nothing to do with the individual's personal experience of aging. Some today say that 80 years is a better age to speak of as "old" because so many people remain robust until then and even beyond.

While the opinion polls record the conscious views of Americans, it is possible that in our inner experience we first sense attainment of later-life status when we're about 50. The transitions to later-life status are gradual. They often pass with little notice even in the face of birthday celebrations and major biological changes. Still, even though individuals don't feel particularly old and may continue to function as they always have, within themselves ("subjectively"), many appear to recognize attaining an advanced stage of life around the half-century mark.

Perhaps this subtle, internal recognition of aging explains the increasing attention given by the popular press to well-known personalities as they reach 50. These include such figures as Jane Fonda, Burt Reynolds, Gloria Steinem, and Bill Cosby, all of whom have been starry symbols of youth, vitality, good looks, and success. The message seems to be that reaching 50 is not bad at all, and that it may even be a mark of superiority. All these beautiful persons are getting old but staying beautiful—we can do it too. Perhaps a new maxim, "life begins at 50," will enter everyday speech if the publicity about achieving that age becomes accepted.

When do we become old, then? Looking at the polls, the publicity, and the observations of gerontologists, the definition seems to be changing and moving upward on the chronological scale. Because the characteristics we relate to advanced age may have more to do with health than with years, the chronological definition of *old* climbs upward as good health lasts longer. In this respect, the personal experience of aging needn't translate into being old, and it's possible that some time the word *old* itself may lose the unattractive overtones it has now.

ARE OLDER PEOPLE HAPPY?

The best way to find out whether life is bleak for older persons is to inquire about their general happiness, or "global happiness," as the researchers call it. To get at this in any useful way, it's necessary to have a standard of comparison: Are older people as happy as other people are? If they are as happy as anyone else, then life can't be any more weary for them than it is for anyone else.

The General Social Survey (GSS) has included a question on global happiness ever since 1972. The interviewers have asked people this: "Taken all together, how would you say things are these days—would you say that you are very happy, pretty happy, or not so happy?" This type of question gets at how people feel now but not necessarily how satisfied they are with life. We address overall life satisfaction later in this chapter.

The straightforward answer to the global-happiness question is that older persons are happy, because they generally ranked at the top of the GSS happiness scale. Of all the age groups, 18 to 85+, the 65- to 74-year-olds took first place in happiness, and the 75- to 84-year-olds took second. This seems to shoot down the idea that life is bleak for older people.

HOW THE INFORMATION IN THE GSS IS REPORTED

Understanding the GSS may help you to understand the results of this important poll and provide a background for discussing what the data mean. It is technical information, but it's a little like having the same slant as the author of a mystery novel—you have a better grasp of what's happening.

One task in presenting the GSS data is to ensure that we can compare the different age groups. To do this, it's necessary to cluster the ages into sets of years, and to arrange the sets so that people don't get counted twice. The sets of years are 18–24 (like many polls, the GSS only surveys adults 18 years and up), 25–34, 35–44, 45–54, 55–64, 65–74, 75–84, 85+. These age intervals may seem odd because they begin at the middle of a decade and end just before the middle of the next (e.g., 55–64), but that's required to avoid overlapping ages (e.g., 55–65 and 65–75 overlap at age 65, and persons that age would get counted twice).

The reason for breaking the ages into fifth-year intervals (i.e., at 25, 35, 45, etc.) is that this is the way it's usually done by the U.S. Census, and most reports of age data follow the U.S.

Census system. Besides, data on the older generation is often based on age 65 because this age is the general standard for retirement under the Social Security system.

In some cases, it was necessary to arrange the ages into other groupings: 18–29, 30–39, 40–49, 50–59, 60–69, 70–79, 80+. This occurred when an interview question was only asked for a few years, causing the number of people included in the upper age groups to be small. Small numbers make percentage reports meaningless—when you say 20%, but only 10 people are in the sample, you're talking about only 2 people, an insignificant number in a national survey. Consequently, it was necessary in a few instances to group the ages so that the percentages would refer to a reasonably large number of individuals. To do anything else would be to distort the statistical picture.

Another technical point is that the annual GSS surveys have been combined into a single pool covering the years from 1972 through 1986 (in 1979 and 1981, no surveys were conducted, so this makes a pool of 12 years). This worked well because there was usually little change over the years. Whenever noticeable change did occur, the data was organized into sets of years: 1972–1976, 1977–1981, and 1982–1986. The period from 1977 to 1981 included only 3 survey years, but this doesn't cause problems because the changes in opinions were generally quite small, and occurred only when comparing the earliest set of years (1972–1976) to the latest set (1982–1986).

One last point concerns the question of whether small annual samples of people really represent the entire population. Some years ago, it would have been necessary to explain how a small, scientifically chosen sample can accurately reflect the national picture. Today, we're familiar with the voting polls taken on election day, when it's often possible to predict who will win when only 1 or 2% of the votes have been tallied. The same principle applies to a survey like the GSS—it involves predicting within a narrow range of error, maybe 2 or 3 percentage points, what the results will be for the whole population. Incidentally, we can add that people who are polled in a survey are called "respondents," which is a term we use frequently in this book.

The evidence shows that older people are considerably more happy than younger ones. The 65- to 74-year-olds recorded the most frequent choice of "very happy"—nearly 40% selected it. Next in rank came the 75- to 84-year-olds, with 36.5% "very happy." The 85+ generation wasn't as high as the previous two, but it did score 33.5% "very happy," which put it above the average for all the age groups from 18 to 44. According to the Harris poll, most of us think the teens and 20s are the best years, but the 18- to 24-year-olds were at the bottom of the happiness list, with only 27% saying they were "very happy." In conclusion, eliminating any possible remaining doubt about the comparative happiness of the older generation, 85% of the 65+ generation responded as being either "very happy" or "pretty happy."

The reports of happiness among the elderly are certainly heartening, but some readers may still have questions about the evidence just presented. Because the findings on happiness are so significant, it's important to answer these questions. Besides, it gives us another chance to look at the technical issues in social science research.

One question might be whether you can believe public opinion polls: "Do Americans answer polls truthfully?" We believe that they do. The poll question on happiness has been asked every year since the survey began, and more than 24,000 persons have responded to it with consistent results. Further, the GSS is known to represent American opinion (it passed scientific criteria for being a "valid" sample of the American public). Besides, there's little reason to think that the American public answers poll questions about happiness untruthfully, particularly when the respondents are assured that their individual identities are kept confidential—which they are in the GSS. This means that respondents are not identified by name, and their private opinions may remain private except in the general tabulation of the survey as a whole.

But, what about the 2–3% margin of error that often arises in public opinion polls—doesn't that change the results? No, not really. Even if the 2–3% error meant that 3% fewer of the elderly were as happy as was shown in the survey, they'd still be happier than some groups and match the average for all of them. Besides, the GSS results are consistent with other smaller-scale surveys that have shown older persons to be happy. It seems quite unlikely that the foregoing figures are significantly in error.

Another question might be, "Is the question about happiness poorly worded?" Can you reduce happiness to just three answers—"very happy," "pretty happy," and "not too happy"? A related question might ask whether there are subtle elements to happiness that must be spelled out in survey questions before the results can be taken seriously. Social scientists have thought of these questions, too. With over 50 years of experience in writing survey questions and taking opinion polls, they've experimented with various types of questions and scales for rating happiness. They've found that the simple, direct question used in the GSS works as well as anything. More complex questions don't change the aforementioned results.

A third question might be, "Do people agree on the meaning of the word *happiness*?" Or are persons talking about different things when they answer questions about happiness? Can we ever really know what happiness is? These questions do not stand up to analysis either. Though we may not agree as to what would make us feel happy, there's really not much ambiguity about how we feel when we call ourselves "happy." People living in different countries may have different ideas about happiness, but within a particular country, they largely agree among themselves—opinion is homogeneous. A question about happiness is one of the easier kinds of questions to answer; persons don't even have to think to answer it.

Also, a branch of psychology, sometimes called "self-psychology," emphasizes the way that each of us interprets things. Self-psychology holds that persons carry meaning within themselves, so you can accept their definitions. If people say they're happy, then it means whatever they mean by the word. You don't have to argue with them or get into philosophical debates about it. When a very large group of older people—85%—say they're "pretty happy" or "very happy," you can believe them. Though their ideas of happiness may differ from yours, their answers are good enough evaluations of their own feelings of happiness.

ARE OLDER PEOPLE BORED?

Another way to look at the question of whether later life is bleak is to find out whether older people feel bored. A great many people think that older people are bored, but do the facts support their opinion? The GSS asks, "In general, do you find life exciting, pretty routine, or dull?" Of those over 65, 33% say they find life exciting, and this pretty well matches the average for those who say they're "very happy." Only 10% overall find it dull, with the highest proportion of dull lives among the 85+ group, and even there, a mere 13% choose "dull." Finding life dull is rare among the older generations.

On the other hand, the older generations do *not* find life as exciting as the youngest age group. Over 52% of the 18- to 24-year-olds find life exciting. After this age, there's a steady downward trend in the percentage of people who say they find life exciting. At ages 25–34, it's 49%. By 55–64, it's down to 40%, and at 85+ it's fallen to 33%. It seems that youth and excitement in life are related. Still, it may surprise some people that one third of those over 85 find life exciting.

Now, contrast the evidence on excitement with the previous information on happiness. The 18- to 24-year-olds, who find life the most exciting, are also the *least* happy. Only about 27% of them report being "very happy," compared to over 33% of the very old. This suggests that happiness and excitement in life are different things, and even that having an exciting life does not necessarily make people happy. Certainly the GSS figures show that older people are not bored, and possibly that they get along quite happily without a lot of excitement in life.

ARE OLDER PEOPLE LONELY?

The statistics on excitement in life suggest a kind of tradeoff. Younger people may have more excitement, but they're not as happy. Older people find life less exciting (though very few find it dull), but they're happier. What about loneliness—are older people lonely? The GSS includes a series of questions on social activity that provides evidence relating to loneliness. The responses to these clearly show that younger people get together socially more often than older people do.

Does this mean that older people are lonely? Not if we look to the Harris polls for an answer. The Harris Associates divided the respondents into two groups—under 65 and over 65—and asked both if loneliness is a very serious problem for the older generation. Of the persons under age 65, 60% thought it was, but only 12% of the elderly thought so! This means that 88% of the older generation did not think loneliness was a problem for them. It's possible that younger people attribute loneliness to older people because they can not imagine that one can avoid loneliness without intense social contacts.

To put the issue in another perspective, is there an association between contact with other people and happiness? The GSS shows that usually there is. At every age, the people who report the highest levels of social activity also report the highest levels of happiness. But the story doesn't end there. The link between social activity and happiness grows weaker as you go toward 65–74 years on the age scale. Whereas only 21% of the 18- to 24-year-olds who socialize infrequently report being "very happy," 39% of the 65–74 group, 23% of the 75–84, and 27% of the 85+ who report infrequent socializing say they're "very happy." These figures for the older group fluctuate quite widely, but still the older generation as a whole does not depend as much on contact with others for happiness as the younger generation does.

Some might point out that the difference between young and old has little or nothing to do with age. Rather, it reflects a change in social customs over history. Perhaps the older generation grew up with values that placed less emphasis on social contact than the present younger generation does. There's a technical name for this sort of explanation: a *cohort change*, or a *cohort difference* (*cohort* refers to persons born within the same year or within a few years of one another). A cohort change reflects historical changes rather than changes caused by aging.

There are many such cohort changes, one of them being the differing attitudes about divorce between young and old.

However, it seems unlikely that the decline in the relationship between socializing and happiness is a cohort change rather than a change that comes with advancing age. If the 65+ age groups all grew up with similar values regarding social activity, you could say they were a "cohort" so far as social activity is concerned. They would be consistent among themselves. All of the age groups over 65 would show about the same relationship between happiness and social activity. But the percentages vary up and down when it comes to the relationship between happiness and social activity. This means that they aren't a cohort when it comes to the feelings of happiness they derive from social activity.

That is, if the 65+ age groups are a cohort when it comes to the importance of social activity to them, then the percentage of low socializers who report being "very happy" ought to be alike for every age group over 65. But they aren't alike. Recall that 39% of the low socializers at 65–74 say they're very happy. At 75–84, however, the rate drops to 23%, and then it bounces back up to 27% for those over 85.

We can not say what causes this variation. For example, it could be due to illness or recency of widowhood among the respective older groups, but that's not what we're concerned with here. We're concerned with cohort differences, which do not seem to explain the declining relationship between social activity and happiness as people age. Older people don't seem to depend on socializing to be happy as much as younger persons do.

Looking back, then, are older people bored and lonely? No. The overwhelming majority do not find life dull, and even one third of the very oldest group find it exciting. The Harris poll shows that the vast majority of older people do not find it lonely. Even though there is a connection between social activity and happiness, the GSS tells us that the connection shrinks as life progresses.

These findings differ greatly from what younger people think about the lives of the older generation. However, those who are actually experiencing later life undoubtedly give the most reliable testimony about it. It seems fair to draw a conclusion: Older persons take life as it comes and manage it well. We'll discuss this more fully later in the book.

DO OLDER PERSONS FEEL THAT THEY HAVE SERIOUS FINANCIAL PROBLEMS?

We've seen that older people aren't unhappy, lonely, or bored, but do they think that they aren't too well off financially? After all, most retired people do have lower incomes than those who are working. Besides, the pay scales were lower in the past than they are today, so it may be logical to think that older people could feel that they're not well off. This is precisely what the majority of people under age 65 do think—the Harris poll showed that over 62% of the public under age 65 believed that "not having enough money" is a very serious problem for older people. What do older people themselves think?

The Harris poll again showed a striking difference between the generations—only 15% of those over 65 thought that finances were a very serious problem. To turn the figures around, 85% didn't think that finances were a very serious difficulty for older people. Still, someone might hold that the words *very serious problem* are misleading. Older people might think that finances are a serious problem, but not a *very* serious one. This is extremely unlikely because nearly 50 percentage points separate young and old—no difference this great would likely result from the way a question is asked. Further evidence from the GSS supports this observation.

The GSS has included a question that reads, "We are interested in how people are getting along financially these days. So far as you and your family are concerned, would you say that you are pretty well satisfied with your present financial situation, more or less satisfied, or not satisfied at all?" The percentages choosing "satisfied" among the older generation were 40 at 65–74; 47 at 75–84; and 52 at 85+. Compared with these groups, the younger generations were much less satisfied. The 25- to 34-year-olds, for instance, ranked at the bottom, with 32% "not at all satisfied."

According to social scientists, the relatively greater dissatisfaction of the young with their financial situation grows out of
their heavy financial responsibilities and their relatively low
income at a stage of life when they are starting families, buying
and furnishing a residence, and so forth. Older people have left
these burdens behind. They still have financial needs, but these
differ from those they had when they were younger, and they
may not cause as much dissatisfaction.

It's also possible to allege that the older generation is comparatively satisfied because it lives in a dream world—the old
might think that they're well off when they actually are not. After
all, the elderly have often been depicted as bumbling, out of
touch, and somewhat weak-minded. If true, those charges could
be serious because they call into question the competence of the
old to give testimony. They could undermine the aforementioned
statistics, as well as other data in this book.

There are several ways to examine these charges. The first
is to look at the GSS data on how people think their incomes
compare with those of others. The relevant question reads,
"Compared with American families in general, would you say
your family income is far below average, below average, average,
above average, or far above average?" The majority of every age
group thought its income was average when responding to this
question. Thus, the answers of the elderly don't differ sharply
from those of other age groups.

At the same time, though a majority of each elderly group
said their incomes were average, larger percentages of two of the
three older groups felt their incomes were below average. The
keenest sense of having a below-average income may have been
due to a reduction in income following retirement, because it was
the postretirement 65- to 74-year-olds who most often said they
had below-average incomes—a sizable 35% of this group rated
their incomes as below average. Next to them were the 75- to 84-
year-olds, for whom 31% chose below average. Of the 85+ group,
27% also selected below average, but this figure differed little
from the rest of the groups, ages 18 to 64. Because many older
people do actually rate their incomes as "below average," it seems
unlikely that they are blinding themselves to the truth. We can
conclude, then, that the old are as realistic as any other group.

But what about the known financial disparities between women and men in the older generation? It's known that women, many of whom are widowed and living alone, have lower incomes than men. How did women rate their incomes? Most of them chose "average" just as did the men, but they also expressed somewhat less satisfaction with their incomes than men did. This apparent discrepancy might be explained on the ground that women compare themselves to other women rather than to men when they rate their incomes. Consequently, they consider their incomes to be average for their peer group, but many still feel that this is unsatisfactory because it is too low. Given this possible explanation, women also may be considered realistic.

The GSS data on satisfaction with income is consistent with the results of the Harris poll. While census records do show that older people, especially older women, have somewhat lower incomes, the majority still manage to find satisfaction with their financial situation. Again, the older generation seems capable of viewing life in a positive way.

ARE OLDER PEOPLE UNHEALTHY?

So far, we've seen that older people have a positive outlook on life. But does this outlook hold up when it comes to health? Everyone knows that people are usually healthier in their 20s than in their 60s, 70s, 80s, and beyond. What they don't know is that older people are still quite healthy and that they're pretty well satisfied with the state of their health. Besides this, older people feel that the health of their generation is better now than it was for a comparable generation 20 years ago—at least two thirds of them answered accordingly in the Harris poll.

To understand how older people can be less healthy than the young but still be quite healthy, it's necessary to look at four essentials. The first is that health remains fairly good for most people throughout their lives. Prolonged serious illness is the exception, not the rule. When serious illness does strike, it is usually quite short in duration and ends in either recovery or death. The use of physician and hospital services is indeed higher for the old than for the young (actually, the very young also have a high rate because of childhood diseases), but the use of these services is concentrated among the most seriously ill. The average older person does not continuously suffer serious ill health, and the majority of persons remain reasonably healthy until experiencing a final terminal illness.

Second, the typical health problems of older people are likely to be quite different from those of the young. Younger people are more likely to suffer from acute infectious diseases such as measles or mumps, but older people more frequently suffer from chronic conditions, such as high blood pressure, rheumatism, and hearing loss. However, some types of health care, such as dentistry, are more commonly used in youth than in old age.

The chronic conditions of the elderly are so widespread that they probably account for the general impression that sickness is normal in later life. For example, many persons reading this book who are over 40 years old have a touch of arthritis in the joints. In fact, 90% of all persons have some type of joint degeneration by the time they're 40! This isn't intended to advise anyone to neglect arthritic conditions—merely to point out that chronic conditions are common. Even more important, chronic health problems tend to be fairly passive. They are more of a nuisance requiring compensatory actions than an immediate, disabling threat to life.

Further, the chronic conditions of older people are not necessarily disabling. In fact, at no age does the likelihood of disability become universal for all. This has been thoroughly documented by extensive studies of America's health carried out by the National Institutes of Health (NIH). These studies have focused on activity limitations, such as inability to drive a car or to bathe, because these are the most liable to result in a demand for health and home services.

The NIH studies show that the majority of people under age 80 have no limitations whatsoever due to disability. After 80, most of the limitations that do occur are quite moderate and do not affect major activities that a person normally performs for him- or herself, such as dressing, cooking, and eating. The point is that even though chronic conditions and disability do become more frequent in later life, they are not major problems for most people.

Besides, the rates of chronic illness after age 65 are lower than might be expected, and such conditions are by no means exclusive to the old—the younger population experiences them too. Among the elderly, about 8% have diabetes, 10% have arteriosclerosis, 13% have substantial joint impairment, 14% have vision problems, 28% have heart conditions, nearly 30% have hearing difficulty, and 40% have high blood pressure.

What do older people do about these chronic conditions? Actually, they cope with them about the same way that most of us cope with problems throughout life—we overpower them by sheer grit, we tolerate them or we compensate for them. We rarely give in so long as we have the power to counterattack. Older people manage vision problems by wearing eyeglasses. They compensate for hearing loss by using hearing aids. They maintain mobility by walking with canes or walkers. They control diseases such as hypertension and diabetes by adjusting their diets or taking medications. In some cases, they undergo surgery to correct chronic health problems, resorting to artery bypasses for chronic heart problems or to insertion of prostheses (artificial replacements) for arthritic joints.

The Harris poll is not exceptional in supporting the contention that reasonably good health is the norm in later life. The NIH has reported that more than two thirds of the population over age 75 describes itself as in good health. The GSS, which is given only to persons who are not institutionalized, shows that nearly 50% of those over 85 say they are in good to excellent health, and that less than 20% say they're in poor health. To alleviate any doubt about the accuracy of self-reports of health, the Duke University Longitudinal Study of Aging has compared self-reports by individuals with physician ratings and has found that they match one another closely.

A third point comes from a different kind of survey question, involving a person's satisfaction with his or her health. Personal satisfaction with health differs from self-described health because self-described health involves standing apart and making a diagnosis, like a physician, from the outside looking in. Rating personal health satisfaction is the opposite—it involves being inside and looking out. Consequently, it's possible for a person to accurately rate his or her health as "poor" but still feel satisfied with it. For example, some people with hangovers may still feel satisfied because they know that their friends who enjoyed the same party have headaches that are even worse. People answering health questionnaires sometimes do affirm contradicting assessments of self-described state of health versus personal health satisfaction.

When asked about health satisfaction in the GSS, more than three quarters of the 65+ generation said "fair" or better. The specific percentages for each older age group who answered "fair" or better were 65–74, 82%; 75–84, 75%; 85+, 70%. Quite large percentages of all three groups reported the highest levels of satisfaction—"a great deal of satisfaction," or "a very great deal of satisfaction"—with these results: 65–74, 48%; 75–84, 41%; 85+, 39%. It seems reasonable to conclude that the GSS firmly supports other studies of health attitudes among the elderly: Many older persons have a chronic condition that causes them to say that their health is only "fair," but they are not so unwell as to feel dissatisfied.

None of this should encourage us to neglect the state of our health. Common sense dictates that health problems should receive prompt attention and that a healthful life-style promotes longevity. Nor does it minimize the catastrophic costs of illness when it does occur, as the recent debates over national insurance for devastating illnesses and long-term care demonstrate. What this review does say is that people can expect fairly good health in later life. We may not have the health we once did, but it is definitely not normal to experience constant poor health in old age.

This leads to the fourth point on health in later life: People do seem to earn it rather than just encounter it by chance. Good health doesn't just happen along accidentally even though there's some evidence that long life and good health may be hereditary. The best genes in the world won't save an intemperate fool from an early grave, and those who enjoy satisfactory health in later life generally maintain a life-style that promotes good health. This can be illustrated in a number of ways, but the GSS offers some enlightening figures on two relevant topics: drinking and smoking.

While nearly three quarters of the under-55 population drinks alcoholic beverages, the percentage of drinkers shrinks as we age. Between ages 55 and 64, the percentage of imbibers stands at 66. At ages 65–74, it drops 10 percentage points to 56%, then it falls to 44% at ages 75–84, and to 31% at ages 85+. This falling rate can be explained in part by the increasing representation of women, who report lower percentages of drinkers at all ages; but men also contribute to it because fewer of them report being drinkers at later ages. Also, the reduced level of drinking among the older age groups could be a cohort effect, perhaps having originated as a habit of abstinence during Prohibition, when it was hard to get alcohol, or the Great Depression, when few could afford it. Whatever the explanation, the evidence shows that those who are now living longest are comparatively abstinent.

When it comes to smoking, the relationship is even stronger. Until age 55, nearly half—45%—of the GSS respondents say they're smokers. By ages 65–74, the percentage has fallen dramatically to 26. Among the 75- to 84-year-olds, it's 15%; and for the 85+, it's down to 5%. Again, these falling rates are undoubtedly due to the increasing proportion of women among the elderly, and possibly also to some cohort effects. Still, it's worth noting that one of the current explanations of longer life among women has to do with their lower rates of smoking in past times. The proportion of younger women smokers is increasing just as it's falling among men (the GSS shows that the highest rate of women smokers—39%—is among the 18- to 24-year-olds, but that only 44% of the 18- to 24-year-old men smoke, as compared to 53% of the 45- to 54-year-olds). Again, whatever the influence of gender and cohort, the GSS figures show that the overwhelming majority—95%—of the survivors in later life are nonsmokers.

This review of health information tells a most remarkable story about health in later life. First, at *no* age, even past age 85, is more than a minority of the population acutely ill and receiving treatment. Second, persons who live many years can assume they will remain in reasonably good health; although 80% do experience chronic conditions, these are not usually severely disabling. Next, most persons rate their health as "good," most proclaim themselves as fairly satisfied with it, and a large proportion of every older age group feels quite highly satisfied. Finally, persons who survive to old age generally have some better health practices than nonsurvivors and than the average younger person.

In spite of this generally positive picture of health among the elderly, no one can afford to be casual about their physical condition, nor can anyone afford to neglect the need for insurance to pay for correcting health problems that do arise. The miracles of modern medicine can be very costly. The discussion of the preceding pages simply means that we need not be depressed or riddled with fear of illness in later life. We need not be hypochondriacs, but good health does require good sense.

ARE OLDER PEOPLE MENTALLY FEEBLE?

Probably the most pervasive fear about age concerns senility, or what used to be known generally as "senile dementia." In recent years, the specific term "Alzheimer's disease" has dominated the language we use for severe loss of mental function. When someone exhibits signs of mental problems in later life, people are quick to proclaim them the result of "Alzheimer's," and smugly believe they've made a correct diagnosis. However, only about 5% of persons over age 65 may actually suffer from Alzheimer's disease. In fact, at present, Alzheimer's disease can only be diagnosed by means of an autopsy conducted after a person's death. Clearly, not even a physician can say with certainty whether an afflicted person has Alzheimer's disease.

But the loose usage of this term only underlines the common fear of mental problems in later life. We can neither underestimate the personal tragedy of senile (meaning "old age") dementia nor underrate it as an epidemiological problem. The rate of senile dementia (some of which can be attributed to Alzheimer's disease) does increase to reach 20% after age 80, and it may grow in the future as even more people live to very advanced years.

What we should realize, though, is that a senile demented mental condition is by no means normal or to be expected. It is not inevitable and not always irreversible, and it is often due to treatable ill health or depression. At present, about 80% of the population over 80 does not experience senile dementia. The majority of people have normal mental function throughout life.

Even if most persons don't have to endure senile dementia, do older people become mentally dull? Popular remarks about older people certainly suggest this. One of the favorites (intended as a compliment) is, "She [or he] is still [surprisingly] sharp as a tack!" This presumes that most persons lose their cleverness and clarity as they age, and that those who retain keen wits are exceptions. Well-intended remarks about brains and intelligence are patronizing. They're rather like the exclamations made about growth in children—the recipients tolerate them, but they don't welcome them. In fact, the research shows that mental acuity in age is not at all unusual.

The psychology of aging is addressed in some detail in later chapters, but two observations on mental acuity can be made at this point. First, even though psychological and neuropsychological research shows that specific functions do slow with age, mental function remains intact for most people. For instance, though reaction time may drop, "crystalized intelligence," based on accumulated learning, persists. Also, mental growth through education can occur across the entire life span. The human brain can be stretched at any age, and has been called "plastic," meaning stretchable—we retain mental plasticity throughout life. The maxim, "You can't teach an old dog new tricks," may be good advice for dog trainers, but it doesn't apply to humans.

Second, a major problem in looking at mental function in old age is that the attitudes of the public in general and of gerontology researchers in particular are frozen by the notion of decline. As a result, nearly everyone seems to think in terms of loss of mental function rather than of *retention* of mental function in later life.

To defrost these attitudes, it might be admitted that the young do excel in terms of speed in handling cognitive tasks.

Having given the young their due, a few psychologists observe that the elderly excel in subtlety and finesse in solving problems. These psychologists cite studies showing that older people handle ambiguous situations imaginatively and use socially centered reasoning more effectively than younger persons. A study of the fate of legislative bills introduced into the Vermont legislature illustrates this point. It was found that the younger legislators introduced twice as many bills as older ones, but that the older legislators were twice as successful in getting their bills through. The young generated quantity, but the old generated results.

In earlier times, older people were sometimes believed to be sorcerers and witches because of their seemingly cunning powers to control life events. Some psychologists today have recognized the unique characteristics of intelligence in older persons, and they are trying to describe and analyze those features. They see the thought processes of the old as being governed by choice rather than by necessity, as being aware of subtle features within situations, and as being independent of mind. The old, they argue, are not as locked into formulas or as bound by conventions as younger persons. Most older people, they say, not only retain mental power, but also continue to grow and remain creative. It is not surprising to these psychologists that Pablo Picasso continued to paint in his 90s, Michelangelo was working until 2 days before he died at age 92, and that Agatha Christie continued to publish detective novels in her 80s.

DO OLDER PERSONS REMAIN SOCIALLY ACTIVE?

Activity is such a fundamental characteristic of human life that some researchers consider it a basic biological drive similar to hunger, thirst, sleep, or sex. Within the social realm, specialists have debated the relative importance of active contact with others for older people. For a time, one of the prominent theories in gerontology, known as "Activity Theory," posited that higher levels of activity lead to greater life satisfaction and that types of activities change as people age. Others found that some people are perfectly content with little or no activity of any kind. The present resolution of the debate is a compromise—most, but not all, people need activity in later life, and activities do change as people grow older.

A major reason that social activity is considered important for most of us is because it ties us to society so that we are socially integrated. "Ties that bind" conveys this idea of social integration. Most of us need connections, relationships, and contacts with others to obtain support and to experience a vital, stimulating life. Though some waning of activity occurs normally with age, a level of activity that dwindles away to nothing is a likely sign of trouble for most of us. Contact with others is essential to sustain life.

Just how much do older persons socialize, then? A series of questions in the GSS probed this topic by asking how frequently an individual spends a social evening with relatives, friends, and neighbors. This is not the best wording for the elderly because they are much more likely to socialize in the daytime than in the evening. The question also excludes casual contacts, such as informal chats at the supermarket or with the pharmacist at the drugstore. Studies have shown that such contacts often serve as supportive interaction for older people, so their answers to the GSS question probably represent the rock-bottom picture of their activity.

In any case, the responses show that the older generation certainly socializes, though not as actively as the young. The numbers of social contacts reported in the GSS can be classified as "very frequent," "frequent," "occasional," and "rare." Of the 18- to 24-year-olds, 70% report having "frequent" or "very frequent" contacts. In contrast, the rate for the 65+ age group is 35%, just half that of the youngsters.

At the same time, the percentage of older (65+) people reporting "rare" contact is quite low—13.5%. Over half of every group of older respondents had at least "occasional" evening social contact with others. Furthermore, the 85+, who might be expected to have very little social contact in the evening, had as much as the 35- to 44-year-olds—55% of each group reported "occasional" evening socializing. Perhaps more striking, there's a steady downward trend in the rate of socializing for all age groups over 18–24. It becomes noticeable at ages 35–44 and persists thereafter.

Do older people remain active, then? Compared to young adults, no; but compared to those 35–64, yes. This suggests that older people who wish to remain active do so. They maintain ties that bind, and they are not socially isolated. This information is consistent with the earlier discussion of social activity and happiness—most older people are neither isolated nor lonely, and some can be quite happy without much social activity.

DO OLDER PEOPLE THINK THAT OTHER PEOPLE ARE FAIR?

One of the most severe tests of the experience of aging concerns the question of whether older people believe that they are treated fairly by others. Do older people have a sense of unfairness that arises from the simple fact of being old? Do older people look back on the passing of youth, beauty, and vigor and become disillusioned and misanthropic? Do older people sense unfairness due to actual discrimination against the older generation? This discrimination is well documented enough that the U.S. Congress has adopted legislation to combat "ageism," a term coined to refer to discrimination against the old.

Groups such as the Gray Panthers have declared war on "ageism" and forcefully demanded civil rights for the elderly. A noted champion of the cause has been Maggie Kuhn, an impassioned militant. Other groups, such as the AARP (American Association of Retired Persons) and the National Council on Aging, have worked successfully to gain favorable public response to Social Security, Medicare and Medicaid, housing programs for the elderly, laws against job discrimination, senior centers, food and nutrition programs, and other services. Still, with all the publicity about discrimination, how does the older generation feel about people? Do they think people are fair to them?

The GSS asked, "Do you think most people would try to take advantage of you if they got a chance, or would they try to be fair?"

A strong majority of the older generation answered "try to be fair," with 70% of 75- to 84-year-olds choosing this—the highest rating for this choice. The older age groups chose this far more than the youngest generations—only 47.5% of the 18- to 24-year-olds and 57% of the 25–34 age group rated other persons as fair.

Another GSS question also asked about the older generation's feelings about others: "Would you say that most of the time people try to be helpful, or that they mostly just look out for themselves?" The media frequently point to neglect and abuse of the elderly, so a negative response could be expected. Nonetheless, the older generation again topped every other group in saying that people are helpful, though by not quite as wide a margin as was the case for fairness. Over 58% of the two oldest groups thought people are helpful, followed by 54% of the 65- to 74-year-olds. The youngest again proved the most cynical, registering only 40% for "helpful" at 18–24 and only 49% at 25–34.

Whatever disadvantages older persons suffer because of their years or status in society, they come out on top in their attitudes toward others. This may be a cohort effect, a response to generosity toward them, or a consequence of something else; but it does show that a positive and generous attitude flows from the elderly toward others.

DO OLDER PEOPLE HAVE ANY SPECIAL ASSETS?

In view of the evidence presented so far, it seems timely to ask *why* older people have a generally favorable outlook on life. The French philosopher Voltaire, who lived at the time of the American Revolution, wrote the play *Candide*, casting the elderly Dr. Pangloss as a cockeyed optimist who misled the young Candide into a series of calamitous, but nonetheless quite hilarious, adventures. Are old persons merely giddy optimists, or does age somehow give a person assets with which to address life positively?

Although a considerable amount of research has gone into the subject of successful aging, no one has yet unlocked the secrets to it. Perhaps this is because early studies focused on decline, and today there's still a primary emphasis both on changes that occur with age and on comparing later life with youth. Apart from considerations of decline, the characteristics of age have received too little attention. The question should be, What is special and unique about later life?

Certainly it is not that older people enjoy a positive outlook because they become passive. Nor is it that their emotions become blunted, as some have suggested. Research on the intensity of emotional reactions shows that, if anything, the elderly experience emotions more intensely than the young. Older people are not passive in their feelings.

The explanation for the relative happiness and good feelings of the older generation can be summed up in a word: experience. Older people have witnessed much in life, including change, sad events, and happy events. They've survived the good times and the bad ones. As a result, they know how to take things in stride. It would seem that they are not passive and remote, but that they have seen many things and understand many things.

Further, research has shown that older people are generally confident about their competence. This is true even though the young may actually be more competent in some respects. For instance, it would be hard for most 60-year-olds to beat a 20-year-old in a 100-yard dash, and professional athletes who compete beyond age 40 are prodigies. But sprinting and other high levels of physical performance are no longer important to older people. They have alternatives to replace outstanding physical performance, and they can function effectively in their own spheres because of years of practice.

Dr. James Birren, former dean of the Andrus Gerontology Center at the University of Southern California and a leader in the psychology of aging, has addressed the characteristic potency of older people. He observes that they can size up a situation and pick out what's important in it. They see the whole picture better even though the younger person may more quickly distinguish the parts. It may be inferred that this gives the older generation a greater capacity for leadership.

Another outstanding gerontologist, Dr. Robert Butler, former head of the National Institutes on Aging and presently in charge of geriatric services at Mt. Sinai Hospital in New York, points to other qualities of age. The elderly, he observes, experience a personal sense of the life cycle beyond the grasp of young persons simply because the young have not lived a long lifetime. This inward sense of the life cycle, Butler continues, creates a profound awareness of change and evolution. The result is a deep realization of the precious and limited quantity of life that makes older people appreciate the world. Butler's own words are worth quoting: "For older people [the inward sense of the life cycle] is not the same as 'feeling old'; it is instead a deep understanding of what it means to be human."

Perhaps the best way to close this chapter is to return to the theme of sympathy for older persons mentioned at the very beginning—the old seem to appreciate that people care. Still, there's more to it than that. They genuinely have a positive outlook about life that goes beyond mere gratitude for avoiding the alternative—death.

It's also wise to remember that in some societies, persons look forward to being old. They consider age to be a time of dignity and refinement. The last years of life are the best, according to their view. In America, the elderly feel much better about themselves and may share more of the outlook held in these other societies than any of the younger Americans can imagine. Anyone who understands this has a good chance for making their final years into their best ones.

This book is dedicated to supplying information on aging so that seekers in later life can reach their goal successfully. The positive and individualistic tone that it reports should not suggest that we can abandon social concern for older people. Planning for the well-being of older persons is like storing up for the winter—the store will be there when it's needed. We need not fear aging. We must reach out, seize hold of it, and plan ahead so that we can live our last years to the fullest.

3

Scholars, Poets, and the Vision of Aging

Most Americans perceive old age only dimly, like the headlights of an oncoming car seen through a shroud of fog late at night. A myopic fixation on youth limits our sight even more. We magnify youth so that it alone seems beautiful and magnificent. How can we clear away this dark cloud and widen our perspective?

One way to see more accurately is to study the history of human thought about growing old. The science of aging may be new, but thinking about aging is not. The present book emphasizes modern research to provide the reader with up-to-date information, but a journey back in time offers us refreshing enlightenment drawn from the well of ancient human wisdom.

Surprisingly, modern scientific theories still echo ideas expressed long ago. One of these is the view that life involves a series of stages—a prominent theory in modern explorations of the psychological experience of growing old. The biblical book of Ecclesiastes first recorded a similar kind of insight about 150 years before the birth of Christ. One of the superbly poetic works of the ancient Jewish religion, Ecclesiastes may have been expressing ideas that were already hundreds of years old.

What did thinkers in the past say about aging? Is aging good? Is it bad? Pleasant? Unpleasant? How did scholars and poets of yore describe it? How did they explain it? What kind of psychological experience were the old believed to have? In what ways did the ancients think young persons differ from the old?

We answer these questions and more as we review some of our heritage of human thought about old age. For the moment, however, we make this observation: Two opposing viewpoints have stood out in this long history. For some great thinkers, old age is the best of times. For others, it is the worst. This *dichotomy*, or two-way split in attitudes, persists even today. There seem to be only two sides, with little middle ground between them. Age has either been deplored for its failings or praised as the only time of life when humans attain wisdom and rise above greedy ambition. In either case, ideas about age have had a profound grandeur.

HOW WAS OLD AGE VIEWED DURING BIBLICAL TIMES?

We begin with the book of Ecclesiastes because it may represent the oldest written record of ideas and feelings about old age. It appears in the Jewish *Megilloth*, still read at Purim (a holiday festival) today, and was bequeathed to Christians in the Old Testament. Ecclesiastes represents a negative view, most mightily expressed in intense and profoundly moving language that lends the book a spirit of torment. In fact, it stands as one of the most crushing statements about old age ever made.

Age is the worst of times. The speaker implies this in one devastating allegory at the close of the book. The major part of the work, however, expresses his writhing despair as an old man. A pessimist, he sees utter futility in all things. "Emptiness, emptiness," he cries, ". . . all is empty!" "All things are wearisome. . . . What has happened will happen again, and what has been done will be done again. . . ."[1] There is nothing new under the sun, no hope for improvement, progress, or betterment.

The speaker has searched for something worthwhile through an entire lifetime. In vain, he has seen everything and tried everything. At one time, he acquired wisdom, but wisdom

---

[1]Samuel Sandmel, M. Jack Suggs, Arnold J. Tkacki (eds.) *The New English Bible with Apocrypha; Oxford Study Edition*. New York, Oxford University Press, 1976, p. 708.

brought only anguish because the more he learned, the more he came to see the folly of life. A metaphor appears repeatedly throughout the book, describing the search for wisdom as "chasing the wind."

Later, abandoning wisdom, he gave himself over to pleasure, laughter, and wine, but these too brought only folly, emptiness, and madness. Feverishly, he turned to building great works; planting vineyards and orchards; digging water systems for irrigation; acquiring male and female slaves, cattle, flocks of sheep and goats; and amassing silver and gold. But what good was all that? One only dies and leaves riches behind for wastrels to consume. When he reviewed all his labor, he saw that it led to emptiness and chasing the wind. He surrendered to despair—there was no other choice!

During this pursuit of restless emptiness, the speaker described life as having seasons, which laid the foundation for the later idea that life is a series of stages: "For everything its season, and for every activity under heaven its time—a time to be born and a time to die—a time to weep and a time to laugh—a time to love and a time to hate—a time to tear and a time to mend . . . ." The profound truth of this idea has become part of the human tradition, and it still finds expression in the scientific field of gerontology. Not long ago, author Gail Sheehy popularized the same idea in her best-selling book, *Passages*.

Near the close of Ecclesiastes an allegory of old age appears:

> Remember your Creator . . . before the sun and the light of day give place to darkness, before the moon and the stars grow dim, and the clouds return with the rain—when the guardians of the house tremble, and strong men stoop, when the women grinding the meal cease work because they are few, and those who look through the windows look no longer, when the street-doors are shut, when the noise of the mill is low, when the chirping of the sparrow grows faint and the song-birds fall silent.

This and other passages carry so haunting a strain that religious scholars sometimes have attributed the occasional more hopeful references to God in the book to editors who aimed to relieve the overwhelming tone of despair. Whatever the truth of this view, Ecclesiastes is one of the world's most powerful characterizations of old age as the worst of times.

Yet, anyone familiar with the Bible knows that older persons were highly respected among the ancient Jews. The charge to "honor thy father and thy mother" in the Ten Commandments has been considered a general directive to respect the older generation. In the Old Testament as a whole, there are close links between regard for the old and respect, or fear, of the Lord. Those who fail to show esteem for the older generation suffer punishment by rejection.

Further, the biblical book of Proverbs is filled with respect for age. A long life, it says, is the fruit of wisdom. Those who attain old age do so by their own effort rather than by accident of good biology. "Gray hair," says Proverbs, "is a crown of glory, and it is won by a virtuous life." Reverence for the past accompanies respect for age. Tradition dominates life.

Comparatively speaking, Americans today have little reverence for the elderly, an attitude that many attribute to a vulgar decline in our national character. But historian W. Andrew Achenbaum of Carnegie-Mellon University has traced the development of attitudes in America and has shown that the older generation has never been greatly venerated here. Modern Americans have not suddenly developed defects in their national character. Rather, we started out as a country of the young, and we quickly became the leader in a worldwide trend toward modernization, leaving old traditions behind.

It seems that veneration for the elderly belonged to a time when agriculture and pastoral life determined the status of the generations—a time long gone when the American nation was founded. For example, the admonition to "honor thy father and thy mother" appears in the biblical book of Exodus along with the provision "that you may live long in the land which the Lord is giving you." The land, agriculture, animal husbandry, and respect for the elderly went hand in hand in ancient times. It was in part their mastery of agricultural technology, which could only be acquired slowly over a lifetime, that accounted for the importance of the old.

The Bible ties together the land, the past, tradition, and

respect for the old with this command to the younger generation: "Do not move the ancient boundary stone, which your forefathers set up." In societies where farming and animal herding were the way of life, the elderly were in command. Most people were illiterate. Formal education and science had just begun. Skills lasted for life and were learned painstakingly over many years with the changes of the seasons and from the timeless biorhythms of plants and animals. Experience reigned supreme, and older people had more of it.

Added to this, the older generation owned the land and the flocks. As the Bible shows, this was crucial in a religious as well as an economic sense. Land passed from one generation to the next by a special blessing rather than by the simple modern process of legal inheritance. In some Bible stories, such as that of Esau and Jacob, it is the blessing itself that designates an heir. Once given, the blessing is fixed as if by God, irrevocably.

Little wonder that the biblical patriarchs like Abraham and Jacob could direct the lives of their sons and daughters and could expect economic support once they transferred the tilling of family garden plots and management of flocks to the younger generation. Such customs persist today in lands where agriculture predominates, as in China and Africa. Americans sometimes envy the status accorded to the old in these developing nations and wonder why we don't offer more respect and economic support to the old. The answer is that no modernized nation gives the elderly as much status as they held in the past, not even Japan.

In some contemporary developing societies, people still consider old age the greatest time of life and look forward with pleasure to becoming old. Americans have never held such views. Today, however, Americans face the challenge of the Aging Boom: to forge conditions that make old age become one of the greatest stages for modern humans.

WHAT DID ANCIENT GREEKS THINK ABOUT OLD AGE?

The Greeks held a fairly optimistic view of life, especially so during their early history. Yet, they too exhibited a certain degree of bipolar thinking when it came to age: It was the best of times or the worst of times.

It was the Greek custom to glorify physical beauty and powers of youth. These were celebrated in the Olympic games and with magnificent statues of men and women, often nude or only lightly draped. Some societies have esteemed the old because they considered them about to enter a higher and more spiritual life, but not so the Greeks. They had no such reason to admire the old, for they believed that the present life alone holds joy. Death meant consignment to a dark, gloomy underworld where souls lived a half life in a half light.

Not surprisingly, some Greek thinkers held a dreary view of old age. Among them was Aristotle, who lived in about 350 B.C. and is said to have been the first scientific student of human society and experience. He believed that young persons fall into permissible errors because they incline to enthusiasm and excess. The old, however, have more serious faults that grow out of their experience with the inevitable misfortunes of life. They are suspicious. They live by shrewdness and calculation rather than by moral values. They are rigid, small-minded, cynical, ungenerous, cowardly, and shameless. They appear self-controlled only because they lack passion, not because they have become wise. Aristotle concluded that such faults should disqualify the old from holding political office. (Step aside, Aristotle—the pounding footsteps you hear behind you may be Maggie Kuhn and the Gray Panthers!)

Greek mythology, too, showed the younger and older generations in conflict with one another—an extreme expression of the generation gap. In this conflict, the young rose against the old while the old tried to maintain control. The outcomes of the struggle were grim. In one case, the aged god Cronus ("Saturn" to the Romans) ate his own children. The offspring of the god Uranus turned the tables, though they weren't quite so violent— they merely castrated their father!

Sigmund Freud, the father of psychoanalysis, recalled a Greek legend in which King Laius and Queen Jocasta gave their newborn son, Oedipus, to a shepherd to forestall a prophecy about their future—that their son would kill his father and marry his mother. When the son grew to become a princely adult, he visited his father's palace, and there, unaware of his true origins and unrecognized by his parents, he did indeed kill his father and marry his mother. Freud drew on this Greek idea of intergenerational conflict when he employed the myth of Oedipus to explain antagonism between fathers and sons. He coined the term "Oedipus complex" to describe the phenomenon, and he attributed it to competition between the male family members for the affection of the wife, who was also the mother.

But negative views about age don't give a complete picture of Greek life, where the senior generation held much the same status as it did among the biblical Hebrews. Like the other civilizations of the ancient Mediterranean region, Greek civilization subsisted on farming and herding, and it followed the common customs of respect for the old. Greek law actually granted political and economic power to the older members of the most influential families, and older men were appointed to draw up the fundamental constitutions of new cities, somewhat as modern experts in political science or law might be called upon to serve as consultants on political affairs. Add to these the folk belief that the old enjoyed abnormal, even magical powers, and it becomes obvious that the ancient Greeks granted a high status to old age.

It must have been these latter considerations that inspired the philosopher Plato when he wrote of the superiority of the aged in his chronicles of the life and thought of his great teacher Socrates. Considered by some to be the greatest philosopher of all times, Plato held views quite different from those of Aristotle, who once had been Plato's pupil.

Plato argued that there should be an ideal society, a kind of utopia he called "the Republic," which only the eldest and best members of society could possibly govern. The young are courageous and spirited, Plato thought, but it was only the old, including older women, who could take charge of a perfect society. The following brief passage relating a conversation between Socrates and his friends gives the gist of Plato's ideas:

"What is the next question? Must we not ask who are to be the rulers and who the subjects?"—asks Socrates

"Certainly!"—answers a participant

"There can be no doubt that the elder must rule the younger."—Socrates

"Clearly!"—participant

"And that the best of these must rule."—Socrates

The last sentence explains why Plato thought the old must rule—only those who have spent years in the study of philosophy can become the best. He reasoned something like this. We live in a cave where we cannot see the real world. We see only shadowy images like those cast by a flickering fire against a rugged, cavelike wall. The shadows merely reflect an ideal world, which stands beyond our daily vision and experience. Through very long study, however, we can acquire the deep philosophical knowledge required to see the ideal world. Therefore, people become fit to rule in late life, when they have obtained wisdom through study of philosophy. Plato thought that old age is the best time of life. Only then can persons have acquired the wisdom essential to aspire to the total selflessness that rulers must have.

Those of us with gray hair may enjoy Plato's point of view, but we should also consider a few of his other ideas regarding the requisites for this selflessness. These ideas may not stir as much enthusiasm. For one, he called his aging rulers the "guardians," and he proposed that they should live in a military-like camp isolated from everyone else. The guardians should pursue a vigorous regimen of physical exercise to maintain a high level of fitness. Their lives were to be communistic: They were not to own their homes, have property, or possess money; silver and gold would not even be allowed in their camp. The rules Plato described might well have suited monks and nuns in later Christian times, for he believed that only those who had given up all material desires could possess the freedom of will and virtue necessary to rule.

HOW DID ANCIENT ROMANS VIEW OLD AGE?

By the time of Julius Caesar, who lived just a few decades before the birth of Christ, the Romans had become the dominant society of the Mediterranean region. Even though the elderly still presided over daily life, some Romans clearly thought of old age as the worst of times. Frequently the butt of ribald and cruel satires in Roman theatrical productions, older people were portrayed as silly, foolish, and lecherous —as dirty old men and dirty old women, to borrow contemporary terms. The modern musical burlesque show "A Funny Thing Happened on the Way to the Forum" followed actual Roman plays. In this farce, old Eronius is the ultimate dupe. On the advice of Pseudalus, a sly slave masquerading as a sorcerer (wonderfully played by Zero Mostel), he spends the entire play jogging around the city of Rome because he's been told that this will bring back his children who were kidnapped in their infancy. At the close Eronius is still jogging around inanely even though his children were restored to him during the wild climax of the farce.

But the negative views of the Romans didn't appear in plays alone. Seneca, a major Stoic philosopher who tutored the emperor Nero, declared that old age was a disease. Even at that, things had changed for the better by Seneca's time, because the custom previously had been to seize feeble old people and unceremoniously throw them to drown in the river Tiber that flows through the city. Happily, this brutal form of euthanasia was abandoned early in Roman history.

Perhaps it was because of persistent negative attitudes toward the elderly that one of the most distinguished of all Roman statesmen felt compelled to compose a defense of old age. Cicero (known as "Tully" to generations of school boys from his middle name Tulius), a distinguished lawyer and essayist, actively engaged in politics during the life of Julius Caesar, who forced him into exile at one time. After Caesar was assassinated, Cicero made the mistake of backing a losing political faction opposed to Mark Anthony, (immortalized to us for his love affair with Cleopatra in Shakespeare's *Antony and Cleopatra*). He suffered a fairly common fate of those defeated in politics during his time—he was executed. The sentence was carried out even though he was 63 years old—quite old for anyone during that era.

Just a year before his execution, Cicero had composed a splendid essay, *de Senectute* ("about Old Age"), in opposition to prejudices against old age. His masterly defense reveals a great legal mind presenting a case that might have been argued before a supreme court. His ideas about age remain as profound and fresh today as they were when set forth more than 2000 years ago.

Cicero cast his essay in a popular form of the time: It involved having some respected savant of earlier ages present the writer's ideas to a few interested inquirers—a literary device intended to add distinction to the arguments about to be presented. For his spokesperson, he chose Cato the Elder, another distinguished Roman statesman who had lived about 200 years before. Cato answers the following four charges against old age: (1) Old age prohibits great accomplishments; (2) it weakens the body; (3) it withholds enjoyment of life; (4) it stands near death.

Cato is 84 years old. He rambles into leisurely reminiscence at times, but the essence of his defense of age rests on two general propositions: Old age, he argues, is better than youth because the old are wise, respected, and influential. Second, old age is superior to youth because the development of one's inner being, the soul, in advanced maturity stands above the trivial pursuit of pleasure typical of the early years of life.

But a good old age doesn't just happen to everyone who lives many years. Not at all—it depends on a well-spent youth and a purposefully designed and well-planned life. Enjoyment of maturity comes only to those with the will to live virtuously by conscious choice and deliberation. Defects of character, not physical deterioration, cause illness and mental decline in later life. People with trivial personalities fail in life, and therefore they fail in old age. A poorly arranged life is the cause of unhappiness in old age.

Cicero then has Cato set forth a maxim that could easily serve present-day militant advocates for the elderly. "Old age," he says, "is held in esteem only if it defends its own position, lays claim to its own rights, is beholden to no man, and exercises its authority over those properly under its control until the last breath of life." But, he adds, old age most of all must remain in control of itself. To accomplish this, one must understand the particular attributes and unique gifts of one's advanced years. Like every other age, late life has special endowments that one can use to achieve success.

Learning stands out as one of these special attributes. Even though the old can continue to enjoy pleasures, pleasures are minor when compared to the power to continue to grow in spirit. And, the spirit is fed by learning. The spirit never needs to age if persons continue to grow within themselves, so Cato argued.

Echoing the wise writer of Ecclesiastes, Cicero has Cato say this:

> There is a fixed course for life's span and a simple path . . .
> for Nature. A fitting timeliness has been allotted for each part
> of the journey, so that the helpless dependency of infancy
> and the fiery intensity of youth, the dignity of the established
> years, and the maturity of old age have each a certain natural
> endowment, which must be perceived and fulfilled in its
> own season.

Altogether a powerful set of observations: Life is a set of passages, and each person must understand the special qualities of each passage in order to live the passages well.

The discourse closes with interesting reflections on death. Cato (still speaking for Cicero) says that he finds comfort in the thought that great philosophers (Plato among them) have argued in favor of immortality. He has no desire to return as a babbling baby to a cradle and relive life. He is happy, instead, to go forward to the life after death, the future, where there is no hardship.

But, suppose there is no life after death? Well, then, Cato is still satisfied. "I have no regret at having lived, for I have so conducted my life that I do not feel that I was born to no purpose, and I cheerfully depart from life as though I were leaving a guest chamber, not my own house. Nature has granted us an inn for a moment, not . . . a permanent dwelling." Through Cato, Cicero proves that he has come to terms with his own life. He experiences a sense of completeness, of fulfillment.

He faces whatever the future may hold with composure— a prophetic state, considering his death just barely a year later. Among his concluding thoughts is the idea that he will have nothing to fear after death even if he is mistaken in his belief in immortality. If there is no experience after death, then he will be conscious of nothing and has nothing to fear. Old age is the last act of the great drama of life, a marvelous stage to be in, the richest one of them all. Cicero closes the discourse with a kind of benediction for his two young listeners: "May you both live to attain that state [old age], so that you may test by your own experience what you have heard from me."

Cicero wrote this essay about 44 years before the birth of Christ, when philosophers more openly speculated over the question of life after death, and before religious faith had settled the issue with certainty for many religious persons. His discourse stands as an eminent expression of the view that age is the best time of life. It towers above most writings on being old, offering insights that continue to be the subjects of scientific inquiry even today. The passage of 2000 years has not dimmed the value of this great statesman's ideas. They can still guide anyone who wants to get the most out of old age in our time.

WHAT VISION OF AGING HAVE MORE MODERN WRITERS HELD?

An ancient writer like Aristotle could write about old age with a measure of detachment not unlike that of present-day gerontologists, but not so two of the greatest poets of more recent times— William Shakespeare and William Butler Yeats. Both spoke about old age with an emotional intensity that recalls the spirit of Ecclesiastes.

Shakespeare composed most of his plays during the reign of Elizabeth I, not long before the Pilgrims came to America. He portrayed old age quite frequently in his plays, even building an entire drama around an older person, in the tragedy of King Lear.

At other times, he depicted the old as useless fools, or as imperfect advisers to the young, or he just included them in his cast of actors.

In *As You Like It*, he showed that the negative ideas of ancient times had remained alive. Here, he drew on the insights of the ancients to describe life as a series of scenes in a drama—one that culminates in decrepitude. In the famous speech beginning, "All the world's a stage, and all the men and women merely players," he described seven acts to the human term on earth.

With powerful, even repelling imagery, he pictured the first stage as the infant, "mewling and puking [spitting up] in the nurse's arms." Next came the whining school boy, creeping unwillingly to school. Then followed the young lover, sighing like a woeful furnace. The young lover became the bearded soldier, full of strange oaths and seeking reputation even in the cannon's mouth, and he was succeeded by the justice and then by the scholar. These two usher in the last scene of all, which could have been inspired by Ecclesiastes. Old age "ends this strange eventful history—is second childhood and mere oblivion—sans [French for 'without'] teeth, sans eyes, sans taste, sans everything." Shakespeare intended to create drama with this singular portrayal of life, but he saved his most biting images for the last years.

With nothing positive to say about old age, it's little wonder that King Lear, which many critics properly consider Shakespeare's greatest play, should be the tragedy of an old man who is trapped by his own pride. Lear became the victim of ingratitude from his two older daughters; they manipulated him by pandering to his pride and then used him for their own advantage after he had rejected his loving youngest daughter in their favor. Sadly, like most persons of his time, Shakespeare died quite young, at 54, denied the long life that is common for us today.

Other poets and writers in modern Western literature have held a more happy view of age than Shakespeare. Some have spoken of a good old age, an old age serene and bright, and of people who are beautiful and free in later life. In praise of old age, one writer said older is better in four things: old wood to burn, old wine to drink, old friends to trust, and old authors to read.

William Butler Yeats, however, expressed thoughts more like Shakespeare's as he struggled through negative feelings about old age. A great poet of the late 19th and early 20th centuries, he belonged to the lyrical Irish tradition and was a contemporary of George Bernard Shaw, James Joyce, and Sean O'Casey. As Yeats aged, he became discontented with his inability to maintain emotion in his poetry, and he was distressed that his mental energy exceeded his physical capacity for work. When only 57, he wrote, "I am tired and in a rage at being old. I am all I ever was and much more, but an enemy has bound me and twisted me so I can plan and think as I never could, but no longer achieve all I plan and think." Seeing age as the worst time of life, he wrote scathingly of it, "this caricature, Decrepit age that has been tied to me, As to a dog's tail."

Later he overcame these negative feelings. He lived to age 73, and by his last years, he had come to terms with old age, writing his greatest poetry during his late seniority. Just 3 years before he died, he said in a letter to a friend, "I have no consciousness of age, no sense of declining energy, no consciousness of need for rest. I am unbroken. I repent of nothing but sickness."

He expressed his feelings in a poem which triumphantly declared that one can overcome decrepitude by a spirited intent to live old age well. These were his words:

> An aged man is but a paltry thing,
> A tattered coat upon a stick,
> Unless
> Soul clap its hands and sing, and louder sing
> For every tatter in its mortal dress.

Contrary to Shakespeare and to Yeats's earlier works, a robust vision of age comes to us from a quite unexpected source—the novel *Moll Flanders* written by Daniel Defoe. Also the author of *Robinson Crusoe*, Defoe tells Moll's ribald tale with serious and humanitarian overtones, and he depicts her scandalous early life as one that is redeemed by her old age. He traces her hardships as a prostitute and adventures with dissolute husbands and lovers in an unsavory career that ends with thievery and a sentence to Newgate prison in London when she reaches her 50s. From there, she is shipped to serve an 8-year term in Virginia.

Now in her 60s, Moll is too old for prostitution, but her life becomes vitalized in the New World. She retrieves an adored husband from whom she had been separated by poverty, and this helps to set the stage for a fruitful old age. Together they brave out difficulties to become prosperous plantation owners. Contented, they return to England, where Moll becomes like her mother, who was "a mighty cheerful and good humored old woman."

Almost 70, Moll triumphs over her past. Defoe caps her life with a fine old age and has her close her story with stalwart words. She avows that she and her husband have resolved "to spend the rest of our lives in sincere penitence for the wicked lives we have lived."

An even more affirmative approach to old age appears in Robert Browning's long poem, "Rabbi Ben Ezra." One of the premier poets of Victorian England, Browning was married to dark-haired, dark-eyed Elizabeth Barrett, who composed the superb series of "Sonnets from the Portuguese" that inspired the song "How deep is the ocean, how high is the sky." The two lived a considerable part of their lives in Florence, Italy. Browning died there and was returned to Westminster Abbey in London, to rest in Poet's Corner.

A man of exceptional sensitivity to human character, Browning himself was beginning to perceive his own old age when he set down the reflections of Ben Ezra. Unafraid to face the realities of human experience, the rabbi was a resolute philosopher who found spiritual purification in hardship. Long life, said he, gives one the chance to witness the unfolding of God's plan. If one has experienced pain or failure, then they illuminate one's joys because they provide a contrasting experience. All creatures with feelings go through struggles, the more so human beings because of their superior awareness and understanding. Old age, however, is a period of wisdom and repose, so the rabbi enters upon it with a note of triumph, thinking that early life is but a prelude to the richness of late maturity. He speaks these memorable words:

> Grow old along with me,
> The best is yet to be,
> The last of life,
> For which the first is made.

But many in modern times have failed to maintain such optimistic views, as we can see from the work of Simone de Beauvoir, the most recent literary figure to take on the challenge of aging. De Beauvoir was associated with French existentialist Jean Paul Sartre, and she is most famous for her book *The Second Sex*, which helped to launch the feminist movement worldwide. The title of her book, *La Vieillesse*, means "Age" or "Agedness" in her native French. Though she began by addressing the biological aspects of later life, her major concern was with the social status of old people. She surveyed this subject from the ancient past to the present, and she closed with biographical commentaries on literary and artistic figures in their senior years. As a whole, her work on aging is monumental and has profoundly impressed gerontologists.

In her book, de Beauvoir viewed age as the worst time of life. She painted its portrait in severely gloomy tones—colors so dark that no other writer, not even the spokesperson of Ecclesiastes, has matched them. There is little in her book to offer relief from her perspective of degradation in old age.

She pointed to the tendency of young persons to shrug off old age as a cause for lamentation rather than what it is: the expression of an innocent lack of foresight. She charged that society's failure to make an organized effort to improve the lot of the old resulted from this youthful indifference to age.

But, let her own words and ideas tell her story. After describing how the old in past societies were put to death or expelled to live out their doom alone, she describes old age in human societies as a "natural curse"—implying that apes do better. Men in age are treated as a "sous-homme"—subhuman, she once told a *Newsweek* correspondent. Although older women are not well treated either, she said in her book that their condition is less burdensome than men's because they can offer "bed-service" and housework to their families whereas men can offer nothing.

Early in her book she remarks, "the vast majority of mankind look upon the coming of old age with sorrow and rebellion. It fills them with more aversion than death itself." Later, she intensifies this viewpoint when she observes that age is "a degradation or even a denial of what (previous life) has been." Her despairing prose at times has the ring of poetic ruin. She writes, "When memory decays . . . former happenings . . . sink and vanish in a mocking darkness; life unravels stitch by stitch, leaving nothing but meaningless strands of wool in an old person's hands."

She even manages to extinguish a beam of hope found in the proposition that old age is a period when one may enjoy leisure. "Lessened, impoverished, in exile in the present day, the aged man still remains the man he was"—and so can find some solace in the enjoyment of leisure. No sooner said, she takes away this small hope of relief with the argument that "it is doubtful that the enjoyment of the present moment is very great." In reality, society has allowed old people leisure only to take away the means to enjoy it, she says. "Those who escape utter poverty or pinching want are forced to take care of a body that has grown frail, easily fatigued, often infirm or racked with pain. Immediate pleasures are forbidden or parsimoniously measured out: love, eating, drinking, smoking, sport, walking."

De Beauvoir's approach is just plain wrong. The charge that society causes bodily frailty in age is just one instance of the deliberately negative outlook that shapes her vision. It takes a very considerable stretch of mind to allege that modern society causes physical decline, an almost absurd viewpoint. Life now is longer and healthier than ever before, and only de Beauvoir's melancholy perspective can compel her to say otherwise. De Beauvoir merely proclaimed theories that she spun out of personal observations and supported with slanted research. She did not have access to solid gerontological data or the findings of polls like the GSS, which reveal the greater happiness of older people.

The problem with *La Vieillesse* is not de Beauvoir's skill. She is powerful in both style and thought, a major writer of our century. The trouble is that her book is a social protest written during the 1960s when protests virtually swept the world. Its aim is to indict society, not to inform us about our later years. As a result, she surveys age from a perspective of decline, with little attention to its richness. Her philosophical and historical approach allows her to tell the story from her chosen point of view while overlooking the solid facts uncovered by modern research.

At times, she even twists neutral or affirmative statements that various figures have made about age in order to ring out her constantly plaintive chant. This is especially true in her biographical reviews in later chapters, which contain hardly even a hint of affirmation or success in later life among the cases she cites. They become supporters of her theory rather than independent spokespersons with their own thoughts.

The truth is that one could take the same biographical information about major artistic and literary figures and interpret it in an entirely different light than de Beauvoir does. Most of her examples were known to have been reasonably happy and well adjusted. They took their age in their stride, and they made the best of it. Interviews with de Beauvoir herself in late life show that she did the same. She died in 1986 at age 78 after a long and productive career, which she could look back on in satisfaction, knowing that she had won celebrity worldwide for her important work.

La Vieillesse has a depth and quality that commands attention from any serious reader. It needs a strong antidote, however. Anyone who hopes to enjoy later life has to dwell on the book's more positive aspects (if that is possible) and to venture far beyond it to explore the great reaches of the modern science of maturity, to get real information on the way we experience old age.

Theorists, Researchers, and the Experience of Aging

Our retrospective survey of aging continues with the birth of social gerontology, following on the rise of the modern social sciences. Economics and political science led the way, but it was only when sociology and psychology had broken new ground that the roots of gerontology could flourish. The first of the two sciences had placed the broad picture of human experience at center stage, while the second provided a focus on individuals, which in turn made research on aging feasible.

Interestingly, the issues of the past have continued to maintain an astonishing hold during our scientific era. Even in gerontological research, the dualistic vision of old as the best of times and the worst of times lingers. Lamentations about the hardships of old age abound, and old age is frequently compared, to its detriment, with youth. The difference is that we're making progress today in studying these subjects. The American public needs to know what the researchers are learning. The later years—one third of our lives—deserve this much attention.

HOW DID THE FIRST AMERICAN GERONTOLOGIST VIEW OLD AGE?

"With mixed feelings" is the best answer. G. Stanley Hall was the first modern American psychologist to seriously study later life. President of Clark University in Massachusetts, Hall concentrated most of his inquiries on childhood and adolescence, and he wrote his best-known works in these fields. In spite of this major commitment, he considered the study of middle and later life an important sequel to his first work. He devoted his final explorations to these mature stages, publishing his last book, *Senescence*, in 1922, just 2 years before he died.

Hall was inspired to write the book by a favorable public response to an article on aging he had written for *Atlantic Monthly* in 1921. Hall attached a rather surprising subtitle to his book: "The Second Half of Life." The full title may suggest why the book never received much public acclaim—people probably just didn't like to think they'd be senescent for half their lives. Also, despite his efforts at scientific detachment, Hall viewed old age as decline—the worst time of life. He tried in a late chapter to offset the overall negative tone of the book by exploring the advantages of old age, but the dominant message remained cheerless.

Hall had intended the word "senescence" to have a scientifically neutral tone, just as he had earlier used the word "adolescence" as a scientific classification for the teen period of life. But the unenthusiastic response to his book on aging suggests that the public wasn't ready to accept such a term with neutrality.

Hall had made a sweeping review of past writing and contemporary data, and he questioned people on what later life was like. He ranged over the history of aging, copiously reporting accounts of primitive customs and ethnographies of past tribal and agricultural societies. He examined literary works; presented current American and world statistical data on aging; reviewed the biological, psychological, and medical aspects of growing old; presented his own survey of older persons; and concluded with a chapter on *thanatology* (the study of death).

A thorough scholar, Hall's work merits attention at the very least because he dispelled the myth that the old were universally revered in times past. In doing so, however, he became preoccupied with gruesome accounts that supported his own negative outlook on old age. He accepted uncritically a number of descriptions of barbaric, grossly inhumane treatment of older persons. To him, neglect, disrespect, and outright brutality toward the elderly were typical of past times. Among other things, he reported that the old were deserted and left to die; left to be killed by enemies in times of war; buried alive; slain or burned alive; and, last but not least, put high in trees to be violently shaken to fall to their deaths, torn to pieces, and eaten raw by cannibalistic fellow community members.

Horrible as these examples are, Hall missed the point that customs of *geronticide* (we might call these past practices of elderly euthanasia) took place in a state of society that engaged in *infanticide* (killing of infants) also. The old were not the only victims of cruel treatment. Children were also slain if their social groups couldn't support them. In some societies, children were the sacrificial victims in religious rites, a custom related to the story of Abraham and Isaac in the Bible. Brutal treatment of the elderly was especially likely in nomadic groups, but this was not out of cruelty. It occurred most often during migrations when hunters had to travel to new hunting grounds or herdsmen moved with their animal stock to greener pastures in the spring and fall. The old simply could not keep up on these nomadic journeys and had to be left behind. Geronticide reflected a state of human development when food supplies were limited and social groups simply couldn't afford to support large numbers, particularly the weak and disabled. Hall overlooked these points.

Another instance of Hall's perspective on old age appeared in his comments regarding a questionnaire he administered to residents of an old age home. He resorted to a modern research method by personally going to visit the home. When there he conversed with the "inmates," as he called them, and then gave each a "tiny blue book" in which to record answers to his survey questions. Hall neglected to mention whether the elderly residents may have had difficulty writing answers on the tiny pages in the books.

In any case, Hall viewed their efforts with contempt. He described his subjects as poorly educated, and said, quite unabashedly, that their answers were trivial, tedious, irrelevantly reminiscent. In his view, they simply recorded information about early surroundings, complaints, wishes, and fears. "There was," he concluded, "pathos and pessimism galore, while disciplined tranquility and serenity were rare." Today such views are never found in the frequent research carried on in nursing homes.

Spurred on by his negative reactions to the first survey, Hall decided to administer his questionnaire to a "few score" distinguished older persons who presumably would give more enlightened answers. He knew that this second group was not representative of the elderly population as a whole—they were mainly well-educated, upper-income people of white, Anglo-Saxon descent—but he felt that they would give interesting answers that he could use to make observations about how people age. It's worth looking at these because they represent one of the first systematic efforts to present a scientific picture of the way people experience and lead later life.

The first of the 14 topics in his questionnaire asked at what age his subjects had realized that they were growing old. Based on the responses given, Hall concluded that midlife was the time when individuals usually recognize the onset of old age. He described this period as the "dangerous" age, a time when one might kick over the traces and run off into unknown, untried regions. For women, he said, this age comes in the mid-30s, but for men it comes between 40 and 45—an interesting observation, which no one so far has bothered to disprove.

Does it seem surprising that anyone might date the start of old age from midlife? Well, Hall went even further. He dated the second half of life from this time, and termed existence from then on as "senescence." The very last stage of life he designated as "senectitude," with the additional label of "post-climacteric."

A second series of questions dealt with the physical reasons why the respondents had successfully achieved old age: Was there something about their life-styles, their health regimens, or their reliance on physicians that accounted for their longevity? In general, the respondents ascribed their long life to virtuous behavior in terms that Cicero would have approved. They had followed a course of moderation, avoiding excesses, relying on temperance, and in general living according to the "golden mean"—all with reference to diet, physical and mental hygiene, and the pursuit of personal interests. As to physicians, the survey group said they customarily took care of themselves and resorted to physicians only in emergencies.

Another set of questions addressed the activities and enjoyments of their present lives. One of these concerned their greatest source of pleasure. Most answered "reading." When asked if they preferred the society of children, youths, adults, or of their own age-mates, "more or less than formerly," they stated that they liked the company of their own age group best, though they certainly didn't shun the others. About interest in public and community affairs, some said they were more involved now because they were no longer tied down to business, while others said they had narrowed the scope of their activities.

Hall asked, "What duties do you feel that you still owe either to those about you or to the world?" The respondents generally said they felt a sense of obligation to educate, admonish, and exhort others to better and wiser living. Some of them advised acquiring knowledge. Others recommended cultivating peace and amity. Many urged building up good habits, and leading strenuous, simple, and efficient lives.

One question used imagery, which again revealed Hall's underlying attitude about age—"Did you experience an 'Indian Summer' of revived energy before the winter of age set in?" Describing age as "winter" hardly represents a detached, scientific approach, but the response was interesting. Most said that they had not experienced an Indian summer—continuity was the key note. However, one who was a scientist said he was accomplishing his most productive research during his senior years. Hall added an interpretive comment to the effect that women did experience an Indian summer. They grow serene, liberal, tolerant, and devoted to good causes in their last years, he said.

Three questions called for varieties of reminiscence. Would the respondents want to live the same life over again? All but three gave a resounding "yes!" Were they troubled with regrets for things done or not done by or for them? No, they were not. Hall commented that age is not a time of regrets. It is, he thought, a time of satisfaction in knowing that life could have been worse.

The third question that called for some reminiscence was, "What temptations do you feel, old or new?" Most of the respondents didn't answer the question. Hall commented that they resisted using the questionnaire as an instrument of "confessionalism." Then, as if he suspected that his subjects had sinful urges that they preferred not to reveal, Hall said that everyone carries many secrets to the grave. It is best for them and for the world that they should carry their secrets to the grave, he added omnisciently.

A final pair of questions explored religious attitudes and feelings about death. About religion, the respondents said they now felt less dependent on the clergy, and that the clergy held less appeal for them than when they were younger. They had also become more skeptical about religion as they aged. This finding, Hall thought, was contrary to the conventional idea that people become more religious as they age.

The closing questions addressed concerns about death. "Do you think or worry about dying or the hereafter more or less than formerly?" The answer was that his subjects were not worried about death, nor were they thinking about the hereafter. Hall used his research on adolescents to generalize that the young fear death more than the old. The old don't worry about death, he said—they worry about the next meal. Their belief in an afterlife doesn't increase either. Some, however, feel serene, at rest, and at peace.

Hall has received scant attention from modern gerontology. Possibly the reason is that he generalized too broadly and expressed his prejudices too openly. The 19th century, when he received his training in psychological research in the German universities in Berlin, Heidelberg, and Leipzig, was not a time of inhibitions or restrained observations. Certainty was the tone, whether it was in the thinking of scientific figures like Karl Marx and Sigmund Freud, or of a popular leader like Teddy Roosevelt. All the same, Hall was a harbinger of things to come—his work on aging was prophetic of the growth of gerontology in the second half of the 20th century.

IS AGE A PERIOD OF DECLINE?

The initial answer of some gerontologists was, "Yes." After Hall, studies of aging slowly gained momentum in the 1930s and 1940s. By the end of World War II, the American Psychological Association had established a Division of Later Maturity and Old Age, a move that set the stage for an explosion of research after the White House Conference on Aging, sponsored by President Harry Truman in 1951.

During these early years, one of the challenges was to develop a theory of aging. The first to respond were Elaine Cumming and William Henry, who published their book, *Growing Old*, in 1961. The book described age as a steady and progressive detachment of individuals from active participation in the surrounding world. Individuals decreased their social interaction with others. They reduced the level of activity in whatever functions and roles they had performed—jobs, family life, organization memberships, and so on. They cared less about things, and they were less personally committed to the things they did. Although older people might take on some new activities, they no longer took part in those of their earlier lives.

"Disengagement theory," as it came to be known, seemed plausible on the surface. Cumming and Henry considered it normal to disengage. As a result, they defined successful aging as a process of withdrawal. Society, they said, supports withdrawal by recognizing such roles as widowhood, by providing for retirement, and by freeing older people from the usual social standards. Disengagement was mutual: society withdraws from the individual, and the individual withdraws from society.

They considered this process beneficial. Disengagement was a prelude to death. It prepared the way, and it was inevitable because death is inevitable.

Instead of winning a favorable reception as the first attempt to offer a theory of aging, disengagement touched off a furor in gerontological circles that lasted for 10 years. Today, disengagement theory is barely acknowledged, and no one conducts research under its banner. Why was the theory so controversial?

Basically, the reason was that the authors failed to find out if people who had disengaged were happy. Were they really satisfied with this state of life? According to the theory, disengagement was good, so people who had gone furthest along that path should be happier than people who hadn't gone as far. Gerontologist Bernice Neugarten and her associates decided to test the connection between life satisfaction and disengagement, using information on the same set of persons (older residents of Kansas City) as Cumming and Henry had. Instead of confirming their observations, the Neugarten group found exactly the opposite. People who exhibited the highest levels of disengagement were the *least* satisfied with life.

The idea of disengagement does seem to run counter to intuition. Some people undoubtedly are happier if they seal themselves off like hermits, but energetic old people who remain active and engaged with life—the George Burnses—aren't that unusual. These people just go on and on being themselves, and they're happy that way. Activity theory, mentioned in an earlier chapter, challenged disengagement on precisely this ground.

The dictum of gerontology is that a description of aging as being simple decline doesn't adequately explain the experience of later life. We need to look elsewhere than disengagement theory for answers.

DO OUR PERSONALITIES CHANGE OR STAND STILL IN LATER LIFE?

Most of us think that some sort of change does occur. For example, we usually think that people become more conservative as they grow older. What do the researchers think?

When Bernice Neugarten and her associates reviewed the Kansas City study, they looked at the issue of personality change specifically. They concluded that people become more introverted as they age. She described four kinds of personalities in late life: (1) integrated, (2) defended, (3) passive dependent, and (4) unintegrated. These types could be used to predict the likelihood of a successful old age, but, most important, they all shared a shift toward internality—a heightened level of introspective reflection and interest in things close at hand.

Other researchers, however, have disagreed strongly with the idea that personality changes. Foremost among these are Paul Costa and Robert McCrae, principal investigators at the Personality, Stress, and Coping Section of the Francis Scott Key Medical Center at the National Institute on Aging. They've developed a trait description of personality around three dimensions: (1) neuroticism, (2) extroversion, and (3) openness to experience (designated by the acronym NEO). They claim that once we develop these traits we do not change.

The diagram in Figure 4.1 gives us a look at the NEO model. Note that each major trait is shaped like a diamond (because it rests on the idea that personalities have facets just as diamonds do). The following are the substructures of each trait:

- Neuroticism (N at the top of the diagram) is made up of anxiety, depression, self-consciousness, vulnerability, impulsivity, and hostility.

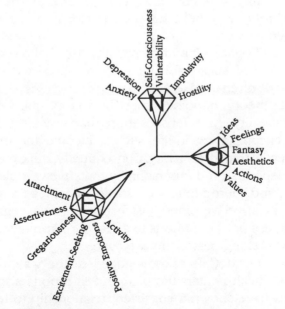

Figure 4.1. The NEO model of personality. (From P. T. Costa, and R. McCrae. "Still Stable After All These Years: Personality as the Key to Some Issues in Adulthood and Aging." In P. B. Baltes, and O. G. Brim, Jr. (Editors) *Life–Span Development and Behavior* (vol. 3). San Diego, CA: Academic Press. 1980.)

- Openness (O on the right-hand side) is made up of ideas, feelings, fantasy, aesthetics, actions, and values.

- Extroversion (E at the bottom) includes attachment, assert-iveness, gregariousness, excitement-seeking, positive emotions, and activity.

(The authors might have made this a more appealing model of personality if they had reversed the order of the letters and put neuroticism at the bottom rather than at the top. The resulting acronym, EON, wouldn't have been too bad either.)

In opposing the idea of change in personality, Costa and McCrae have sharply attacked the developmental school of psychologists (discussed later in this chapter), labeling the notion of maturational change as the "El Dorado of developmental psychologists." Contrary to the developmental school, they argue that personality is made up of a set of dispositions that endure throughout life—a theory that conforms with the ideas of Sigmund Freud, who held that one's personality becomes fixed by the teen years.

The trait conception of personality has vital consequences for the issue of successful aging. A sense of well-being, or happiness, is often used as an indicator of such success. Accord-ing to trait theory, happiness must be a consequence of one's fixed personality characteristics more than anything else. Even practical circumstances in life, such as income and friends, are less influential than personality. Consequently, our experience of old age depends on the personality traits we've developed in early life, and there's little we can do to achieve a successful maturity. Relative happiness just happens to us, regardless of circumstances or of our efforts to affect our happiness, depend-ing on the lifelong personality we have.

Costa and McCrae acknowledge that the way individuals report their health enters the picture. Self-reports about health conditions have shown a consistent relationship to feelings of well-being. Specifically, individuals who say their health is poor also report low levels of well-being. But self-reports of health, Costa and McCrae have found, are closely linked with neuroticism. Someone who's spent a lifetime as a neurotic is likely to experience more acute feelings of ill health than someone who's a happy extrovert. It's really one's degree of neuroticism that accounts for feelings of health, not health itself. Their conclusion, then, is that a happy extroverted type of person will probably feel less of a sense of ill health and will age successfully also.

Costa and McCrae, working with David Arenberg and other associates, made an interesting elaboration of their views on the stability of personality traits. They examined the "subjective well-being" of a group of 5000 persons over a number of years (longitudinally). Parallel to the idea of happiness, subjective well-being is often included in studies that assess the quality of life in terms of the relationship between the individual's subjective feelings and her or his measurable affective states such as freedom from health worry; energy level; interest-filled life; cheerful mood; and emotional and behavioral control.

The study found *no* decline in levels of subjective well-being during mature adulthood. The authors observed that the quality of people's feelings about life neither improve nor worsen with the years, and that individuals quickly adapt to whatever circumstances they find. Still more, their data showed that older people do not become hypochondriacs, as some researchers have charged, even when health problems actually increase with age. Psychological well-being, they concluded, is relatively free from objective life circumstances—once an optimist always an optimist, according to Costa and McCrae.

IS THERE REALLY A MIDLIFE CRISIS?

As part of their research on trait stability, Costa and McCrae looked at evidence concerning the midlife crisis. This, they said, had attained the status of a folk concept, "freely invoked by novelists, commentators, and neighborhood gossips." Hall had expressed a variant of the idea when he asserted that midlife was the time when people first sense the onset of age—the "dangerous" age, as he called it.

To conduct this research, Costa and McCrae used an inventory they had developed by analyzing the content of writings about the midlife crisis. The kinds of qualities that appeared in their inventory included inner turmoil, inner orientation, change in time perspective, sense of failing power, marital dissatisfaction, life viewed as tedious and boring, disharmony with offspring, sense of separation from parents, and rise in repressed parts of the self. They used the inventory in interviews with a sample of 233 men ranging in age from 35 to 79 years.

What did they conclude following the interviews? Few of their men showed any clear sign of a crisis at *any* age. More importantly, they found no relationship at all between midlife and crisis. In fact, they made a specific statistical test for such a relationship, and found that it went in the wrong direction! There was less of a sense of crisis during middle age than there was at other times!

Struck by the importance of this finding, Costa and McCrae decided to repeat their study with another group of men. This time, they examined a second set of 315 men also ranging from 33 to 79 years of age. Once again they found no relationship between midlife and crisis, leading them to conclude with mild sarcasm that, "The mid-life crisis, whatever it was, did not appear to be confined to mid-life."

This evidence against a male midlife crisis obtains confirmation from the GSS, which is a national sample that accurately reflects the American population. The relevant question is the one concerning happiness discussed previously. The percentage of men in the midlife years (ages 35–44 for our purposes) who say they are "very happy" is 31%. That's higher than that for the 18- to 24- and 25- to 34-year-old age groups, which each report about 25% "very happy" respondents.

Not to neglect women, the GSS shows that 34% of the 35- to 44-year-old women report being "very happy," a percentage that matches the average for the more than 13,000 women surveyed so far. Not even those in the menopausal and so called "empty nest" years, 45–54 and 55–64, report lower levels of happiness. In general, happiness increases throughout life for both women and men.

DO OUR PERSONALITIES CONTINUE TO DEVELOP AS WE AGE?

Some gerontologists think that Costa and McCrae's trait theory leaves us with a dilemma because it doesn't account for all the facts. It's obvious to anyone that the young and the old differ in the way that they think and behave. It's equally obvious to us as individuals that we are not the same persons we were even a few short years ago—people in their 30s and 40s know they have changed dramatically since their childhood and teen years.

It is just this type of difference that Aristotle sought to describe and explain more than 2000 years ago. These differences provoke some to think that old age is the best time of life and others to believe the opposite. We know that old age differs from youth. But, precisely how does it differ? That is the question.

Stability of personality traits seems to tell us that we don't develop. We are doomed, prisoners of our personalities laid down by heredity and the events that shaped our early lives. We experience personal histories of inner feelings quite beyond our control, neurotic or extroverted, happy or unhappy, condemned to play out an unavoidable destiny.

Another theory of human experience, however, holds that development occurs throughout our lifetimes. It was first set forth systematically by Charlotte Buhler, a Viennese-trained psychoanalyst who joined the faculty of the University of Southern California, the location of the Andrus Gerontology Center, during the 1930s. Her idea was that there are progressive steps to human life, a view that was first suggested in the biblical book of Ecclesiastes. G. Stanley Hall had suggested the same idea in modern terms when he briefly sketched out five periods: childhood; adolescence—from "puberty to nubility"; middle life, which he called "the prime"; senescence; and senectitude, or "old age proper."

Buhler's theory was especially noteworthy because she tied the phases of life to biological development, a kind of linkage that later fell under a cloud when social scientists came to reject past ideas about biologically inherited racial superiority and biologically determined social roles for men and women. She defined five periods in life: (1) birth to age 15, with a biology of "progressive growth"; (2) age 15 to 25, a time of continued growth with ability to reproduce biologically; (3) the first phase of adulthood from 25 to 45, characterized biologically by stability in growth; (4) the second phase of adulthood from 45 to 65, with loss of reproductive ability; (5) the last period of life, from 65 on, with regressive growth and biological decline.

In later statements of her theory, Buhler emphasized the relationship of biological growth to the task of setting goals. She said that we only begin to determine goals for ourselves following childhood, so childhood can be described as a period of preparation and experimentation. During the first phase of adulthood, individuals complete goal development and settle on a specific set of purposes. The second phase of adulthood is one of assessment, when individuals evaluate their success or failure in striving to reach their goals. In the last phase of life, there's not much left to accomplish, so we experience either a sense of fulfillment or failure. This phase is spent in continuing previous activities or in returning to the "need-satisfying orientations" of childhood.

Buhler emphasized the parallel between the biological and psychological realms of life. The two fit together. In the biological area, we experience a pattern of physical growth, stability, and final decline. Psychologically, we follow a parallel pattern characterized by expansion, culmination, and contraction in setting and accomplishing goals. She also believed that biological change can sometimes outstrip psychological change, just as it had for William Butler Yeats, who was still growing as a poet at a time when he was declining physically.

Unlike some stage theorists, Buhler did not rigidly divide life into patterns that were universally experienced by everyone. Rather, she recognized individual variations. This was especially true, she thought, with regard to mental powers, where some people have achieved a peak quite late in life. For her, stages of development represented a broad outline of how we change, and biology contributes a general structure to this experience.

DOES GROWING OLD CAUSE US TO EXPERIENCE A PSYCHOLOGICAL CRISIS LATE IN LIFE?

Costa and McCrae thought not, but Erik Erikson, probably the best known of the developmental psychologists, holds a different view. For him, crisis occurs whenever we have to meet major challenges in life. It is a fact of all stages of human development. We are challenged to grow at every phase of our lives, and age is no different in this respect than any other time. Growth, not decline, is the main issue in late life. We need to change in order to meet new conditions and experiences, whatever they may be.

Erikson was trained in Vienna like Charlotte Buhler and came to the United States in the 1930s where he had an outstanding professional career. During the 1960s, he captured the public mind with his book *Identity and the Youth Crisis*, a work that boldly proclaimed, right in the teeth of the youth rebellion, that young people experience an "identity crisis." His reason for describing this period as a time of crisis? The young face a severe challenge in establishing their psychological identities, and they go through a personal rebellion in the process.

What are the challenges of the years after youth? The first is to achieve "generativity," which means becoming capable of producing something that will last beyond one's own lifetime. Most often, persons accomplish this by raising a family or achieving success in an occupation, but creativity in the arts and altruistic service to others also represent possibilities. According to Erikson, this stage of life begins quite early and lasts longer than any of the others—from ages 35 to 55. Failure to achieve generativity results in an impotent slide into stagnation—a state of boredom, psychological poverty, and sometimes excessive concern about physical and psychological decline.

Each stage is turbulent, a difficult turning point in the jungle of experience. All changes are fraught with the risk of failure, but a successfully negotiated change creates the desirable inner quality of the new stage, whether it be identity, intimacy, generativity, or some other quality. Some individuals only partially accomplish a developmental task at a particular stage, but they manage to struggle on in spite of it.

On the other hand, people who totally fail to achieve a particular goal of development face serious problems. They collapse toward the opposite pole, and they experience acute difficulties in meeting the challenges of later times.

Erikson's most significant contribution to the study of aging lies in his description of the eighth, and final, stage of life. In his view, this is not a period of motionless stability, nor is it one of automatic decline. It is a time of growth like all the others. We continue to go forward during our last years.

Whereas generativity moves outward socially, our final stage of growth becomes more internal and personal. External accomplishments have little importance at this point. The task is to achieve a sense of inner integrity, of wholeness.

During this stage, we experience retirement and recognize the finitude of life, dual events that provoke individuals to retrospectively examine and evaluate their lives. What have I done? Was it good or worthwhile? Cicero had asked himself this question and had answered it affirmatively. A successful life review results in accepting the life we've lived.

This stage is as affirmative as any other. In fact, it is the fulfillment and crown of the seven previous stages. A person who experiences a sense of integrity feels that life has had meaning and value. Failure to grow toward integrity causes collapse toward the opposite condition—despair. It results in the desolate cry of Ecclesiastes: Existence has no meaning. The post–World War II existentialist movement in Europe illustrates the state of despair that Erikson described. Life had become absurd, even sickening. It had been a waste, and it should have been different.

Erikson developed his theory of critical stages in personality development from his psychoanalytic background and from observations made during conferences with his patients. His anecdotal method of study does not satisfy psychologists who demand rigorous proofs from statistical studies or strictly controlled experiments. In fact, Erikson's theory has proven difficult to translate into research models, and this type of failure accounts in part for the contempt exhibited toward developmental psychology by Costa and McCrae.

All the same, these criticisms need not obviate Erikson's thinking. There simply have not been enough reports about people who have successfully negotiated the changes of later life. What about Mary Brasch, who graduated from college and received her bachelor's degree at age 87? What about Grandma Moses, who only began painting at 78 and was a smashing hit in her 80s? Are these persons rare exceptions? Or do they demonstrate one kind of resolution of a normal crisis of later life? Did a psychological crisis and a life review precede these remarkable accomplishments? Is late life a unique stage in which learning, creativity, and new adventures not only are possible but also become sheer pleasure as never before? We don't know yet.

Whatever the validity of the criticisms, therapists and counselors of the elderly, faced by the practical task of helping people who do experience psychological crises, have successfully adapted therapy to older adults. Among these therapies is a structured procedure for review of one's life. A variant, known as reminiscence therapy, allows a leisurely ramble through one's past. Both undoubtedly owe a debt to Erikson. While we may not have hard evidence to support Erikson's idea of crises and growth at all times of life, his work remains a valuable contribution that individuals can look to as they go about the task of achieving a successful old age.

WHAT HAVE DEVELOPMENTAL PSYCHOLOGISTS SPECIALIZING IN AGING THOUGHT ABOUT LATE LIFE?

They hold the view that personality is not just a set of traits that remain stable throughout life. Rather, growth continues even to the time of death. Although they don't deny the existence of personality traits, the developmentalists insist that we constantly remake ourselves. One approach to describing this process starts with the proposition that we interpret our experiences in order to give meaning to them.

This branch of lifetime development theory emphasizes the idea of the *self*, a concept that grew out of a tradition shared by both sociology and psychology and that dates back to the work of American psychologist William James in the 1890s. Linda Breytspraak of the University of Missouri in Kansas City explored the concept of the self in age in her book, *The Development of the Self in Later Life*.

What is the self? According to one definition, the *self* is the individual's conscious experience of a distinct, personal identity that is separate from all other persons and things. Perhaps not unlike the idea of the *soul*, the concept bears similarity to the term *inner being* referred to in the New Testament portion of the Bible.

The self is what makes it possible to judge our own appearances critically when standing in front of a mirror. It's as if we were other persons looking at ourselves. We rely on the self when we evaluate our behavior as if we were our own parents. We resort to it when we attempt to control the impression we make on others, when we argue with ourselves, admonish ourselves, or feel guilt.

It is through the self that we are capable of carrying on a dialogue within ourselves as if we were two different people talking back and forth to one another—sometimes with odd consequences if we do it out loud. At times, this inner experience of the self seems quite beyond our own control, as when we feel inexplicably and buoyantly happy. Equally, it can command us when we become inconsolable, bowed down by an inward wound caused by the death of someone we love. Karen Horney, one of the distinguished proponents of the psychoanalytic school of psychology, once described the "real" self in this way:

> The palpitating inward life, the engenderer of spontaneity of all types of feelings, the source of spontaneous interest and energies, and the part of the self that wants to expand and grow and fulfill itself. The real self at its best enables one to make decisions and to assume responsibility for them, and it leads to a genuine integration and wholeness of the person.

A key feature of the self is that it is the instrument through which we attach meaning to the events of life. We are not passive or submissive like a clam resting on the ocean floor. We carry around meanings within ourselves, and we use them to interpret events. For a newborn baby, most events have no meaning whatever even when they register in the senses. A mature person, however, creates meaning out of the flow of events. Each of us uniquely experiences life because we attach meanings to happenings. We also negotiate with events and people, and then we act as we see fit.

A corollary of the idea of an active, "palpitating," self is the fact of continuing growth over the entire lifetime. There is no period when one comes to a standstill or falls into total decline (except, of course, if mental function becomes inhibited). If nothing else, we struggle to maintain our self-consistency, our self-esteem, our wholeness. According to self psychologists, this may explain the consistent research finding that the old experience greater self-esteem than the young.

The idea of continuing lifetime development has been expounded effectively by psychologist Carol Ryff of the University of Wisconsin in Madison, who has done outstanding work on research techniques to measure developmental phenomena. Ryff has composed a model of personality growth that brings together the work of an impressive list of psychologists in the fields of lifespan development, personal growth, and mental health. They include figures known to the public—among them Carl Jung, Gordon Allport, Abraham Maslow, Carl Rogers, and Erik Erikson. Others, such as M. Powell Lawton, James Birren, Charlotte Buhler, and Marie Jahoda are better known to gerontologists than to the general public. Ryff identifies six themes that appear repeatedly in the work of these individuals: self-acceptance; positive relations with others; autonomy; environmental mastery; purpose in life; and personal growth.

The key idea for us is *personal growth*, but because its meaning depends in part on the other concepts, two or three that may have an ambiguous meaning require prior explanation. The first of these is *autonomy,* which refers to a dual set of abilities: (1) the capacity to resist social pressures; and (2) the power to judge oneself by personal standards rather than by seeking approval from others. The same kind of idea surfaced years ago in David Reisman's *The Lonely Crowd*, where he described persons as "inner directed" or "outer directed." An autonomous person is inner directed.

Environmental mastery refers to an executive process in which a person manages a complex array of activities—family life, work, personal relations, and so forth. *Purpose in life* has a reasonably clear meaning, but it is noteworthy because it has recently attracted attention as a possible measure of well-being in late life. Researchers are testing the possibility that loss of purpose may occur near the close of life and could foretell the approach of death.

Ryff observes that *personal growth* includes the qualities of generativity and integrity described by Erikson. Besides these, it includes openness to experience and a willingness to develop, features identified by Carl Rogers. Well known for his nondirective counseling technique (in which a therapist assists a client to work through a problem by exhibiting an affirming attitude toward the client's statements), Rogers held that those who continue to grow will experience positive mental health and a greater richness of life. Ryff notes that we can realize ourselves by "losing ourselves"—in work, play, contemplation, and loyalty to others. All of these can produce personal growth.

The importance of each of these six themes may differ at various times of life, she says. Environmental mastery, for example, may climax during the middle years when one is employed, raising a family, or building resources for retirement. The need for positive relations with others peaks for most people at the time of choosing a marriage partner. Purpose in life may become most crucial at retirement, when it's necessary to find new goals. The several themes, says Ryff, may also have different consequences for the sexes throughout life—men may achieve autonomy more easily than women, and women positive relations with others more easily than men.

Ryff vigorously defends developmental psychology against Costa and McCrae's criticisms, and she counters by pointing to flaws in their research methods and the concept of traits. It's her own approach to developmental theory, however, that's of most importance. Instead of concentrating on traits such as neuroticism, she looks at each individual's actual life experience to explain success or failure in aging. She searches for root causes in day-to-day events that could affect our inner being. Her idea is that a life plagued by misfortune will cause a person to become neurotic, whereas a successful life will produce feelings of well-being. Both neuroticism and well-being grow out of the same thing—previous life experience. They are not fixed or permanent traits of personality. According to Ryff, it is the flow of experience in life that constantly challenges us to grow. Personal development must occur at all times.

HOW DO WE EXPERIENCE LIFE AS WE GROW OLD?

When all the debates are set to rest, what do they tell us about the way we experience aging? On the one hand, Costa and McCrae have shown that our fundamental personality traits remain stable. This is a comforting thought. We do not undergo major changes in later life. We don't shift from optimism to pessimism, or vice versa. We don't suddenly trade one kind of self for another.

This news about the stability of personality is good. There's no evidence that people generally go through an inner collapse in later life. Rather, our inner being has strength—it is something that we can count on. Our personalities in old age are probably as comfortable as an old shoe.

But developmental theory also makes sense, so why not accept the ideas of both schools of thought? The two may actually be reconciled with one another because they address different aspects of personality. One is concerned with traits and the other with growth within our inner selves. Development of the inner being doesn't necessarily require a change in personality traits, but rather continued growth, whatever one's traits might be. There's no necessary conflict between these theories.

Besides, Costa and McCrae have left an opening for the idea of development. They say that trait theory is most useful for broad descriptions. It is of little use in predicting the unique responses of an individual at a particular time. If this is so, it's likely that we continue to grow in our psychological capacities throughout life without altering our core personality traits. We may retain stability in our personalities but we don't stand still. We learn new tricks. Our experience, whatever our traits may be, flows into new channels. The experience of life, the new stages in the cycle, serve as catalysts. Whatever our personalities, we have to rise to new challenges, and this adds new dimensions to our inner being.

The idea of stability leavened by change seems reasonable. Old age is like any other period of life: Older persons need to adjust to retirement and other circumstances, but all periods challenge us to adapt and adjust. Just as infants use their existing personality resources to communicate, despite their inability to use words, so the old call up from their personalities whatever resources they possess to deal with change.

Sometimes the process may be stressful, as the rise of male suicide in old age attests. But even then, the occurrence of suicide is very rare—less than one-tenth of 1% of the over-65 male population—and the vast majority remain serene. Studies have claimed, in fact, that serenity is the characteristic feature of later life.

Let's summarize what we've learned from the GSS and from these two psychological theories to describe the way that we experience later life. First, the experience is positive. A large percentage of the old are happy. Their self-esteem is high as compared to other age groups. They maintain good morale. They're equipped with well-established personality traits on which they can draw as they continue to grow and develop.

Beyond these basic considerations, we can look once more to Linda Breytspraak's review of research on the self, which cites a number of studies of the way that the old experience life. One of these based on a nationwide survey directly contradicts the 2000-year-old observation of Aristotle: It shows that the old are more likely than the young to be concerned with morality, ethics, and virtue as elements of inner being. Younger people stress achievement in the occupations and family roles rather than these deeper qualities.

Some recent national studies using adjective checklists to

record inner feelings have disclosed remarkable findings about the strength and composure of old people. When respondents fill out these checklists, they pick out adjectives that they feel apply to themselves. We report Breytspraak's summary of these studies because they throw further light on the way that people experience later life.

In spite of less concern for work, older people feel more competent than the young. They sense that they have the ability to get things done, and they describe themselves as hardworking, well-organized, tough, strong, and intelligent.

One might not expect it, but young people are more likely than the old to describe themselves as absentminded. Besides that, they confess to being disorderly, lazy, and restless. Older people are more likely to have a sense of self-control and self-reliance. They're less likely to describe themselves as timid, helpless, indecisive, and dependent.

In social situations, the old experience less discomfort. The young experience more inner turmoil than the old. They're more likely to use such adjectives as "emotional," "shy," "frustrated," "nervous," and "embarrassed" about themselves.

The old feel less vulnerable and less of a need to manipulate and misrepresent. Again, contrary to Aristotle, the old are less compelled to be guileful, shrewd, dogmatic, and sarcastic. They express thoughts that show more socioemotional support for others.

Within themselves, the old have an overall sense of effectiveness in achieving goals. They experience a definite sense of ease in the presence of others. Poor health, as we have seen, can inhibit the sense of inner well-being, but it need not obliterate it. The old successfully overcome contrary external circumstances.

In sum, these studies reveal an unexpectedly high level of psychological strength in late life. We can look forward to old age, and that's good news. Has this review of modern theories and research on the experience of aging seemed to close with a too-glowing account? Does it seem overstated? Overblown? Too good to be true? Remember that this glowing account was based on real surveys of real subjects of every age. Further, we can test its credibility as we pursue our journey through later life.

Conservatism, Politics, Religion, and Sex

Not long ago, economist Robert Samuelson asked an intriguing question in his column for *Newsweek* magazine: "Will older Baby Boomers mean more conservative politics and less economic vitality?" With this question, Samuelson ventured into one of the oldest debates known to humankind—do persons become more conservative as they grow old? Samuelson wasn't convinced that they do. Samuelson's answer: "Don't be so sure."

The differences between the young and the old have gripped the minds of sages and ordinary mortals at least since the time of Aristotle. It's generally assumed that differences do exist, that they are substantial, and that they influence social events as well as personal behavior.

During the 1960s, for instance, the Baby Boom generation ballooned the youth component of our population to 40% of the total, and gave us the Woodstock concert, the age of Aquarius, nationwide demonstrations against the Viet Nam War, and a hippie life-style in the Haight-Ashbury district in San Francisco. Commentators on the social scene concluded that these events showed profound differences between the generations, and they quickly contrived a sobriquet to describe the supposed phenomenon: "the generation gap."

The idea behind the generation gap is that people grow more conservative as they age. Presumably, they join the Republican party, become neoconservatives, staunchly support their church or temple, condemn permissive sex, lose their sense of adventure and inventiveness, and so forth.

But, do older people really stand so far apart from other age groups? Do they think like everyone else on some things? Are they more liberal than others in some cases? Does conservatism start earlier in life than we think?

Possibly, too, the conservatism of the old is more of a cohort difference than one of chronological age (see Chapter 2 for more on this). Maybe conservatism in older Americans reflects the times when they grew up rather than their years of age. They may have started life with more conservative attitudes than the younger generation today. If so, it may not be that increasing age has raised the level of conservatism, but that social attitudes have become more liberal. As serious students of aging, we have to look at the real facts and accept what they tell us one way or the other.

In the past, the common opinions and theories rested on general observations, but no one had the kinds of facts required for scientific proof. Until now, we haven't been able to go much beyond good guesses, hunches, and speculation when it comes to describing the characteristics of older people. Does the idea of a generation gap hold up to close study?

Today, we can test the longstanding suppositions about differences between youth and age because the GSS gives us the hard data to do so. Even more, we can make some realistic predictions about how things will be in the future. In 30–40 years, the Baby Boomers will have reached their seniority, and the population picture of the 1960s will reverse—the 50+ generation will constitute about 40% of our nation's inhabitants. After 2030, we'll hit the peak of the Aging Boom. Will Robert Samuelson's optimistic suggestion, "Don't be so sure," prove true, or does some other more gloomy scenario lie ahead?

We return once more to presenting detailed statistics because this is the best way to see the facts for themselves and to answer the following questions: Do older people describe themselves as conservatives more often than the young? Do they differ in political outlook? If so, do the old exert a strong political influence that's opposed to the will of younger people? Do older people become more religious as they age? Are they more moralistic and opposed to permissive sex? Do their experiences and feelings in regard to specific problems, such as crime, differ from those of the young? Answers to these questions give us a clear picture on the issue of conservatism, help us to understand how people experience age, and provide a basis for predicting the future.

DO PEOPLE BECOME MORE CONSERVATIVE AS THEY GROW OLDER?

We look at this question in a number of ways, beginning with the way that older people describe their general political leanings. When interviewers for the GSS bring up the subject of politics, they show the respondents a card with a scale on it and ask; "We hear a lot of talk these days about liberals and conservatives. I'm going to show you a seven-point scale on which the political views that people might hold are arranged from extremely liberal to extremely conservative. Where would you place yourself on this scale?"

For our purposes, we don't need to know more than the broad categories that people have checked off, so we've grouped the answers into conservative, moderate (or middle-of-the-road), and liberal. When we look at the results, we see at once that the older generation is indeed more conservative than the younger one. As age advances, fewer people describe themselves as liberal, while more describe themselves as conservative.

Because this pattern shows up repeatedly in this chapter, we now give the results in Table 5.1, to show a clear picture of the trend. (We omit the "No Answer/Don't Know" column in this particular table because it doesn't change the pattern. This means, though, that the figures associated with each age won't add to 100%.)

The columns labeled "Age" and "Conservative" on the left

Table 5.1. Which Age Group Is Most Politically Conservative?

Age	Conservative	Moderate	Liberal
18–24	22.4%	37.1%	36.6%
25–34	26.5%	37.2%	32.9%
35–44	34.7%	35.8%	25.8%
45–54	36.7%	39.6%	19.3%
55–64	35.3%	41.2%	18 %
65–74	33.6%	38.5%	20.2%
75–84	33.6%	37.1%	17.8%
85+	34.7%	38.3%	10.8%

side of the table show that at ages 18–24 and 25–34, only about one quarter (22 and 27%) of the respondents say that they're conservative. After those two age groupings, the figure for conservatives leaps to 35% at ages 35–44. After that age group, the proportion of conservatives stays just about the same, with minor fluctuations, as we go up the age scale. The peak percentage of conservatives shows up at ages 45–54, with close to 37%, but it drops again and closes at about 35% at age 85+.

When we look at the figures closely, we see that the trend toward conservatism starts at ages 35–44! In fact, the very old are not even the most conservative. It's the 45- to 54-year-olds who show the most conservatism, people whom we often call "middle-aged!" This suggests that we may have to revise our thinking about the age in life when people become conservative.

Look at it from the other end of the spectrum—the liberal end. It's definitely the young who most often describe themselves as liberal—at 18–24 about 37% do so, and at 25–34, 33% do too.

The largest single drop in the percentage calling themselves liberal comes at ages 35–44, when there's a fall of over 7 percentage points from the 25- to 34-year-olds. At 35–44, too, there seems to be a switch toward conservatism because there's a jump of more than 8 percentage points from the previous group who give themselves the conservative label. The proportion who adopt the liberal label declines over life, and the decline begins quite early.

When we look at the moderate column, one other thing becomes clear. It shows that the largest proportion of people at all ages describe themselves as "moderate." At age 18–24, 37.1% call themselves "moderate," while 36.6% describe themselves as "liberal" and 22.4% say "conservative." Later, when conservatism reaches a peak of 36.7% at ages 45–54 and liberalism drops to 19.3%, the proportion of moderates stands at 39.6%

At most later ages, the preponderance of moderates persists. In fact, we can even suggest that if there's a shift away from a liberal outlook, it is toward a moderate one. This seems true because the highest ratios of moderates appear in the older age groups (45–54 and up) with only one exception.

Careful observers may see other facets to this table, but one thing seems clear: It's wrong to conclude that we steadily become increasingly conservative in our political views as we age.

To summarize, we learn from this table that the largest proportion of older people think of themselves as moderates. Any shift toward conservatism starts in midlife. It is the middle-aged population that most often describes itself as conservative, not the oldest generation. Let's test these preliminary findings by examining the way that persons at various ages identify with political parties.

DOES PARTY AFFILIATION SHIFT FROM DEMOCRAT TO REPUBLICAN AS PERSONS GROW OLDER?

Most of us would agree that the Democratic party in national level politics favors more liberal social policies than does the Republican party. The traditional view that older people are conservatives suggests, therefore, that the elderly would probably affiliate with the Republican party more often than do the younger age groups. But, do they? And, if they do, does this fact support the idea of increasing conservatism with age?

The GSS figures do indeed show a higher proportion of Republicans at the more advanced ages. The peak Republican affiliation comes after age 75 (41% at 75–84 and 47% at 85+), with a low of 29% at 25–34. The high point in Democratic party affiliation comes at ages 25–34, when 53% say they're Democrats. The low for the Democrats is at 85+, when 41% adhere to the Democratic party label.

These differences in party identification at various ages, however, may have very little to do with age itself. Though the GSS figures are accurate, they could represent either a cohort phenomenon or a reflection of the social class standing of the older age group. As a cohort, people over 85 were born around the time of the very popular Republican president Teddy Roosevelt. They reached maturity when the Republicans won most presidential contests, before the Great Depression. It's also known that most people who affiliate with the Republican party come from above-average income groups. Those who survive to very old age also usually come from above-average income groups, so many of the elderly could have been lifelong Republicans.

Further, when we look at the statistics on 18- to 24-year-old party affiliation, we discover something even more interesting. We see more evidence that increasing age may have little to do with party affiliation. At this young age, a smaller percentage (49%) are Democrats than at any age until 75–84 (again 49%). From ages 25 to 74, the majority (about 55%) of the population interviewed for the GSS thinks of itself as affiliated with the Democratic party. Not so the very young. If there's a tight link between age and political liberalism, then the highest level of affiliation with the Democratic party would occur among the youngest Americans. But it doesn't!

Some might argue that the 18- to 24-year-olds haven't made up their minds yet. That seems unlikely, however, because only about 4% of them answer the question on party preference with the "No Answer/Don't Know" response. Besides, only 18% specify a preference for "Independent" (unaffiliated with any party).

The youngest age group, at 49% Democrat, definitely stands in contrast to their nearest cohorts—most people in the GSS (55%) say they're Democrats and appear to stay that way throughout their lives. At age 75+, however, the population seems to have more in common with the 18- to 24-year-olds than with the ages between. Some years ago, a political scientist named Angus Campbell observed that people may form commitments to a political party when young and remain with them throughout their lives. The GSS figures confirm this view. Doesn't this confound the view that people become *more* conservative as they grow older?

HOW ABOUT SPECIFIC POLITICAL ISSUES—ARE OLDER PERSONS MORE CONSERVATIVE THAN THE YOUNG?

Generally, the answer is no, but it depends a little on the particular issue we're discussing. The GSS includes questions on 15 specific areas of the federal government policy. These address such things as space exploration, arms, foreign aid, education, welfare, health insurance, and improvement of the living conditions of black persons.

The GSS interviewers open their questions on specific political issues this way: "We're faced with many problems in this country, none of which can be solved easily or inexpensively. I'm going to name some of these problems, and for each one I'd like you to tell me whether you think we're spending too much money on it, too little money, or about the right amount." They then name the issue and follow up by asking, "Are we spending too much, too little, or about the right amount," about each of the 15 issues. (As you look at the figures, keep in mind that there are three possible choices. If the answers were evenly divided, each choice would get about one-third, or 33%. Any choice that gets more than 33%, then, is attracting stronger support than we might expect.)

The answers to these questions further confound the theory of increasing conservatism with age. For 10 of the 15 issues, there's almost *no difference* between the answers of any age group. Neither the young nor the old appear more liberal or conservative than the other.

The largest proportion of each group takes a similar stand on spending for each of the following: space exploration (55% say "too much"); crime (65% "too little"); drug control (55% "too little"); helping black Americans (42% "about right"); spending on arms (40% "about right"); foreign aid (70% "too much");

welfare (45% "too much"); national highways (average of 46% "about right"); social security (average of 57% "about right"); national parks (57% "about right"). Every age group expresses similar views about these 10 key political issues.

Differences among the age groups do arise in regard to four subjects: education, the environment, aid for cities, and national health insurance. (Mass transportation represents a special case, which we discuss here later.) It's a good idea to start with education because many people assume that the generations differ strongly on this subject. They picture the older generation as voting down school budgets over the pained outcry of young parents.

The subject of education shows the greatest contrast between young and old, but the difference between them centers on a question of whether we're spending enough or spending too little. Very few people at any age think we spend too much on education, and a third or more at each age feels that spending is about right. Differences arise regarding whether there is too little spending. Here, 60% of the under-55 age groups think we spend too little, while only 36% of the 65+ think so. The 55- to 64-year-olds fall between these two groups, with 46% saying too little is spent. Evidently, older Americans support present levels of spending for education, but they may be more reluctant than the young to spend more.

National health insurance exhibits somewhat less of a difference between the age groups. More than 60% of the younger ages feel that too little is being spent, whereas only about 45% of the 65+ generation think so. This difference most likely reflects appreciation of the federally insured Medicare program by older persons—a program that isn't available to most people under age 65. The generations probably don't oppose one another. It's just that the elderly feel some degree of satisfaction, whereas the young feel some dissatisfaction.

Of the 18- to 24-year-olds, 73% also feel that we spend too little on the environment, while only 34% of the over-65s share this view. Still, the older group doesn't condemn environmental spending. Of the three possible answers to the question ("too much," "too little," "about right"), the largest segment of the older population (38%) thinks that spending on the environment is about right. About 35% favor more spending, and fewer than 20% want less.

As to spending to improve American cities, close to half (45%) of the youngest age group feels that the level is too low. Only 27% of the 65+ share this view, but 27% of the older generation don't want to commit themselves—they give no answer or say they don't know.

What can we conclude about these four instances of differences between the generations? First, they don't show strong evidence of increasing conservatism with age. Second, they suggest that generational differences of opinion on public issues primarily express the special requirements and perspectives of each stage of life. If age alone dictated our political opinions and made us liberal or conservative, the differences among the generations would stand out more sharply and cut across all issues, not just these four.

We can use the idea of particular requirements and perspectives at different stages of life to explain the differences that do arise among the generations. The concern of the young for the environment and the cities probably reflects a heightened consciousness brought about by studies in school. For national health insurance, the reason for the difference seems obvious— the elderly benefit from the Medicare program, but most young persons don't. When it comes to education, the elderly have passed beyond the years of child-rearing when the cost of educating children is important and sometimes burdensome. Besides, the older generation grew up at a time when education was less widespread and necessary. Overall, life experience and cohort effects rather than chronological age itself seem to explain differences in attitudes.

Of the 15 questions on political spending, the last is the question of spending for mass transportation. The response of the older age groups seems ambiguous because nearly one quarter of the 65+ age group gave no answer or said they don't know when asked whether spending on mass transportation is sufficient. The 85+ in particular showed the highest level of uncertainty. At the same time, nearly 45% of this same age group feels that we spend "too little."

Compared to this, the younger ages now seem more conservative—they averaged almost 50% saying "about right" and only about 33% "too little." The striking reversal that turns up on the issue of mass transportation probably grows out of the serious transportation difficulties older people have. Going out even to perform simple chores, such as grocery shopping and getting to the hairdresser, can become a serious problem in the later years.

To summarize, we see little evidence to support the idea of growing conservatism with age when we look at specific issues of public policy. Young and old agree on two thirds of the issues presented to them by the GSS interviewers. Cases of lesser unanimity seem related to the individual's stage of life or age cohort, and not to chronological age itself.

The notion of growing conservatism over life appears to be a fallacy. We've accused the elderly of hardening of attitudes along with hardening of the arteries, but we may be guilty, instead, of "hardening of the categories." Older people have been categorized as unyielding and unimaginative, but it's evident that the idea doesn't fit with the real facts. It's time to adjust our notions about growing conservatism in old age.

DO OLDER PEOPLE HAVE MUCH INDEPENDENT POLITICAL INFLUENCE?

Even if people don't become more politically conservative as they age, their special interests as voters may have begun to dominate political decisions in the United States already, and they may grow stronger in the future. For example, the *Wall Street Journal* not long ago pointed to the AARP's (American Association of Retired Persons) political clout in an article about two Super Tuesday Democratic primary hopefuls in Florida. Put deep concern over the costs of health care for the elderly together with voting power, said the *Journal*, "and, boom, a political issue is born."

With over 28 million members, AARP may well become the greatest force in politics since the heyday of the AFL/CIO. Besides this, voting records clearly show that larger proportions of older people vote than do younger people. According to the GSS, the peak years for voting in presidential elections occurs between ages 45 and 84. During these years, 75% or more of the respondents say they voted in the last presidential election. In 1968 and 1976, the 55- to 64-year-olds ran ahead, with 80% voting participation, but the 65- to 74-year-olds nosed them out 80% to 78% in 1984.

With their winning percentages, it looks as if older people might become a dominant force in politics some time in the future. A problem arises, however, when we ask whether older people stick together on issues and vote regularly as a political bloc. For instance, do older voters in a presidential election tend to vote for the same candidate any more than the rest of the population does? Do they band together on the five specific age-affected issues we discussed in the previous section? To put the question another way, do we need to fear the specter of senior political power?

Gerontologist Robert Binstock thinks not. Co-editor of the *Handbook of Aging and the Social Sciences* and a professor of gerontology at Case Western Reserve University in Cleveland, Binstock has observed that the older age groups (65+) so far have made up only a small proportion (about 20%) of the electorate. Under these circumstances, they can hardly dominate the political process no matter how active they may be as voters. In addition, older people differ as much from one another as any other segment of the population does—whether black or white, rich or poor, north or south, male or female. Their interests as a social group rarely coincide.

To this, Binstock adds that the major legislative gains on behalf of the elderly have come through the work of others rather than through their own efforts. The one exception was the Townsend Movement in the mid-1930s. Led by an elderly California physician, this movement frightened politicians by advocating a tax on all businesses to finance an unheard-of pension amounting to $200 a month. The result was the adoption of the Social Security program in 1935, which at first paid much less than $200 per month.

With this one exception, Binstock holds that the improvement of federal programs for the elderly between 1930 and the 1970s didn't rest on their own political power. Rather, it rode the wave of the prevailing political philosophy of the times—the theory that spending on behalf of individuals stimulates the economy. Leadership for this idea came from people of middle age, so that the best advocates for older people came from the ranks of younger generations.

Voting in presidential elections as recorded in the GSS tends to support Binstock's thesis. Generally, older people vote along with the rest of the population—when the tide goes Democratic, older voters swim along with it. When it goes Republican, they're in the swim too. The one partial exception is the 1984 election, when the older voters gave Ronald Reagan the lowest level of support of any age group; according to the GSS, an average of 55% of the 65+ voted for him while close to 60% of the others endorsed "the Gipper."

There's no telling for sure what may happen in the future. Perhaps older voters will become a solid political bloc that can dominate national policy. Until now, though, the public has supported programs for the older generation because they have considered them deserving. Maybe this is what accounts for the older generation's positive attitude toward others. They're grateful.

ARE OLDER PEOPLE TOUGHER ON CRIME AND CRIMINALS?

Attitudes about punishment of criminals offer another test of the idea that people grow more conservative as they age. Presumably, conservatives favor harsher punishment than do liberals, so older people should favor harsh punishment if they truly hold conservative views. Historic experience, too, should make the elderly favor harsh treatment because they grew up when the death penalty was more common and attitudes generally more harsh—for example, schools before the 1950s freely meted out corporal punishment. How do older people feel about the treatment of criminals?

First, the GSS shows that older people clearly don't want to risk becoming victims of crime, and they tend to fear it more than younger people. When asked if they feel safe walking in their neighborhoods at night, a majority of the older respondents say that they don't. At every age, concern about the safety of one's neighborhood is quite high (40% on the average), but at 65–74, it reaches 50% and then climbs even higher at 75+ to nearly 60%. Women show nearly double the rate of fear when compared to men, but men also show increasing fear with age (18% at 18–24 and 40% at 85+). Fear of walking in one's neighborhood at night is common in America, but it's most severe for the elderly.

Fortunately, there are some breaks in the cloud of fear that hangs over crime. The great majority of people at every age feel safe and secure in their homes at night. Under age 65, the proportion who feel safe fluctuates from 84% (at 18–24), to 89% (age 35–44), and back to 86% at 55–64. Of the 65- to 74-year-olds, 85% feel safe, but the rate drops to 77% at 75–84 and then climbs back to 80% at 85+. Women feel unsafe more often than men, especially so after 85 when they exceed the men by 15%. In general, a substantial majority of the elderly feel safe at home, but they feel less safe than the younger population.

Interestingly, the older population actually experiences less violence and criminal victimization than do the young. Young people report being victims of crime and violence far more often than older people do. Nearly half of the 18- to 34-year-olds say they have ever been "hit" (the GSS uses "hit" as an indicator for violence), but less than 20% of the 65+ age group say so. For women at 65+, the rate is less than 10%, but for men it's 30 or more from 64 to 84, and 15% at 85+.

The proportion of people 65+ who've experienced a burglary (someone entering their home to steal during the past year) is 5%, generally less than the rest of the population and half the rate for 18- to 24-year-olds. Fewer old people report robbery (having had anything stolen during the previous year)—less than 2%, compared to 4% at ages 18–24 and 3% at 25–34. A surprisingly high percentage (20% overall) of the GSS population reports having been threatened with a gun or shot at. The average for 18–64 stands at 35%, well above the rate for men over 65 (20%) and women (10%).

Why do the elderly, who experience lower rates of violence and crime, express greater fear than the young? One reason undoubtedly relates to the greater costs of victimization in later life. Recovery from bodily and financial injury becomes more difficult as one ages. Possibly, too, the greater cautiousness of older persons, recorded in numerous psychological studies, contributes to their greater sense of unease at home and their fear of venturing out.

More importantly, though, does their greater fear provoke a search for stronger defense measures? Does it intensify their desire to prevent crime, or their wish to punish criminals harshly? The GSS includes questions that relate to each of these topics. By comparing attitudes on gun control, treatment of criminals by the courts, and the death penalty, we can estimate who's more tough on crime—the young or the old.

Gun ownership represents a possible form of self-defense reported in the GSS. Whatever the differing sense of fear of young and old, about half the men in all age groups say they have guns in their homes. From one third to one half of each group of women under 75 report the same, though their husbands may own the guns. After age 75, 21% of the women at age 75–84 have guns at home and 14% of the 85+ do also. So far as gun ownership is concerned, there's no evidence that the older generation arms itself in fear of crime any more than any other age does. There is a strong gender-linked difference in gun ownership, however, which exaggerates age differences among older persons, among whom women predominate.

Nor is there any difference of opinion among the age groups on the need for gun laws. The GSS asks whether persons favor requiring permits for guns. Close to 70% or more of each age group answers affirmatively. Few persons have any doubt (say "don't know" or have no answer) about the issue, but most of the opposition (about 28%) to gun permits comes from the 35–64 age bracket. Women at all ages favor gun laws more than men do.

Furthermore, little difference or doubt exists about the need for more governmental spending to control crime. Just about the same percentage (60% or more) of most age groups think there's too little spending to halt crime. The low actually appears at 85+, where only 54% favors more spending, while the high of 68% shows up at ages 55–64. The rest of the age groups hover around 65%. There's no evidence here of an unusually high law-and-order mentality among the old. The same applies to government spending on drug addiction.

The most severe test of the theory of conservatism regarding crime, however, comes in the responses to two questions: whether the courts treat criminals harshly enough; and whether capital punishment should be used. "In general," asks the GSS interviewer, "do you think the courts in this area deal too harshly or not harshly enough with criminals?" "Not harsh enough" is the response of the overwhelming majority of all ages. Of every age group from 24 to 84, 80% or more gives this answer.

Again, the very young (18–24) and the very old (85+) have more in common with one another than they do with the other ages. Neither group gives as much support to harsh treatment as the others do—67% support at 18–24 and 73% at 85+. The very young also express the most opposition to more harsh treatment. Nine percent of the young are opposed, while less than 5% of the other age groups share this view, and 15% of the 85+ say they don't know or give no answer.

The final area, capital punishment, asks about the death penalty for convicted murderers. The responses here strongly confirm what we've seen so far. There's no evidence of any more severity among the old than among the young—approval for capital punishment fluctuates narrowly between 63% and 71%. The strongest opposition to the death penalty appears among the 18- to 24-year-olds (32%), but after that, the age brackets range from 23 to 27%, a negligible variation. There's no evidence whatever that older people take a more harsh or unyielding attitude toward criminals. In fact, it's the middle-aged population that expresses the most unforgiving attitudes.

In one area alone—the legalization of marijuana—does one find a marked difference between the young and the old. A majority of every age group actually *opposes* the legalization of marijuana, but the difference rests with the extent of opposition and the proportions who favor legalization. In terms of opposition, for instance, 56% of the 18- to 24-year-olds and 64% of the 25- to 34-year-olds disapprove of legalization. But 76% of the 35–44 bracket disapproves. The rate climbs sharply from there on until it reaches 85% at 65+.

On the other side of the coin, 41% of the 18–24 population and 33% of the 25- to 34-year-olds favor legalization of marijuana. By the next age decade, the proportion favoring legalization falls to 21%. It hits bottom at 75+, when it sinks to 10%. Once more, both sets of figures show that familiar phenomenon: Older people may indeed seem more conservative, but the trend toward conservatism starts early in life—somewhere in the 35–44 age bracket.

DO PEOPLE BECOME MORE RELIGIOUS AS THEY AGE?

So far, we've seen little evidence that the oldest Americans constitute a hard-shell, obtuse conservative group. If anything, conservatism starts quite early in life, at ages 35–44, and it remains fairly constant from there on. Moderation may more accurately describe the attitude of the oldest members of our population, especially so when compared to their immediate juniors, the 55- to 64-year-olds.

But even though the oldest generation may be moderate in regard to politics and crime, perhaps it is immoderate in other crucial areas of social behavior and attitudes. What about religion, for instance? Previously, Gallup polls have shown a strong connection between religious commitments and a conservative outlook. Does the older population exhibit characteristics of intense belief and commitment that might betray an underlying conservative bias regarding everyday social behavior? The GSS directs a series of questions toward religion.

One of these questions concerns strength of religious belief, showing a considerable difference between the youngest and the oldest Americans. In fact, the American population falls into three separate classes when it comes to religious belief. The youngest group, from 18 to 34, shows the lowest level of religious conviction, with less than 35% expressing strong belief. The next category, from age 35 to 64, shows a middle level, ranging from 41 to 47% strong believers. The 65+ show the greatest conviction, with over 50% in every group specifying strong belief. At 85+ the population of strong believers reaches a high of 66%.

One might conclude that these figures provide convincing evidence of a relationship between long life and strong religious conviction, but they don't tell the whole story. What about attendance at religious services, for instance? It's true that older people state more often that they attend services weekly, but if we take attendance at least once a month as a standard, we find that the age groups don't differ much.

Over half of the 18- to 24-year-olds (55%) say they attend at least once a month. The proportion increases to 69% in the middle years from 45 to 54. From there, it climbs 4 points to 73% at 55–64, where it remains for the 65–74 and 75- to 84-year-olds. At 85+, there's a decline to 64%, presumably related to transportation and other difficulties rather than lack of conviction. Whatever the differences in strength of religious commitment, the young don't fall far behind the old in regular church attendance.

Belief in life after death practically wipes out the differences between the ages. One might expect that people with mild religious convictions wouldn't consider life after death a credible idea. Not so. Though young people don't usually express strong religious conviction, they nearly match the old in belief in an afterlife. Only 3 percentage points separate the young and old— 67% of the 18- to 24-year-olds believe in an afterlife, while 70% of the 85+ are believers. At 25–34, the young even outstrip the old— 72% say they believe in life after death.

We see that the gap between young and old narrows when

we look beyond simple differences in strength of religious conviction. We can't simply conclude that religious faith increases with age, so how can we account for the greater conviction and weekly church attendance of the old? Some gerontologists think it probably reflects the times when the respective age groups grew up and learned their way of life—a cohort difference. Older Americans reached adulthood in a time when religion was a more prominent feature of life than it is today.

Older Americans had more opportunity to absorb religious faith in their youth. Indeed, Andrew Greeley, a prominent sociologist, successful novelist, and Roman Catholic priest as well, has published a study with Michael Hout of the University of California, which illustrates how religious practices of the past have changed with the times. The low in church attendance by Protestants occurred in the 1950s, and among Roman Catholics, attendance declined sharply from 1968 to 1975.

Even today, most of the young report that they had a religious upbringing of some type, but it's apparent that some have abandoned their early religious affiliation. This shows up when we compare the answers to two questions.

The GSS asks, "In what religion were you raised," and then again, "What is your religious preference (now)? Is it Protestant, Catholic, Jewish, some other religion, or no religion?" When we compare the two sets of answers, we see that religious ties drop among the two youngest age groups. For Protestants, there's a fall of 6% at ages 18–24, but only another 3% at 25–34. Roman Catholics start with a smaller decline than Protestants—5% at ages 18–24, but another 5% from 25 to 34. The largest share of these apostasies probably swing to nonobservance of religion. For example, there's a jump of 7% in "no religion" at 18–34, when between 10 and 12% answer "none" when stating religious preference. In contrast, only a tiny minority (about 3%) of the 65+ age group answers "none."

The GSS confirms that older persons do hold stronger religious convictions and attend church more frequently than younger people. But many of these differences may be attributed to cohort experience and not necessarily to chronological age. What the survey does not show is that religious conviction

increases with age or that strength of belief and church attendance are necessarily related to commitment to the idea of
afterlife. As to conservatism, it's true that people who hold strong
religious convictions tend to hold a conservative outlook, but this
does not seem causally linked to age. Religion and conservatism
may be linked, but not necessarily chronological age and conservatism.

WHAT ABOUT SEXUAL ATTITUDES AND BEHAVIOR?

So far, this chapter has not shown much evidence of a great shift
toward conservatism in the later years of life. Older people do
differ in their thinking from the young, but change starts earlier
than was expected and some of it appears to be a cohort
phenomenon. But what about issues involving sex? Major
changes in sexual attitudes and behavior occurred since the
1950s and 1960s, so the older age group might be expected to
hold more conservative attitudes because it grew up before the
time when new thinking evolved.

Attitudes about types of sexual behavior—teenage sexual
activity, premarital sex, extramarital affairs, and homosexuality—
may be more important than attitudes about politics, political
issues, religion, crime, etc. The GSS includes questions on all four
subjects, and respondents state whether they consider the behav-
iors "always wrong, almost always wrong, sometimes wrong, or
not wrong at all." Let's have a look at the answers.

Teen sexual activity (defined as taking place between ages
14 and 16) reaps condemnation as "always wrong" by a majority
of all age groups except ages 18–24. Still, even this young set
registers a 44% disapproval. There are, however, major differences between the young and the old. From 55 and up, "always
wrong" reaches over 80%, compared to only 52% at ages 25–34.
At age 85+, there's a peak of 88% (two thirds of the 85+ respondents are women). The oldest Americans may agree with the
youngest on some things, but not on the matter of sexual activity
for teens. Compared to the young, almost twice as many of them
disapprove.

Is this evidence of conservatism among the elderly? Perhaps. Consider, though, that disapproval suddenly spikes upward 13% at ages 35–44 (52% "always wrong" at 25–34, but 65% at 35–44). Doesn't this show that the trend toward disapproval starts at a time in life when people may themselves have teenage children?

Further evidence for an early shift toward conservatism comes to light when we observe that ages 35–44 seems to represent a dividing point between the young and the old. This age group ranks 21% more conservative than the 18- to 24-year-olds but is 23% less conservative than the 75–84 category. Parenthood more than age seems to underlie attitudes about teenage sexuality. The oldest generation is probably just adding to common parental attitudes by bringing in views that were typical in past times. Once more, age alone doesn't fully explain conservatism. Parenthood (life situation differences) and the greater sexual conservatism of past times (cohort differences) enter the picture.

Premarital sex, though, garners less disapproval than teen sexual activity. From ages 18 to 54, a majority considers it "not wrong at all" or only "sometimes wrong." Even fairly large proportions of the older groups don't consider premarital sex wrong—43% approve at ages 55–64 and even 24% at 85+. Still, disapproval is registered by some. It starts at 13% at 18–24, climbs to 32% by 45–54, and tops out at 59% at 85+.

Extramarital sex attracts widespread condemnation. Disapproval begins with 62% considering it "always wrong" at 18–24, climbs to 72% by 45–54, and reaches 87% at 85+. If we combine "almost always wrong" with "always wrong," there's less difference between the age groups: 80% negative at 18–24 and 90% at 85+.

Only a small minority consider extramarital sex acceptable ("not wrong at all" or "sometimes wrong"). At 18–24, approval is only 20%. This drops to 13% at 25–34, and then falls to less than 10% at later ages. The not-yet-married and the divorce-prone early years of life seem to match up with the higher percentages of approval of extramarital sex.

Homosexuality earns almost as much disapprobation as

extramarital sex. The rate starts at 60% calling it "always wrong" at ages 18–24, rises to 66% at 35–44, 79% at 55–64, and 84% at 85+. In the early years of life, women express less disapproval of homosexuality than men, but the difference vanishes by age 35.

A series of GSS questions on pornography further probes the subject of attitudes on sexual behavior. One of them asks, "Does pornography promote acts of rape?" Of the 18- to 24-year-olds, 45% think so. A moderate, but steady rise follows, until a sudden increase to 58% at ages 45–54. This is the midway point, because the peak, which comes at age 75–84, stands at 72%. In general, sizable proportions of every age group think pornography promotes rape, and women (who form an increasing majority as age increases) hold this view more commonly than men do.

Does pornography promote a breakdown in morals? At ages 75–84, 76% of the respondents believe it does, but at 18–24, 43% *don't* think so. The major change in viewpoint again comes in the middle years—45 to 54—when 62% agree with the statement that pornography breaks down morals.

Does pornography provide an outlet for bottled-up sex impulses? While sizable proportions of every age group think not, about half or more of them think it does. Of the 18- to 24-year-olds, 61% feel it offers an outlet, followed by 56% at 45–54 and 51% at 85+. However, the response on this question has an unusually high rate of "Don't Know/No Answer" replies. The proportion starts out at nearly 10% in the early ages, climbs to 20% by 65–74, and peaks at 32% at 85+. Seldom are so many people unwilling to commit themselves in responding to a survey question.

One set of questions in the GSS taps actual behavior in regard to matters of sex in an interesting way. The first of these asks whether sexual materials provide information about sex— a question the individual can hardly answer without having actually seen such materials. The second comes even closer to testing knowledge by asking, "How much information do you have about the pornography issue?" The third in the series is even more explicit and revealing because it asks, "Have you seen an X-rated movie in the last year?"

COMPARING THE GSS TO OTHER SURVEYS ABOUT SEX

Why are the specific answers to these questions important? In brief, the reason is that they offer insight into actual behavior regarding personal practices, and this is exceptional. Sex is a highly sensitive subject that people do not usually discuss in public surveys. Because of this, there has never been a nationally representative survey of our population's sexual practices. Even the best studies, such as the famous Kinsey report that secured responses from 18,500 people, was not representative because it had to rely on volunteer respondents. The same is true of the scientifically controlled work of Masters and Johnson, as well as a survey of the sexual behavior of older persons carried out by *Consumer Reports* magazine.

The difficulty with volunteer reports is that the respondents are self-selected. We don't know whether they actually represent the entire American public. They may, in fact, have an unusual eagerness to reveal their private lives in a way that is quite untypical of the general population. Consequently, we don't know whether or not they truly represent the crosssection of public opinion.

One of the more lurid and highly publicized exposés of sex practices is probably especially misrepresentative. This is the national best-selling *Hite Report: A National Study of Female Sexuality*, by New Yorker Shere Hite. Hite adopted a feminist viewpoint after experiencing some of the more degrading sexist experiences all too common in the lives of women, and she later surveyed 100,000 readers of *Cosmopolitan* to explore a number of facets of women's lives, including sex.

But *Cosmopolitan* readers don't make a good national sample of women. The magazine reaches an atypical upper-income audience that feels comfortable with the openly sexy image the magazine projects. More than this, Hite received responses from only 4.5% of the readership. This group does not even represent *Cosmopolitan* readers, let alone American women. Worse still, Hite's respondents may have answered because they felt they had a tale to tell. Later releases of Hite's questionnaire results showed that many were un-

happily married and dissatisfied with their spousal relationship in greater proportions than the wider American population.

The GSS, on the other hand, provides a valid survey of
the entire American public. Even though its questions are
more restrained, the results are accurate. Further, to answer
the questions under discussion, the respondents have to
have information, or they have to have done what the
questions described.

First, "Do pornographic materials provide information
about sex?" At ages 18–24, 69% think that they do. By ages 55–64,
54% still agree, but at 75–84, only 46% agree. Surprisingly, nearly
half (49%) of the 85+ concur, but 27% either don't know or give
no answer.

The second question, "How much information do you have
about the pornography issue?" suggests that the 85+ generation
is the most innocent—50% admit they have very little information
about the subject. The 75–84 follow with 37%, and two other
ages, 65–74 and 18–24, stand fairly close to the 85+, at 30% with
very little information. The 35- to 44-year-olds are the least
naive—only 17% say they have very little information. Perhaps
most intriguing, this question has once more shown some degree
of similarity between the youngest and the oldest generations.

The final question asks for highly specific information on
actual behavior—"Have you seen an X-rated movie in the last
year?" Less than 10% of the over-55 population report having seen
such a movie in the last year. The highest level of X-rated movie
viewing occurs at 18–24, when 37% respond affirmatively. At
25–34, the proportion falls to 28%, followed by 23% at 35–44, and
17% at 45–54.

Shere Hite's best-selling study about female sexuality captured headlines because it implied that the entire American female public engages in rampant extramarital sex and other
libidinal practices. The response to these GSS questions, however, suggests more modest and reserved behavior by three
quarters or more of the population, at least in regard to pornography. The elderly in particular must be exempted from any
characterization of pornographic enthusiasm.

Returning to attitudes once more, one question brings to light very marked difference between the young and the old. The GSS asks, "Should there be a law against distributing pornography?" followed by three choices of response: "at any age," "to persons under 18," or "no laws forbidding distribution." For the first time in the series of questions on sexuality, the young and the old seem radically divided—at 18–24, only 20% answer that it should be illegal to all, but at 85+, 70% favor making pornography illegal.

Still, the oldest age group is not isolated in its views. A trend to say that it should be illegal to all starts quite early and reaches 48% at 45–54. By 55–64, it stands at 56%, climbs to 64% by 65–74, and reaches 69% by 75–84. Nearly everyone agrees that pornography should be illegal for those under 18—roughly 90% of every age group favors such a ban.

Another question about pornography is even more interesting because it deals with willingness to change one's opinion. Are the old more inflexible than the young? The GSS asks, "How firm are you about pornography—would you say you are very likely to change your opinion, somewhat likely to change, somewhat unlikely to change, or very unlikely to change your opinion?" Here's what the different ages say.

At one end of the scale stand the 85+—79% of them say very unlikely to change. At the opposite end are the 18- to 24-year-olds, with only 36% unlikely to change their views. A full 74% of the young might be willing to change, whereas only 21% of the old say they might be willing.

But the tale does not end there. Consistent with other issues, the shift toward conservatism begins at a relatively young age. By 45–54, 61% assert that they would be very unlikely to change their views. The level of unwillingness increases to 65% at 55–64, rises to 70% at 65–74, and falls to 68% at 75–84. The oldest age group, made up predominantly of women, shares a view that's held by almost everyone from age 45 up. When measured by willingness to change one's mind on this subject, conservatism does characterize the thinking of older persons. But it begins in midlife or before.

WILL THE OLDER POPULATION MAKE SOCIETY MORE CONSERVATIVE IN THE FUTURE?

Can we answer Robert Samuelson's question about the future? Will older Baby Boomers mean more conservative politics and less economic vitality? About 10 years from now, in the year 2000, the first wave of the Baby Boom, born in 1946, will wash up on the shores of later life. During the following 30 years, our 50+ population will climb to 40% of our public, while the 65+ age group will increase to 21%. For the first time in history, our population structure will tip toward old age. Will we stagnate in conservatism and apathy?

The answer is no. This chapter has shown that the American population already characterizes itself as moderate at every age. Conservatism even now begins at ages 35–44 in some matters. By late midlife, conservatism is the pattern for the majority. The future population structure won't alter these characteristics very much.

We should also consider another feature of our present development: the increasing level of education of the oncoming generations. Studies have repeatedly shown a connection between flexibility of mind and higher levels of learning. Social scientists have predicted that present levels of education, never before matched in our history, will profoundly affect our national future. They say, in effect, that the unprecedented levels of education among Americans will guard against any tendencies toward stagnation.

But, more important still, the GSS discloses that we have misread the older generation when we charge it with a dreary stolidity. The conventional wisdom about age seriously needs revision. Things are more complicated than they seem, and what has appeared as a characteristic of the old, in reality begins earlier than we think—middle age, a time of life usually seen as filled with vigor. If leadership of our society falls predominantly to those in midlife, then we're already led by moderates and conservatives. Life in the next century will be as it is today—deadening if we let it be so, but filled with vitality if we decree otherwise.

6

Family and Residence
in Later Life

Do you have the impression that families abandon their older
relatives as the years go by? If so, you've probably formed
it from the negative publicity about the family relations of older
Americans. The dominant media message centers on neglect and
abuse. Is this unpleasant image true?

Not for most Americans. Part of the reason for the image
rests with the notion that in the past, the elderly were warmly and
caringly nurtured in the bosom of the family until death did them
part. It's thought that the young of today migrate far from home,
or, if still living in the neighborhood, simply don't bother with
their older family members. This seems believable because the
nuclear family, made up of Mom, Dad, and the kids, establishes
a pattern of family life that doesn't seem to include the old.

As with other myths about age, the contrast between past
and present doesn't stand up well against solid facts. For one
thing, the vast majority of people in the past never lived long
enough to spend a blissful old age with (or without) their families.
We've already seen that the average life expectancy in 1900 was
about 47, which means that most people survived only briefly
beyond their childbearing and child-rearing years. In those days,
the average woman outlived the average man by only 2 years, so
not even women could expect a long period of late-life association with children and grandchildren.

Back then, too, children were far less likely to have the chance to bask in sunbeams of indulgent love from grandparents. As recently as 1920, when life expectancy was about 50, only 40% of America's 10-year-olds had two living grandparents, and only 11% had four grandparents. Today more than 75% of 10-year-old children have two grandparents, and more than 70% have four. Three quarters of grandparents now see their grandchildren every week or two, and half see them daily. We're even up on great-grandparenthood—46% of today's elderly enjoy great-grandchildren.

Besides this, studies of family patterns in Europe and America dating back 200–300 years have disproved the proposition that older parents generally lived with their children or grandchildren. The nuclear, two-generation family was the norm then as now. Older people maintained independent households and continued to do so unless health or poverty prevented it. Social scientists have estimated that less than 1 in 10 older women and fewer than 1 in 20 older men lived with their children. If parents survived, the three-generation extended family existed, but not under one roof.

The facts about shorter life expectancy and the rarity of live-in extended family arrangements in earlier times allow us to dismiss the notion that there's been any great decline in the way that families treat their older members. If treatment of older family members hasn't worsened, just what circumstances determine family contacts in later life today? Answering this question brings up a whole series of connected questions: Where do most older Americans reside? Do they move south when they retire? Is their housing adequate or substandard? What about retirement communities—do they provide a satisfying life-style? What about marriage and marital status? What kinds of family histories have older people had? And, above all, what sorts of relations do they maintain with their children and other relatives?

Some of the answers to these questions appear in the GSS, but others require reference to U.S. Census figures and to the many studies carried out by other gerontological researchers. In this chapter, we survey a wide range of sources to find the information we need. This is useful because it exposes us to the rich variety of information available on later life today.

WHERE DO MOST OLDER PEOPLE LIVE?

If you consider numbers alone, most older people live in the two most populous states of the U.S.—California and New York. California has close to 3 million people over age 65, and New York over 2 ¼ million. But that gives a somewhat distorted picture. To understand where older persons live, we should look at the population *composition* of a state. What proportion, or percentage, of the population of the state is over age 65? Sheer numbers of the elderly within a population don't give enough information. We have to look at percentages along with the numbers.

Take Florida for instance. Florida ranks third in numbers of persons over age 65, with more than 2 million of them. In percentages, however, it ranks number one among the states, with close to 18% of its 11 ¾ million population aged 65 or more. Population numbers and percentages tell quite different stories.

Let's look at the numbers first. In descending order behind California, New York, and Florida are Pennsylvania, Texas, Illinois, Ohio, Michigan, New Jersey, and Massachusetts—all in the top ten states wtih large numbers of elderly. This list shows what you might expect: the greatest numbers of older people live in the states with the biggest populations—excepting Florida again. Florida ranks fifth in total population (counting everyone in the state and then comparing that number to all other states). But, as noted, it stands third in number of people over age 65 and first in the percentages.

Surprisingly, after Florida, the state with the highest percentage of older people is Arkansas! Next comes little Rhode Island. Behind it follow Iowa, Missouri, South Dakota, Nebraska, and Kansas.

Besides Florida, only two states that rank in the top 10 in numbers of elderly make it into the top 10 in percentages of the elderly: Pennsylvania and Massachusetts. California doesn't even come close to the top in percentages—it ranks 34th, making it a state with a relatively young population composition. Even New York, which hasn't experienced the degree of in-migration that California has, drops from number 2 down to 13 when we use percentages.

What's going on here? Why do states such as Kansas, Iowa, and South Dakota have such large percentages of older persons? We might guess that rural and farm life of such states are healthy and peaceful, or that persons live longer in states with a low population density. But neither of these can be the answer, because Rhode Island, with 925 persons per square mile, is hardly rural (it's just about the most densely populated state in the U.S.)[1]—yet, it matches the rural/farm/low-population-density states when it comes to proportion of older people. In any case, longevity based on a healthful country life-style doesn't explain the presence of large proportions of older residents in some states.

Another guess might be that older people have moved into the states with the higher percentages of elderly. But that doesn't seem to be true either. We know that out-migration of the older population has happened in some of the states with the highest proportions of the people aged 65+. Among these are Missouri, Massachusetts, Pennsylvania, and even Florida.

But what about the younger generations? The explanation for the high proportion of older people in a state's population is that the younger generation moved out. The young have migrated to warmer climates and to places where they find industrial, business, and service jobs. Because the young have left certain states, the population composition in these states has thereby shifted toward the older generation.

This is especially true in the rural, agricultural states such as Iowa, South Dakota, Nebraska, Kansas, and Missouri. The steady passing away of farming as a way of life in America has dropped the proportion of farmers in our population from 75% at the time

---

[1]New Jersey, with about 1015 people per square mile, is the most densely populated state. Rhode Island used to be number one, but it's number two now. If we count Washington, D.C., then it's the runaway winner, with 9931 persons per square mile.

of the first U.S. Census in 1790 down to 2.5% today. In the past 50 to 75 years, the young have left farm areas by the thousands to move to sites of high business prosperity while the older population has stayed behind. This explains one of the reasons for high percentages of older people in states where you might not expect them. Later in this chapter, we question whether this leaves the older generation isolated from its children.

DO MANY OLDER PEOPLE MOVE SOUTH?

No, not if we're speaking of the majority. Nearly 80% of the 65+ population stays put. The vast majority of persons even remain in the same homes when they retire. Generally, members of the older population qualify as nonmovers.

Over two thirds of the migrants within the U.S. are between 20 and 40 years of age. Because the older population tends to stay put, we might ask whether it's satisfied with where it lives. It is—more so than the young—according to the GSS. It shows that 63% of the respondents over 65 expressed "a great deal of satisfaction" with their area of residence, compared to only about 35% between ages 18 and 35.

We don't know all the reasons that the older generation finds greater satisfaction with its place of residence. One of them may have to do with the greater composure and imperturbable spirit of the old. Equally possible, a high level of satisfaction with place of residence could occur in later life because people have deliberately set roots down in a chosen community, and they own a home there. The young may be more constrained by problems of income and access to a workplace than the old, so they may feel that the grass is greener elsewhere, and they experience more of a pull to move.

Still, 21% of the older generation does move. This represents almost 6 million people, not an inconsiderable number. What states do they leave, and where do they go?

The statistics on this subject may seem peculiar at first because some of the states that lose older people also attract them. The main reason for this strange phenomenon is that some older people are drawn back to family, neighbors, and scenes of their youth after having moved elsewhere following retirement. Consequently, a few states that lose older population gain it from former residents coming back.

The state that loses the highest percentage of its older folk is New York, with 14.6%. California comes second with 8.5%, then Illinois at 7.2%. Florida, New Jersey, Ohio, Pennsylvania, and Missouri, trail along with between 4 and 6%.

Turning to the gainers, the all-time winner is Florida, which pulled in 26% of the older migrating population by the time of the 1980 census. The figures on the other states show just how powerfully Florida has appealed to the older generation—its closest competitor is California, but it trails far behind with 8.7% of the in-migrants. Arizona and Texas come along next at 5.7 and 4.7%, followed by New Jersey, Pennsylvania, North Carolina, Washington, Illinois, and New York, with between 2 and 3% each.

The U.S. Bureau of the Census has fashioned an Attractiveness Index, which takes into account the in-and-out movement of older people. *Attractiveness* reflects the appeal of the state in terms of its share of interstate migrants age 60+, after you subtract the proportion who leave. The result becomes a point score comparable to a score in a sports event like football. Seen as a competitive event, the Attractiveness Index makes Florida look like the Super Bowl champ, with three to four times the scoring power of any other state including California.

The U.S. Bureau of the Census has drawn up another index using the 1975–1980 period and has called it the "Impact Index." It suggests how much the influx of older people into a state has affected its population composition. Looking at things this way suddenly gives us a new winner. Arizona jumps to the top, with 21.91 points. Florida comes in a close second with 19.40 points, but California loses out to several other states. Behind Florida appears New Mexico, with a 10.42 impact score. Indiana pops up next at 8.8 points; succeeded by New Hampshire with 8.75; Arkansas and Pennsylvania tied at 7.98, Colorado and Delaware tied at 7.7; Alaska 7.7; and Washington, Utah, and Wyoming, all at about 5.5. California sinks to 21st position on the Impact Index.

Because these two indexes show different facets of the same picture, they alter the positions of the states. This tells us that many older people do more than just chase the sun when they move. Do older people move south, then? Some do, indeed, head south to follow the sunshine. But other kinds of attractions than sunshine obviously motivate shifts to states such as Indiana, New Hampshire, Washington, Wyoming, Utah, Pennsylvania, and Alaska. Practical or personal preferences, such as moving to New Hampshire to gain a haven free from income and sales taxes, probably account for these other moves.

As shown earlier, almost 80% of the older population doesn't move at all. Many of those who do move undoubtedly seek out warmer climates, but there are other motives too. Family, friends, neighborhoods, associations with a habitat, and finances all enter into the choice of residence in later life. The old move south when it makes sense, but they stay put more often, and they evidently choose carefully in making decisions about relocating.

WHAT SORTS OF RESIDENCES DO OLDER PEOPLE HAVE?

About three quarters of the older population own their own homes. This puts them ahead of the rest of the adult population, which only enjoys 64% home ownership. Still, the older age groups more often own older homes, over 50% of them built before the 1950s. These older homes lack some of the amenities of newer construction. Younger home owners more often have air conditioning (58% young to 54% old), more than one bathroom (44% young to 33% old), and central heating (56% to 47% old).

High home ownership affords the older generation something more than mere personal shelter. It can provide a ready source of cash at retirement, a potential advantage that may substantially improve the comforts of later life. Lest we mistake our homes for gold mines, however, specialists in personal financial management writing for *Money* magazine cautiously recommend that older owners think about trading down a larger home for a smaller one, rather than simply cashing out their homes. To trade down, individuals would sell their homes; put some of the proceeds into smaller, lower-cost residences; and invest any surplus funds in securities to increase retirement income. Other alternatives (e.g., "home-equity liquefying annuity plans—reverse mortgages," or "sale-leaseback arrangements") may suit some individuals, but they require very careful assessment of long-term financial needs.

Mobile homes provide housing for about three quarters of a million of the older generation. Principally located in the south, these residences were once considered second-rate, but many have been developed in attractive surroundings that offer an appealing life-style to retirees.

Retirement communities, sometimes built as condominiums and sometimes as rental apartments, have had mounting attraction for some, usually the more affluent. In general, though, older persons seem to cherish the independence and sense of security derived from abiding in their own private residences. Moving to a nursing home is a rarity—only 5% of the overall 65+ generation, and about 20% after 85+, make such a move.

ARE RETIREMENT COMMUNITIES GOOD FOR OLDER PEOPLE?

For many years, the common opinion was that older people should live in *age-integrated communities* (i.e., with a crosssection of people of all ages), and this became the federal government policy for public housing projects. Though it was common knowledge that age peers like to associate with one another more than with other generations, nearly everyone seemed to think that there was something unhealthy about having the older generation live by itself.

Until the 1960s, the federal government clung to the idea that age-integrated residences provided the most wholesome environment for the elderly. Once this policy changed, and development of special housing units for older people began, some diehards persisted in the conviction that separate residences for the elderly were undesirable. Researchers who studied the effects of such housing on adjustment, satisfaction, and survival in later life quickly found the doubting Thomases wrong. Most older people thrive when they live in surroundings with their agemates, whether in government housing or other kinds of unmixed units. The reason is that elderly housing includes special services not usually available in other kinds of residences. Too, they offer greater opportunity for friendly companionship and personal support. It's thought that these advantages account for the longer-than-usual length of life experienced by many residents of elderly housing.

One difficulty encountered so far has not had anything to do with ill effects from segregation or overconcentration of older persons. Rather, it has stemmed from financial problems, especially so in the case of some facilities known as "life-care communities." High-minded and excellent in principle, these communities offered apartments for independent living linked to intermediate-care facilities (light assistance with activities of daily living) and a nursing home unit. Residents would make a substantial admission deposit and pay a monthly maintenance charge in return for a lifetime guarantee of care at any of the three levels.

Regrettably, a number of these facilities, including some managed by religious organizations, went bankrupt when they failed to anticipate the longevity of the residents and the increasing costs of services. These misfortunes, which occurred during the inflationary times of the late 1970s and the early 1980s, appear to have been corrected. Still, it's wise for an individual interested in a life-care residence to inquire carefully into the financially viability of any prospective location.

But government housing and life-care communities don't represent the only opportunity for specially designed quarters. Commercial "Retirement Edens" (so titled in an AARP book) also enter the picture. The vast majority who move to these specially designed facilities find the amenities most agreeable.

These communities offer attractively designed housing units, superbly landscaped surroundings, handy resortlike recreational facilities, nearby transportation, access to health facilities, and so forth. Foresighted planners have carefully addressed the requirements of older persons, offering hotel and restaurant services, shopping, sports, and cultural areas, organized activities, and groundskeeping—generally relieving individuals of the more burdensome chores of life while increasing opportunity for socializing, leisure, and healthful activity.

Today, over a million people live in more than 2400 adults-only communities located in almost every state. The communities range in size from the vast Sun City, Arizona, with 45,000 residents, to the medium-sized Heritage Village in Southbury, Connecticut, with 2500 units and about 3500 residents, down to Bermuda Village in North Carolina with a few hundred residents. Anyone seeking information on this kind of living can make a good start by contacting the AARP for its publications on retirement areas and housing.

Are retirement communities good for older people then? The answer is definitely yes. Studies show that the majority who move to them find them most satisfactory, and longevity seems to increase for their residents.

DO OLDER PEOPLE WANT TO LIVE WITH THEIR CHILDREN?

Conventional wisdom holds that parents and grandparents want to live with their offspring. Once more, we are misled if we accept it. The GSS quickly dispels notions about any desire of the older generation to live under the same roof with its children even though the authors of the GSS questions imply that this arrangement is common. They ask, "As you know, many older people share a home with their grown children. Do you think this is generally a good idea or a bad idea?"

The truth is that many old people don't think it's a good idea. More than 8000 people have answered this question since 1972, and there can be no doubt that most older people think it's a *bad* idea, while many of the young think it's a good one. At ages 18–24, 51% of the respondents say they favor intergenerational living. Of the 25- to 34-year-olds, 45% share their view. After these two ages, opposition begins to climb, reaching 55% opposed at ages 55–64 and increasing to 62% at 65–74. At ages 75–84, there's a slight drop back to 60%, and at 85+ an even greater one, perhaps reflecting increasing dependence on children in the more advanced years of life. Even at this advanced age, though, when many of the respondents are quite frail women who live alone, a majority (51%) still remains opposed. The GSS also offers a choice of "it depends," but fewer than 20% at any age choose it.

DO OLDER PEOPLE ACTUALLY LIVE WITH THEIR CHILDREN?

With a very few exceptions, the answer is overwhelmingly no. Research shows that the older generation translates its attitudes in favor of independent living into action—only 6% of older men and 11% of older women share living quarters with their children.

Those few who do reside with their children often do so because of physical or financial incapacity. Some come from cultural traditions, such as the Japanese, where customs support having one or more older parents in one's home. In mainland Japan, authorities attribute this custom to the inadequacy of pensions, not just to filial obedience. They add that the custom is declining as pensions improve.

Does independent living demonstrate a dislike for associating with one's children, or just a desire for autonomy? Autonomy is the answer. Studies by gerontologists show that older people prefer to live near their children even though they don't want to live with them. Travel time, rather than geographic proximity, is the crucial factor. Of the older population with children, 84% live within an hour's distance from a child, and proximity increases with the parents' age. Members of the older generation definitely do not turn their backs on their children—they simply enjoy the freedom of remaining master or mistress in their own homes.

WHAT'S THE FAMILY HISTORY OF OLDER PEOPLE?

Today we know that the nuclear family typically includes mother, father, and children—with an average size of slightly less than four people, or one or two children per family. We also know that families of the past differed from those of today, so it follows that the family history of older people must differ from present family life.

Generally, families in the past were larger than they are now. The 85+ generation, some of whom might have been born as early as 1890 or even before, shows the pattern of the past. Taking into account every kind of residential arrangement—people living alone, newlyweds without children, medium-sized and large families—the average household size in the 1890s was almost 5 persons (4.93 actually). It was not until 1940 that the average family size had fallen below four persons, where it remains at present.

In the GSS, over 43% of the 85+ age group reports having had seven or more brothers and sisters, while close to 75% claims four or more. The 65–74 age group, born two decades later, still shows 40% with seven or more brothers and sisters, and over 60% with four or more. By contrast, only 21% of the current crop of 18- to 24-year-olds say they have seven or more brothers and sisters, while 35% say they have one or two, and less than half have four or more. The differences between young and old reflect the fact that the average mother between 1878 and 1902 had five or more children. Today the average is less than three.

The different generations view the ideal number of children in a family from the perspective of their own experience with family sizes. The GSS shows that more than half of the 18–44 age bracket thinks that two children are ideal. At 45–54, there's an increase of 6% in preference for three or more children, and by 75–84, almost 60% favor this larger number. At 85+, the proportion who favors three or more drops back to 54%, while 10% don't know or give no answer.

Additionally, the family history of divorce has changed. To say that the older generation experienced personal divorce or divorced parents less often than the young is one of the classic understatements of our time. Since the early years of the century, the divorce rate in the U.S. has increased nearly 400%.

In spite of this, there's little difference between past and present in the proportion of people who lived with both parents until age 16. According to the GSS, close to 75% of all age groups have lived with both of their parents until that age.

What's changed, though, are the reasons given for only living with one parent. Three quarters of the people over 65 who lived with one parent say it was because the other parent had died. For the young, death of a parent is a rarity. Divorce has replaced death as the reason for living with a single parent.

Too, contrary to the popular view, many of the old of today married *later* in life than people in recent generations. In the 1890s, the average woman waited until 22 years of age to marry, while the average man waited until 26—so says the U.S. Census. By 1950, the average marital age for women had dropped to 20, and for men it was down to 22 ½.

But now, the trend of age at first marriage is climbing again, so that women marry later than they did at the turn of the century—at 22 ½—while the average man now waits until age 24 ½. Specialists on the family say that the earlier age of marriage caused some of the increase in the divorce rate between 1950 and 1970—early marriages end in divorce more often than later marriages. Because the age of marriage has since gone up, the divorce rate has since dropped.

Another feature of family history may come as a surprise. Staying single for life was more common in the past than it became after World War II. From 1900 through World War II, between 7 and 9% of the population never married at all. This was true of both men and women. As late as 1970, some of the older generation showed the effects of past practices because 7.5% of the men and 7.7% of the women had remained as lifetime singles.

After World War II, a marriage boom accompanied the Baby Boom. Over 95% of the eligible population married, and by 1975, only 4.7% of all men age 65+ had remained single (technically called "ever-single") for life. Women outdid the men in the marriage market. By 1984, the proportion who had remained lifetime singles was down to 3.7%, its lowest point in modern history.

Today the ever-single pattern seems to be creeping back to

its pre–World War II level. More people postpone their marriages, with an accompanying rise in the percentage of singles in the younger age groups. For instance, almost 14% of the 30- to 34-year-olds are single, whereas only about 6% were in 1970. The longer anyone puts off marriage, the greater the chances of never marrying at all. To hazard a forecast, by the middle of the next century, we should see an elderly population with 10% ever-singles.

DO OLDER PEOPLE BECOME SWINGING SINGLES?

Family relationships come about through kinships of several kinds—with parents, children, brothers, sisters, aunts, uncles, cousins, in-laws, and so on—but the fundamental family link is the relationship of husband and wife. As a result, we need to pay special attention to the marital status of older people.

Occasionally, stories appear in the media about lively older bachelors pursued by a bevy of women, some old, some young, living a life of unrestricted pleasure. For women, the merry widow is an image that dates back at least to the last century. Even Benjamin Franklin, whose wise sayings for young and old filled the pages of *Poor Richard's Almanac*, advised young men to establish amorous relationships with single women past the age of menopause because this would offer opportunity for enjoyment of a full sex life without the risk of pregnancy. Today, TV's "Golden Girls" shows older single women with a lively interest in the opposite sex.

Does the swinging single image truly characterize older people? Perhaps it does hold for some. Age in general is a time when people have lived beyond the barriers and inhibitions of earlier life. It's possible that a swinging life-style does prevail, especially so for those in the earlier years of maturity. Generally, though, the evidence from gerontological studies doesn't support a swinging image even for those who remain active sexually or in other respects. The older citizen who haunts the casinos of Las Vegas and Atlantic City, is the life of the party at the country club and on cruises, or chooses an openly scandalous sex life, is the exception, not the rule. Profligate or casual sexual behavior aren't the usual avenues of enjoyment in later life.

HOW DO OLDER PEOPLE FARE IN MARRIAGE?

Are Many Older People Married?

If we're talking about men, census figures show that the answer is emphatically yes. The marital status of older men looks like this: 84% are married at 65–74; about 70% at 75–84; and close to 50% at 85+. We study the marital status of women in more detail in the next chapter, but for now we just note that the percentage of married women after age 65 is about one half of that for men, and it falls as age increases. Married men outnumber married women more than four to one in the most advanced years of life.

Do Older People Marry or Remarry Often?

Marrying and remarrying is rare for older people, so much so that December brides or grooms attract avid attention. Overall, about 5% of the 30 million people over 65 marry or remarry.

Because marriages past age 85 charm our minds, they usually set off a veritable outburst of publicity. Picture what would happen if an entertainer over 85 were to marry a mature lady of stage, screen, and television—it would be a national event. Matrimony after 85 is so unusual that it's scarcely mentioned in scientific studies of aging.

Are Older People Happy with Their Marriages?

According to the GSS, the answer is definitely yes. GSS interviewers ask, "Taking things all together, how would you describe your marriage? Would you say that your marriage is very happy, pretty happy, or not too happy?" Married people over 65 outrank all other age groups in marital happiness except for the 18- to 24-year-olds. At 65–74, 69% report very happy marriages, as do 73% of ages 75–84, and 64% at 85+. The young marrieds aged 18–24 may outrank the middle age ranges, but they don't beat the 75- to 84-year-olds. Only 71% of the youngsters claim "very happy" marriages compared to the 73% for the older group.

The rock bottom of marital happiness comes at 35–44, when only 61% of men and women together say that they are very happily married. After that, the rate of happiness increases slightly, but at ages 55–64, it jumps to 67%. During the next 10-year interval, it reaches 69%.

At 85+, the proportion describing their marriages as very happy dips, but the reason for this may be frailty of one or both spouses rather than interpersonal conflict. Still, a higher proportion at this age reports a very happy marriage when compared to some of the other ages, so marriage remains blissful for a substantial majority even past age 85.

On the basis of this, we might like to think that marriage improves with age, but we have to be careful about jumping to that conclusion. One consideration is that statistics on marriage in late life tap largely those who've had successful marriages and the few who've married recently. Most people who were unhappily married would have divorced long ago, so they don't appear in the late-life population to report on the state of their marriages. This means that the relatively high proportion of people reporting happy marriages in late life may reflect their lifelong experience rather than increasing happiness in their marriages.

There are also other reasons for caution in interpreting these figures. One is a cohort difference: Most people who reached 65 between 1972 and 1986 married before the divorce boom really got under way (it didn't peak until the 1970s). The reason they express greater happiness could be that they expected less from marriage. Too, they may report greater happiness because they're retired and experience less external pressure in life (another life-stage, age-related difference). Last, the greater composure of older people (an age-related difference) may contribute to the explanation. Whatever the contributing factors for these differences, the elderly now lead most Americans in reporting happy marriages.

DOES STATUS AS A MARRIED PERSON IN LATER LIFE AFFECT GENERAL HAPPINESS?

One of the consistent findings of research on marital status is that married people at all ages are happier than singles—not just happy in their marriages, but happier about life in general. This is also true in late life, notwithstanding the stories of gay divorcees and merry widows. Older married people enjoy an advantage in happiness over people who have remained lifetime singles, have divorced, or have become widowed.

The GSS strongly supports the research on the association between marriage and general happiness. At 65+, it shows that almost 50% of the married population describes itself as very happy. In comparison, only 26% of the widowed, 33% of the divorced, and 27% of the lifelong singles report being very happy.

Separation after age 65 ties in with the lowest levels of happiness—only 17% of those who are separated say they're very happy. Correspondingly, the proportion of not too happy persons reaches its highest level among the separated. Of them, 36% fall into the not too happy category, compared to only 8% of the married, 19% of the widowed and divorced population, and 14% of those who've remained lifetime singles.

Do married people in late life have as much fun as singles? We can get some idea of this by reference to the GSS question that asks whether life is exciting, routine, or dull. This data reminds us that an exciting life doesn't necessarily lead to a happy one because older people who are separated from their spouses report the most exciting life of all—80% of the separated persons at 65+ say that their lives are exciting compared to about 75% of the married group. Still, the married population over 65 leads those who've remained single (72% lead an exciting life) and the widowed (under 50% lead an exciting life). In general, then, married people past 65 are happier than anyone else and have a more exciting life than most.

WILL THE GROWING NUMBER OF SINGLES LEAD TO MORE ISOLATION AND LONELINESS IN THE FUTURE?

We've already seen that there's an increasing number of people who never marry. In addition, more couples remain childless than they used to, and this means that the death of a marriage partner will leave the surviving spouse without offspring for companionship or caregiving. Do these trends suggest that a greater number of older people in the future will feel more isolated and lonely than they do now?

Not necessarily. The Harris poll showed that the vast majority of older people don't consider loneliness to be a serious problem for themselves. Besides this, single persons usually form attachments with friends in whom they can confide (confidants), and remain active in social groups (church organizations, unions, clubs, volunteer services, AARP chapters, etc.), possibly more so than married individuals. Confidants appear to fill important gaps in an individual's emotional life. They share interest in a person's well-being and experiences, and they seem to compensate quite fully for the absence of a spouse, children, or relatives.

If we take lifelong singles as a special case, we find that family relationships may be less important for them than for married people. The GSS shows that lifelong singles draw less satisfaction from family life than married people do. This may be because singles never have intimate contacts with a spouse or children, so they simply learn to get along with little family contact in general. About a quarter of the older ever-singles, too, experience as much general happiness as persons who've been married. They appear to rely on friends and distant relatives when their parents or siblings have died (about half of the ever-singles may have physical disabilities).

Some gerontologists have even suggested that friendships may be superior to family relationships in some respects. They argue that friendships rest on mutual, open exchange of sociability between equals, and that this sustains a person's sense of usefulness and self-esteem. Family relationships, on the other hand, may detract from intimacy because feelings of obligation toward spouses and other relatives may prevent openness and honesty.

Some singles maintain close relationships with people who aren't blood relatives. Researchers use the term "fictive kin" to describe friends who have become so close that they speak of one another in the language of family membership. Many people are called "cousin," "uncle," "aunt" who are not actually related to those who call them by these names. Such people are fictional relatives who occupy the status of family members. Researchers sometimes refer to these as "surrogate family."

No one knows how extensively these and other nonfamily

networks serve older lifetime singles. What is known is that older singles manage to get along quite well. It's unlikely, therefore, that the increasing number of singles and childless couples will cause more loneliness in the older generation. Older singles, as well as people in families, should get along fine in the future

DO MANY FAMILIES ABANDON OR ABUSE THEIR OLDER MEMBERS?

The discussion of migration earlier in this chapter suggested that most older people live nearby one or more family members. But does this prove that older people have ties to family that live close by, or that their families treat them with kindness and consideration? Can we dismiss the growing publicity about neglect and abuse of the elderly?

Several years ago, Ethel Shanas answered these questions in a major address to the Gerontological Society of America. An expert on the American family and coeditor of *The Handbook of Aging and the Social Sciences*, Shanas reported that 80% of the care provided to older persons came directly from family members. Families, she said, provide a network of companionship and affection. Older parents step in to support women who are widowed in their 50s. Frail persons who are bedfast depend on family for care and very rarely use social services. Men rely on their wives and wives on their husbands for assistance in late life.

About abuse, the *New York Daily News* not long ago ran a story headlined "Granny Bashing." It reported estimates that 500,000 older persons living with their children had been physically abused. Although these reports are repugnant, is there really an epidemic outbreak of physical or mental violence or financial victimization perpetrated by families against elders? The facts don't suggest an epidemic, but they do show that the rate for all types (verbal and physical violence, neglect, and financial exploitation) may be as high as 4% of persons over 65. This could amount to over 1 million cases across the nation each year.

One national survey of families found that it was difficult to prove cases of elder abuse. Interviewers in the survey could turn up evidence only after in-depth probing. Most often, the instances cited involved screaming and yelling. Some seem to have been related to care activities, such as forced feeding or medication, and to physical restraint. Only 3% reported any physical violence.

Estimates based on a recently completed random sample survey in Boston showed that as many as 13,500 of the city's 346,000 population over 65 may have experienced abuse. Boston is probably fairly typical of large American cities, but it may not represent the situation in smaller cities, towns, rural areas, and suburbs very well. The study found that physical violence had occurred in almost two thirds of the cases, "chronic verbal aggression" in about a quarter, and neglect in the remainder. Contrary to what one might expect, it was the spouse rather than the children who perpetrated the abuse—close to 60% of the incidents involved spouses. Oddly, it was men who were most likely to be abused. They experienced almost double the rate experienced by women.

Even though these figures disclose that abuse is a serious problem, the studies suggest that most cases are caused by the stress of poverty or sickness in families. Abuse could be avoided if it were treated as an illness, through identification of high-risk families, intervention by social service agencies, referral for counseling, and diagnosis and treatment of underlying medical problems, such as hypertension, that may provoke abusive behavior. Furthermore, the studies do not contradict the ideas expressed by Ethel Shanas. The overwhelming majority of families treat their older members lovingly. They remain in touch with them, are concerned about their well-being, and care for them solicitously.

DO OLDER PEOPLE EXPERIENCE THE EMPTY NEST SYNDROME?

The empty nest syndrome, which is commonly considered a phenomenon of midlife rather than old age, deserves attention here because it does fall within the frame of later life. Departure of a child or children from home when parents reach their 40s and

50s most often serves as the triggering event for this syndrome. Psychiatrists who have diagnosed cases of empty nest syndrome say that it afflicts women more often than men, and that it disrupts relationships between husband and wife. Marriage becomes tedious. A sense of purposelessness accompanied by depression may pervade life. A loss of intimacy often follows, with less confiding, hugging, and kissing. Family counselors prescribe development of new activities as an antidote to the empty nest. They point out that once life becomes fulfilling again, spousal relations usually return to normal.

No one should underrate the unpleasant effects of the empty nest syndrome for those who do experience it, but there's little evidence that the condition is widespread. The GSS, for example, shows no evidence whatever of any decline in happiness among either men or women during the 40s and 50s when the empty nest years are supposed to occur. In fact, numerous studies besides the GSS have shown that the happiest years of life come when parental responsibilities have concluded. Launching children from the nest may involve some adjustments and require initiative to create new commitments, but it does not usually cause severe stress. On the contrary, aging married couples today often experience greater difficulty in prompting their children to leave home than they do from filling an empty nest.

DO OLDER PEOPLE EXPERIENCE MANY PERSONAL AND FAMILY PROBLEMS?

The GSS provides interesting information on this subject. It asks a series of questions about the number of personal and family problems interviewees have experienced during the preceding five years. The problems named are severe—deaths, hospitalizations, divorces, unemployment—for families as well as for the individual responding. No other single source of data, including NIH (National Institutes of Health) surveys, presents such a comprehensive picture of the troubles of life as the GSS.

Nor does any other source present such an unexpected set of findings. When all four kinds of difficulties are totalled, the GSS shows that the elderly actually experience *fewer* family problems than other age groups! To understand this, we first rank these problems: Loss of a spouse is the most grievous problem to bear at any age. Divorce ranks second. Hospitalization trails behind, and unemployment follows.

You can almost eliminate divorce and unemployment as family problems for the elderly. Consequently, though older persons experience more woes because of family deaths and personal and family hospitalization, when all problems are taken together, their record of misfortunes is unexpectedly low. They've experienced a smaller number of problems than other age groups. Even more surprising, the elderly are most likely to answer "none" when asked about all four types of problems. From 9 to 20% of the older age groups say they've had no problems at all, whereas only about 6% of the younger groups say so.

None of this suggests that the aged have no problems. It does, however, support other findings in the GSS, Harris poll, and elsewhere, which show that old age is a better time of life than most people suppose.

DO OLDER PEOPLE OFFER ANY HELP TO THEIR CHILDREN AND RELATIVES?

We hear talk today of the "sandwich generation," referring to people in their 50s or thereabouts who must assume responsibility both for children and for older family members at the same time. This doesn't mean that the majority of older persons never give anything in return, however. On the contrary, assistance flows from the older generation to its children and grandchildren, to brothers and sisters, and to other family members.

Gerontologists have studied the kinds of assistance that the elderly provide. Typical examples are financial support, help during illness, care of younger children (most parents are indebted to grandma and grandpa for respite from child care), assistance with household construction and repair jobs, household management, and advice.

The Harris poll documents these examples with specific

statistics. The most common type of aid has been help during illness—67% of the older respondents said they had provided this. Forty-two percent had given financial support, 39% advice, 36% had shopped and run errands for their children, and 26% mentioned making repairs and housekeeping. Other research has shown that more than two thirds of the older population receives help from children and relatives. In three-generation families, 34% of the grandparents received economic help from children and grandchildren, 42% received emotional gratification, 52% obtained help with household management, and 61% enjoyed assistance when ill.

Family assistance is mutual, flowing from parents to children and children to parents, as well as to and from relatives. The older generation can rely on their families. But they give as well as they receive.

HOW DO OLDER PEOPLE LIKE BEING GRANDPARENTS?

Most grandparents take great enjoyment in their status. Interviews conducted by Bernice Neugarten and Karol Weinstein in the 1960s produced statements like, "It's through my grandchildren that I feel young again," or "It's carrying on our family line." This and other research show that most grandparents provide help and are affectionately permissive with grandchildren, but avoid interference with child rearing.

Sometimes, they have a fun-seeking relationship with grandchildren, supplied through games, walks, and trips to the zoo, park, and beach. They continue to play a role in the various rituals of family gatherings even when it is somewhat less central than in past times. Too, grandparents serve as a reservoir of family wisdom and may become substitute parents (parent surrogates).

But not all is hearts and flowers for grandparents. A few resent their status, making statements like, "I'm too young to be a grandmother." Men have been known to refuse the title of "grandpa." Persons who express these kinds of attitudes see the grandparent role as alien to themselves.

Even the most loving grandparent may sometimes find that their adult children impose on them too much. Too frequent requests may come for grandma to take on chores or an afternoon or evening of child care when parents want to work late, shop, or just play. Grandparents may feel that they have finished their child-rearing days and greet what they consider excessive calls for help with little pleasure.

These problems, however, are the exception rather than the rule. The vast majority of older people relish the grandparent role and manage it without serious difficulty. They can relax more with the grandchildren than they could with their own children. They don't have direct responsibility for daily care, training, and discipline, so there's a measure of ease and freedom in their relationships with their grandchildren. According to numerous studies, the great majority of older people find grandparenthood satisfying and fulfilling.

DO GRANDCHILDREN CONSIDER THEIR GRANDPARENTS GROUCHY?

While we only have a small number of studies on the subject, the answer is definitely not. Grandchildren view their grandparents favorably and look to them for love, help, understanding, and friendship. They don't think of them as too old-fashioned or as very likely to spoil them. They usually don't think of them as old people, but rather as friends.

Studies show that grandparents offer an informal, easygoing relationship. This sometimes includes a kind of privilege of irreverence that they wouldn't have tolerated in their own children. Grandchildren reciprocate their grandparents' love. Many feel an obligation to go and visit with them, to offer them love, and, when necessary, to help.

WILL FAMILIES MEAN MUCH TO THE ELDERLY IN YEARS TO COME?

Ever since the sexual revolution of the 1960s, media experts and other authorities alike have wondered about the future of the

American family. Some toll the death knell of the family, citing the climb in the divorce rate, the growth of "alternative life-styles" (such as live-in boyfriends or girlfriends and openly homosexual relationships) and the Baby Bust of the 1970s. The last of these trends may well pose the most serious problem because it threatens to leave future members of the older generation without young persons on whom to call for help.

They note, too, that women have traditionally served as the family caregivers for the old. Because of the growing employment of women outside the home, they may not have time for the caregiver role in the future. Even now, they say, the family doesn't offer older persons much in the way of a sense of prestige.

No one can deny the reality of the trends cited. The doomsayers could be right.

But predicting the future is risky business—about as bad as trying to forecast the weather or the stock market—and there are reasons to believe that the family will continue to perform its vital role of supporting the elderly. Today, the divorce rate is down and more families are staying intact. Ties between husbands and wives, parents and children, appear to be reviving and remaining strong. The birthrate is up. Evidently, the Baby Boom generation only postponed childbearing and rearing until they could afford to have children.

Besides, the family has always been the basic unit, the mainstay of human society everywhere in the world. It seems that we cannot exist without it. The reasons for its crucial role may be biological (involving sex, reproduction, and care of offspring). Or they may be psychological, such as in the attraction generated by differences between men and women. They grow out of our need for intimacy, best achieved through long-term relationships and the simple pleasure of seeing a familiar face daily. The exchange of care and concern thrives best in the warmth of the family. All these factors suggest that the family will persist. They lead us to predict that this institution will remain as vital for the elderly in the future as it is today.

7

Retirement and Personal Economics

Nowhere does the knowledge gap about aging have more serious practical consequences than in the sphere of economics. This is true for American business as a whole as well as for personal financial planning.

Consider, for instance, the question of older consumers. Consumer spending is one of the major forces that keeps our economy going, yet few businesses realize that people aged 50 and up now represent 60 million potential customers, and that early in the next century, they'll represent a market of 100 million persons. What's more, advertisers still beam their messages primarily to younger audiences while analysts warn that disdain for the older consumer will adversely affect marketing and could even depress overall business conditions.

For individuals, no subject is more important to enjoyment of the later years than personal financial planning. Besides considering postretirement income, it's important to understand how the circumstances of later life will influence our spending habits, our decisions about living arrangements, insurance requirements, and saving, and investment plans, to mention only a few major aspects of financial planning.

To fully explore these topics would require an entire book, so in this chapter, we focus only on basic facts that may contribute to maximum self-fulfillment in the later years.

AT WHAT AGE DO PEOPLE RETIRE?

Strangely, the popular image of retirement has become entangled with major national publicity about age discrimination and against forced resignation from work. Intense publicity about displacement of older airline pilots, sales executives, state police officials, managers, and workers has focused attention on violation of the rights of senior employees. According to this publicity, many people become victims of discrimination because they are forced to retire. Some years ago, Dr. Robert Butler devised the word "ageism" as an epithet for discrimination against older people. Aptly named, ageism has come under attack because of its similarity to racism and sexism.

The impression generated in the battles to end compulsory retirement is that people leave work because they're forced to, not because they want to. Nothing could be further from the truth. Americans *do not* clamor to stay at work. We're retiring in droves, and we're doing so earlier and earlier all the time. We don't even wait to reach age 65, when we become eligible for full Social Security benefits. A great many of us retire in our early 60s or even before.

In this book, we've used ages 55–64 as one of the key age groups when we've presented GSS data, but this bracket gives too conservative a picture when it comes to retirement. It doesn't show what actually happens because only 26% of the 55- to 64-year-old males in the GSS state that they're retired or out of the work force. The true number of retirees in this age bracket is much higher, and one reason is that the 55–64 set of years that we selected for this book averages together a group of fairly active work years, 55–59, with the next age period, 60–64, when the retirement flood really begins. Combining these two makes the working population in the first mask the growth of retirement in the second. Also, perhaps many people no longer at work in this age group don't think of themselves as retired yet.

In any case, nearly half of the males, and a greater proportion of females, have left the work force by age 65. Early retirements begin in the 50s or before, and then swell up at about age 62, the earliest year for partial Social Security benefit payments for men.

By age 65, retiring and retired employees and business owners look like a stampeding herd. During their 65th year, persons still at work celebrate crossing the threshold of eligibility for full Social Security benefits with a thundering rush into retirement. According to the U.S. Bureau of Labor, 90% of the working population has retired by the end of its 65th year. The bureau estimates that by the year 2000, only about 5% of the population will continue to work past age 65. (A later section shows that high wages in the future labor market may offer strong inducements to stay at work, but for the present, the large number of retirees is striking.)

Even now, only about 10% continue to work past age 65, according to the U.S. Census. Many of these persons do so part-time, or they work in professional fields, such as medicine and law, where they have some latitude to set their own work schedules. Others have businesses of their own and don't have to conform to the structured job requirements of conventional employment.

In the past, most people worked until death parted them from their employment. They had no choice but to keep working because there was no national pension system that made retirement possible. Even to this day in Japan, which relies heavily on a private saving system to supply pension income, more than 40% of the population remains at work past age 65.

An interesting way of calculating the impact of retirement on our lives is to consider that adulthood begins at age 22, and then the average person can expect to live about 55 years of life as an adult. If people retire at age 65, they would spend about 12 years of these years as retirees, and this means that they would live close to one quarter of their adulthood in leisure. Persons who had the good fortune to retire in their early 50s could spend about 25 years free of the obligation of daily work—almost half of their adult lives! Retirement, it's been wisely said, is a new life stage in human history.

WHY DO PEOPLE RETIRE?

Studies of retirement decisions have shown that only 7% of retirees, at most, leave work unwillingly. Some have even shown only 1 or 2% involuntary retirements. Poor health, however, may motivate retirement in some instances. This is especially true of retirements taken by individuals during their 40s and early 50s. By age 60, as many as 30% of working persons have retired, and one third to one half of these may have done so for reasons of health.

It used to be that serious illness was about the only acceptable excuse for retirement at almost any age. Workers felt they had to justify leaving active employment because the powerful American work ethic defined idleness for any reason as a sin, a breeding ground for slothful discontent and mischief. Consequently, workers often used ill health as a feigned reason to retire.

Today, many people who retire for reasons of health aren't severely disabled or incapacitated. Rather, they may have some chronic condition, such as heart trouble or arthritis, that triggers retirement but doesn't necessarily prevent all activity. Such illnesses in the past led from early retirement to an early grave. Today we can alleviate the effects of ill health to the point where a wise decision in favor of retirement can assure a long and happy life.

Still, the majority nowadays retire voluntarily rather than for reasons of health. The main reason people retire now is that they can afford it, and the availability of Social Security pensions rests at the foundation of their decision. Social Security serves as a basic building block for retirement even if it doesn't provide a total retirement income. When combined with private company pensions, personal savings, and other resources, it makes retirement affordable for the millions.

Actually, studies show that many people who continue to work past 65 do so because their financial situation compels it. They have no other choice because their pension incomes would be too low to make ends meet. They work because they must, not because they love their jobs.

These studies reveal that the affordability of retirement is crucial. As a reason *not* to retire, it outweighs the psychological rewards and personal self-esteem that are believed to derive from work. In Japan, as we've seen, persistence of employment past age 65 by over 40% of the work force is due to the meagerness of

pension incomes. In 1980, the most recent year when comparative international figures are available, the U.S. had only 19% still
at work past 65.

Comparison with other economically developed nations
confirms the importance of affordable retirement. Sweden,
which some people consider a model for social programs of all
types, reported 50% retired persons between ages 55 and 64 in
1980. Such countries as Canada, Australia, Britain, France, West
Germany, and Italy led the U.S. in growth of retirement between
1960 and 1980, but the U.S. now matches them closely. With
acceptable pension levels, persons around the world appear
willing to exchange the workplace for a more independent, laid-
back life of retirement.

HOW DO RETIREES LIKE RETIREMENT?

Oddly, the belief that retirees don't enjoy retirement was also
fostered in early research in gerontology. Scientific researchers in
the field adhered to the theory that we acquire our sense of being
and identity from what we do, the roles we play, and especially
so from work. They reasoned that work occupies so much of life,
and is so powerfully founded on the strong American work ethic,
that the daily round of toil supplies our inner sense of self-esteem
as well as our daily bread. Scattered case histories, compiled by
early researchers, appeared to support the theory. They showed
that some people suffered a baneful, withering effect from
retirement that led to early death.

Researchers theorized that decline came on because retirement caused a crisis in personal identity. It compelled people to
modify their entire personalities, to remake themselves. The
process was considered emotionally exhausting, destructive, and
often impossible to complete. The case histories of individuals
who suffered decline after retirement seemed to show loss of a
personal sense of direction. They couldn't find themselves, and
this accounted for their ill health and eventual premature death.

Subsequent research has reversed these early findings. The
GSS, as we've seen, demonstrates that the happiest years of life

follow retirement—almost 40% report being "very happy" at ages 65–74 and 37% at ages 75–84, compared to an average of 32% for the earlier ages. Researchers today say that a positive attitude toward retirement has replaced the once-nagging sense of evading duty. Workers today don't need to feel as if they're "copping out" when they retire. It's no longer a stigma to leave the workplace. Rather than bringing on an empty, meaningless life, retirement has beneficent effects.

The Harris poll unexpectedly illustrates both the old and the new attitudes toward retirement. When asked if they'd like to continue work, one third of the age 65+ respondents seemed to reveal old-fashioned attitudes by answering "yes." However, when later asked if they'd actually consider taking a job, only 11% said they would do so!

The respondents weren't dishonest in giving these contradictory answers. It's not unusual to find people thinking one way when asked about a general attitude and another when asked about its everyday practical application. The GSS offers independent support for the second answer. It shows that only about 12% of the 65+ survey group actually were working full- or part-time.

ARE RETIREES BORED WITH LIFE?

One of the queries in the Harris poll throws indirect light on the issue of whether persons experience boredom in retirement. The interviewers asked, "Do you now think you made the right decision to retire when you did, did you retire too early, or do you now think that you retired too late?" Persons answering this question were divided into groups according to the ages when they discontinued work—55–64, 65–69, 70–79, and 80 or more.

Less than 10% of any of these groups expressed any doubt at all about their decision to retire. They felt that they'd made the right choice. Slightly more men than women (from $1/2$ of 1% up to 2% depending on age) even felt that they'd retired *too late*.

Some doubt about their decision was registered by those who'd retired 3–4 years ago, compared to retirees of 2 years or less—the rate of doubt climbed from 4% for the recent retirees to

8% for the 3- to 4-year group. Awareness of these figures has prompted some gerontologists to speak of the first 2 years as the honeymoon period of retirement, but though the rise to 8% is a doubling of the number, 92% still feel pleased with retirement. Clearly, retirement remains a honeymoon.

The issue of boredom brings us back to the GSS data on how much excitement people find in life. Recall that the proportion of people who find life exciting declines with age. The decline, however, sets in well before people reach retirement age.

The most exciting period of life is ages 18 to 44, when 50% of the population say they find life exciting, but the sharpest drop in excitement occurs at ages 45–54. The proportion at that age falls to 43%, followed by a smaller decline to 40% at 55–64. There's no sharp break downward at ages 65–74, when most people have retired. The decline merely continues slightly to 38%. At 75–84, long after retirement, there's a further slide to 34%, and the figure remains there past age 85. Retirement seems to have little connection with relative boredom or excitement in life.

WILL THE FUTURE JOB MARKET OFFER ENOUGH ATTRACTION TO KEEP OLDER PEOPLE AT WORK?

Although the normal course today is to retire by age 65, future trends in the labor force may modify this. For one thing, eligibility for full Social Security benefits will start a slow rise, beginning in the year 2003. By the year 2027, age 67 will be the year for eligibility for full benefits. But other changes may end up being more important in affecting future labor trends: Opportunities and rewards for work in late life may increase in the future.

The U.S. faces a labor shortage starting about the year 2000. It could boost wages and other incentives to a point where prospective retirees may find the attractions of work more alluring than those of retirement. This could be much more important than any future increase in the chronological age for eligibility for full Social Security benefits.

The statistics on the future are clear. Just as the proportion of the older population will grow, so the proportion of people of traditional working age (20–65) will shrink. The aging of the Baby

Boom generation combined with recent declines in the birthrate will reduce the numbers of men and women traditionally available for work.

We can get keener insight into the future by looking at more detailed figures for the 18- to 34- and 45- to 54-year age groups. By the year 2000 (only a short time from now even though the date sounds like something out of a science fiction novel), the 18- to 34-year age bracket will have shrunk by 20% while the 45- to 54-year-old will blossom by 46%. Until recently, the proportion of younger U.S. workers has been climbing, but that is changing and will continue to change in the future.

While no one can predict future business conditions precisely, it's a reasonable bet that a severe labor shortage is in the offing. Today the U.S. has somewhere around 120 million jobs available during good times. Unemployment has been low because the number of people going to work has almost equaled the number of jobs. As the proportion of younger workers shrinks, older workers will probably be more in demand. Very likely, businesses will have to make special efforts to attract older workers to fill the available positions.

Businesses have already shown some willingness to hire older workers in spots where the young used to fill all the available jobs. Travelers Insurance Company in Hartford, Connecticut, and Corning Glass Works in Corning, New York, are major corporations that have developed policies to employ the talents of older workers. Their personnel practices don't necessarily require older workers to return to full-time work. Rather, they've created job banks of retirees who can come in to handle short-term projects or peak loads of business. The advantage is that the older employees are available, they don't need to be trained, and they enjoy the occasional involvement in work activity, as well as the added income.

It's obvious that if fewer young people enter the work force while the economy stays robust, employers will have to offer attractive incentives to keep older employees at work. Wages and other rewards (more flexible time schedules, health and other benefit packages, etc.) may become so attractive that older workers will find the lure of staying on the job irresistible.

DO OLDER WORKERS MAKE GOOD EMPLOYEES?

Conventional wisdom has it that older workers contribute disproportionately to business costs. For many a worker and executive who's felt the cold breath of pressures for early retirement, this view may have a particular poignancy. Such negative perceptions of older workers undoubtedly had much to do with the antidiscrimination legislation of the 1960s and the subsequent campaigns against mandatory retirement. In view of the possibility that older workers may become an increasingly important part of the labor force in the future, we need to look at their characteristics with some care.

A survey done by pollsters Yankelovich, Skelly, and White (YSW) for the AARP in 1985 revealed the relative value of older workers. Addressed to 400 human resources and personnel executives selected for their role as gatekeepers of employment in medium- to large-size companies, YSW called on the executives to rate their company's older employees. Good to excellent ratings were given in the following areas: good attendance and punctuality (86% affirmed this); commitment to quality (82%); loyalty and dedication to the company (82%); a great deal of practical knowledge (76%).

Between 60 and 74% of the executives also gave "good to excellent" marks to older workers for other qualities. These included solid experience on the job and in the industry; solid/reliable performance record; someone to count on in a crisis; able to get along with coworkers; emotionally stable.

What surprised many people more than anything was the YSW finding that older workers didn't cost more than younger ones. Health benefits and retirement plans, for instance, were no greater for senior employees. Too, YSW heard reports that older workers were more dependable than younger workers.

Other studies have found that older workers outperform

younger workers in several respects. They're more regular in attendance at work, take less time off for illness, and have fewer work accidents caused by bad judgment. They match younger workers in performance, and they tend to be more attached to their work and satisfied with their jobs because they've established their niche in life.

If older workers turned out to be such paragons, YSW naturally asked why many major companies do so much to encourage or even insist on early retirement of employees. The question came down to whether such qualities as loyalty, dependability, and experience are most needed in today's business climate. "Not necessarily," came the answer.

Today, YSW learned, American businesses face intense worldwide competition that favors other characteristics: ability to adapt, to master new technology, to generate new ideas, and to demonstrate a competitive spirit. These were the characteristics that gatekeepers rated highly but found wanting in older workers. They now outweigh the traditionally valued qualities of reliability, dependability, experience, and loyalty in which older employees excel.

YSW saw few signs of overt discrimination against mature employees but acknowledged their need for retraining for the modern marketplace. Further, it said that older employees themselves must play "a significant role in advancing their cause within companies." This they must do within a framework of reciprocity that recognizes the competitive conditions of modern business. Openness to innovation seems to be the key here. YSW concluded that such cooperation would advance the interests of all concerned. In sum, older workers make excellent employees, often better than younger ones. Any investment required to hone their skills for the modern marketplace would seem to make sense.

HOW FINANCIALLY WELL OFF ARE OLDER PEOPLE?

People from age 65 and up have lower incomes than most of the age categories under 65. Why? Because of retirement and the lower lifetime earnings of people in the past.

The results show clearly in the GSS. If we use a $15,000 annual income as a standard of comparison, we see that 70% of the population over 65 had incomes below this amount from 1972 (when GSS began) to 1986. Only 30% of the 65+ respondents were above the $15,000 annual figure. In contrast, only 45% of those in the 18–64 bracket had incomes below $15,000, whereas 55% had incomes above it.

If we use a very low income figure of $5,000, we see that low income becomes more common as age advances. From age 75 on, 35% of the respondents had incomes below $5,000 compared to 27% at 65–74, 13% at 55–64, and only about 10% overall under age 55. (We know that some fudging goes on in reporting income to national survey interviewers—next to sex, income is the most taboo subject—but even with this, considerable differences would remain).

Does this mean that older people are poor? Not really. For some, the answer is "yes," but for most, it's "no." As economist James Schulz of Brandeis University has succinctly put it, "From a statistical point of view, *the elderly in this country are beginning to look a lot like the rest of the population:* some very rich, lots with adequate income, lots more with very modest incomes (often near poverty), and a significant minority still destitute. This is very different from the past when most were destitute" (emphasis in original).

Dollar income figures themselves don't explain why Schulz should make the foregoing statement. Several factors need to be taken into account to understand it. One of these is the high rate of home ownership among the elderly, a fact described in the previous chapter on family and friends. Because most older people have owned their homes for many years, their mortgages are often either fully paid off or require only minimal payments.

Another relates to the various tax exemptions for older persons. These include higher standard deductions for federal income taxes and the exclusion of Social Security pensions from income taxes for married persons with annual incomes below $32,000. Some states relieve older persons with lower incomes from paying state and local taxes. Benefit programs, such as Medicare, also reduce expenses for the elderly.

Other factors enhance available income in later life. An obvious one is elimination of expenses linked with the responsibilities of earlier life stages. Among these are relief from daily appearance at the work place, which can reduce annual outlays for clothing, cosmetics, commuting, meals, and automobile insurance and maintenance. Child-rearing costs, often amounting to thousands of dollars per year during midlife, normally become a thing of the past by retirement. The need to put aside pension savings disappears, and the amount taken out for Social Security alone amounts to about 7.6% of each individual's paycheck. (For small business owners, this comes to 15.2%, as they must also contribute the employer's share of the Social Security amounts.) Company pension plans or other savings can add another 5 to 10%. These and the other differences have led economists to conclude that a husband and wife at age 65 need only 64% as much income as a couple between ages 35 and 54, who have two children.

This elimination of the expenses yoked to early life also means that older people tend to have more *discretionary income*—income that they can spend as they please instead of for necessities. This doesn't necessarily make the old affluent, but it does indicate that they can manage successfully on fewer dollars than the young. Having paid their dues by discharging the duties of early life, they have greater latitude in spending as they wish during their mature years.

WHAT ARE THE INCOME SOURCES FOR OLDER PEOPLE?

The sources of income in later life differ considerably from those at younger ages largely because pensions replace wages and salaries. The Social Security Administration has prepared a chart (Figure 7.1) that shows the combined sources of income of older Americans. This represents all income of older individuals together, not the amounts that each individual actually receives. It's a total for all Americans over 65 rather than for a single person. Still, with adaptation to personal circumstances, individuals can use it to get a rough idea of how much of their income they can

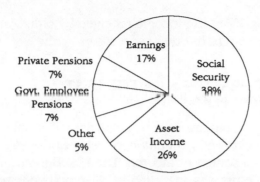

Figure 7.1. Sources of income for older Americans. (From J.H. Schulz, *The Economics of Aging* (Fourth edition). Dover, MA: Auburn House Publishing Company, 1988.)

expect to get from Social Security, pensions, wages, and other sources.

Social Security pensions, which represent 38% of the income that older people receive, lay a basic foundation. Yet this may be well below what many of us would expect—it's commonly believed that Social Security will supply the entire pension income individuals need. For most of us, though, it's by no means the only source of income required, and to think otherwise can lead to regrettably poor financial planning.

Asset income, which represents 26% and arises from rents, stocks, bonds, and interest, seems larger than one might expect. Although it represents a large chunk of the total income of all elderly combined, it's concentrated in the upper income brackets.

Earnings from employment account for 17% of the total income received by the entire older population. The percentage here is large enough to suggest the potential of paid work as a source of income in the event of a severe labor shortage in the future.

Private company and government employee pensions at 14% may seem rather limited. This kind of income, however, is growing in importance and may make a significant contribution to the financial well-being of the present younger generation when it retires.

The remaining 5% of the income received by older Americans comes from a variety of other sources.

WHAT ARE THE FEATURES OF THE BEST PRIVATE PENSION PLANS?

Because private pension plans only began to spread widely after World War II, the present generation of retirees doesn't rely heavily on them as a source of income. The U.S. Bureau of the Census, however, estimates that 76% of all employees today work for employers who offer pension plan coverage, whereas only 12% did so in 1940.

As more and more people have begun to draw on these private sources, an increasing number have had the good fortune (or the wisdom) to get checks from two or three former employers, as well as from Social Security. Retired military personnel who obtained civilian employment following their discharge from the service represent a typical example of this happy situation. Observers, sometimes with ill-concealed envy, have dubbed these people a "pension elite" and accused them of being "double-dippers."

While private pensions offer a vision of a comfortable future, individuals need to become aware of the features of better plans early in their careers. Most often available to employees in government or major corporations, we summarize what economist James Schulz has said about them in his study, *The Economics of Aging*.

Adequacy and certainty of benefits are the number one considerations. *Adequacy* can be illustrated by reference to a fairly common standard in government pension plans. Benefits of this type represent a percentage of the salary an individual earns during the final year (or years) of employment. This percentage often builds up at a rate of 1 to 2% for every year of service up to a specified maximum, such as 50% of the salary the individual earns during the final year of employment.

How do individuals build up to the 50%? It would work this way. A government pension plan might provide that individuals could build up a pension at the rate of 1.25% per year. Someone who worked for the government for 40 years would receive the maximum benefit (multiplying 1.25% x 40 equals 50%). While 40 years may seem like a long time, persons would not have to start to work for the government until age 25 in order to achieve the maximum by age 65. Recall that economists estimate that individuals have an adequate postretirement income if they receive somewhat less than 70% of their final salary. Given this, the 50% of former salary, plus Social Security and private savings, would combine to provide an adequate income.

Certainty, of course, involves the solvency and safety of the pension fund, but it also includes features such as vesting and portability. *Vesting* of a pension means that the individual becomes eligible to receive the pension at retirement age only after a specified period of service with the employer (e.g., pensions in some professional sports vest after 4 seasons of play). The length of time for vesting is usually 5 years, but for a few, it may take up to 10 years.

Portability means that individuals may carry the entitlement to vested benefits with them if they leave one employer and change to another. Vesting and portability may be negotiable when an individual takes employment, an important consideration for anyone who starts work with a new employer after age 40.

Other considerations in private pension plans include the size of the employer's contribution, the rights of surviving beneficiaries, and the relationship of benefits to Social Security. The first two of these need to be reasonably generous—ensuring an employer contribution at about the same level as the individual's, and ensuring payment of benefits to survivors for a period of years at least equal to the number of years payment would have been given to the retiree.

Some public and private employers provide the option of choosing either the company plan or Social Security: one or the other, but not both. The individual must decide which choice will be most beneficial in the long run. Another consideration is the adjustment of future benefit payments for inflation, a feature

offered by Social Security and some public pension plans but not
by private employers. Careful study of the terms of employer
pension plans before accepting a position can go a long way to
assuring a secure and pleasant retirement.

HOW CAN RETIREMENT INCOME BE ESTIMATED?

The key to estimating retirement income is *replacement income*,
which refers to the individual's income after retirement calcu-
lated as a percentage of the income before it. How much preretirement income should be replaced? At least 65 to 70%. Postretirement income need not fully replace preretirement income for
the reasons given before (reduction in taxes, elimination of child-
rearing expenses and pension plans, reduction or elimination of
home mortgage, etc.)

To calculate your own retirement income, add together the
following: the amount that Social Security will provide (the U.S.
Social Security Department will supply figures on the size of your
anticipated pension check); the amounts anticipated from employer pensions and individual retirement savings, annuities, or
other plans; and the anticipated income from assets, if any.
Simply add these amounts together. Then compare the result
with your preretirement earnings (and total expenses) from all
sources. If you wish, you may convert this to percentages, as
follows:

$$\frac{\text{(Retirement income from all sources)} + \text{(Savings due to reduced expenses)}}{\text{(Preretirement income)}} \times 100 = \text{(Replacement income)}$$

Next, calculate the amounts you'll save on expenses (e.g.,
taxes and pension plan savings). A simplified example for someone earning a preretirement income of $50,000 appears in Table
7.1.

DO OLDER PEOPLE DESERVE THE INCOME
THEY RECEIVE?

The fundamental answer is yes, but it needs a careful explanation.
(Much of the following reflects the work of economist James

Table 7.1 Postretirement Income as Replacement for Preretirement Income

Preretiremnt Income Source	Amount ($)	% of Preretirment Income
Postretirement income		
Social Security	7500	15
Company pension	22500	45
IRA/KEOGH	6000	12
	36000	72
Postretirement savings in expenses		
Reduced mortgage costs	6000	12
Reduced business expense	2000	4
Reduced taxes	1000	2
Reduced pension savings and social security	5000	10
Postretirement income plus reduced expense	50000	100

Schulz.) Because critics target the Social Security system more than anything else when they allege favored treatment for the elderly, we begin by describing the development of that program to answer the question fully.

Few people had any doubts about the justification of retirement income for the elderly until the late 1970s and early 1980s, when Congress and the public rudely awoke to the growing crisis in our public pension system. Improvement in benefits brought about by cost-of-living increases in Social Security payments in 1972—along with an expanding older population, earlier retirement, hyperinflation, and a recession—were bringing the Social Security trust fund to the brink of bankruptcy. Higher payroll taxes for Social Security became inevitable though politically explosive. Continued support for programs for the aging, 30% of whom had lived in grinding poverty in 1960, seemed doubtful.

Also, many people realized that Social Security payments to retirees actually represented a transfer of income from those who were working to those who were retired—but the reason for this arrangement had been forgotten. Few knew that Social Security witholding taxes are paid into a trust fund, and that Congress, when framing the law in 1935, had intended to have earnings from this fund serve as the source of payments. The fund was to become a huge loan pool for other government departments, and the interest earned was to be paid out as pensions to retirees.

Congress later abandoned this idea because it was impractical. To make it work, the trust fund would have had to grow for years, and the current members of the older generation would get no pensions. As a result, the legislators adopted a pay-as-you-go plan, which directly transferred tax monies (paid into the trust fund) to retirees. Congress still retained the idea of investing any surplus funds (funds not paid out to retirees) into loans for other government departments, but the amounts were quite small until recently.

The intent of the pay-as-you-go plan was to ensure that the first retiring participants would become eligible for benefits within a reasonable period of years, though they wouldn't have contributed to the Social Security system for as long as today's retirees. Even at that, there were no payments until the first beneficiary, Miss Ida Fuller, received a check in 1940 when she retired from her job as a secretary in a law firm. The check amounted to a monthly pension of $22—hardly bountiful.

Today, some highly vocal critics insistently claim that to be old is to be overprivileged. Their charges of preferential treatment hit primarily at the costs of Social Security and the inequity of having the young support the old. Are the charges of overprivilege true? Oncoming members of the Baby Boom generation need to pay close attention to these allegations because they could influence future social insurance policies—and therefore their own pocketbooks in retirement.

Over the years, Congress, labor unions, and most economists have continued to support the idea that Social Security provides an equitable intergenerational exchange. It makes jobs available to the young by encouraging the old to step down. More older people would have to hold jobs if they couldn't afford to retire. Therefore, while younger workers may bear the present burden of Social Security payroll taxes, they benefit from the system too. Also, present retirees are receiving benefits to which they contributed in the past, and present workers will receive retirement benefits in the future.

But, do benefit levels transform older people into affluent fat cats? Hardly. Social Security provides a floor of protection, and not more. It was never intended by Congress to serve as the entire income for retired individuals. Figures on the percentage of income replaced by Social Security for persons at different income levels readily show this. For those with very low preretirement incomes, $6,500 per year, Social Security replaces only 57% of preretirement earnings, and the replacement rate declines from there. At $10,000 the amount replaced is 49%; 42% at $15,000; 34% at $20,000; 23% at $30,000; and 14% at $50,000. Pensioners don't suddenly reap a bonanza from Social Security when they retire.

Two other features of the Social Security system lend the program legitimacy: its broad base of coverage and its certainty. In terms of coverage, the system is able to give security to individuals with widely differing lifetime work patterns, including interruptions of work for pregnancy and child rearing, for illness, and for unemployment, because it is compulsory and creates a huge pool of people who pay into as well as benefit from the system. It's notable that the governments of most developed nations have adopted a similar compulsory approach. The first was in Germany under Chancellor Bismarck in the 1880s. The U.S., which postponed action until 1935, was a latecomer. Japan, which doesn't emphasize a government pension system, still legally requires workers and employers to set up private plans.

Research shows that individuals, left to their own devices, would not put aside the payroll taxes that now go into Social Security. Besides, individual pension savings would probably not equal Social Security payments because the large size of the program assures that administrative costs—the expenses of operating the system—are low and are favorable to beneficiaries.

In terms of certainty, Social Security creates a lifetime saving system made up of equal employee and employer contributions, backed by the full faith and credit of the federal government. The principle involved is not unlike that of the longstanding mutual benefit societies that were in existence before the program. Among these were the Masons, the Benevolent and Protective Order of the Elks, the Knights of Columbus, B'Nai Brith, and

numerous ethnic and religious organizations dedicated to the
welfare and benefit of their members. The theory behind these
organizations was, and still is, that each member helps the other
and that all benefit by a united effort. Following their philosophy,
Social Security represents a pooled social contribution by individuals. It serves as a shield against adversity and eventually
comes back in the form of a pension to those who pay the taxes.

Social Security doesn't put anyone on easy street. All in all,
it represents a fair and workable system on which individuals can
rely to structure an adequate retirement income. Because people
pay into it throughout their working lifetimes and usually also
build up other pension savings and assets for retirement, it's
reasonable to say that they deserve the income they receive.

HOW DOES THE PUBLIC FEEL ABOUT
SOCIAL SECURITY?

Public opinion surveys have persistently shown overwhelming
public support for the program, even against opposition and
some fears for the future. In 1985, when reforms in Social Security
were still very much on people's minds, YSW pollsters conducted
a survey titled "A Fifty Year Report Card on the Social Security
System," which demonstrated just how powerful this support is.
Using a national sample from every walk of life, YSW found that
almost 90% of Americans hadn't the slightest doubt that the
program should continue, and that only 3% wanted to phase it
out. Americans also thought that the program had been successful (92% "successful" or "very successful"), and that it was important (96% "an important program" or "one of the most important
programs").

Among the reasons given for favoring the program were
these: More people are now living to old age (94% said this);
taking care of parents financially would be a burden without it
(80% said this); and it's an essential source of income for many
elderly Americans (98% agreement).

Other surveys since YSW's have continued to show a high
level of endorsement (90% or more) for Social Security. Some
have recorded a willingness to sacrifice pay increases if it would

mean better Social Security retirement benefits even though YSW had found earlier that 62% considered the present level of taxes "about right." Other polls have proved that 63% of the public would accept higher payroll taxes in order to assure the future of the program.

WILL THE YOUNGER GENERATION GET SOCIAL SECURITY BENEFITS?

The answer is, Yes.

The reason for asking the question at all reflects the recent crisis of public confidence in the system, a phenomenon that economist Schulz explains grew out of the post-OPEC oil emergency and succeeding high inflation and unemployment when benefits were being paid out faster than payroll taxes were coming in. In 1979, a Harris poll recorded the nation as verging on despair over the situation. It found that 40% of the public hadn't any confidence at all that they'd ever receive their public pensions.

Intense media publicity about the specter of the aging Baby Boom generation further fanned the bonfire of uncertainty. The rising costs of benefit increases, designed to keep pace with inflation, added fuel. A new type of anxiety was born: "Social Security Insecurity," as some have called it.

Experts understand that these fears are sincere but consider them unjustified. They point out that of all the public programs in America, Social Security enjoys the most public support. Schulz, who is probably the preeminent national expert on the economics of aging, calls the Congressional commitment to the program "the Congressional pension promise" even though he gives strong warnings about the condition necessary to ensure the future of Social Security.

Among the conditions that Schulz cites are continued national support, steady economic growth, and careful attention to financing over the long term. Already, the reforms of recent years have solved the financial problems for the foreseeable future. Increased payroll contributions, together with an income tax on the Social Security benefits of some (when this book was written,

this involved taxes on up to 50% of the benefits of married couples with incomes of $32,000 or more and single persons with
$25,000 or more), account for most of the improvement. Further,
taxes on Social Security income must be deposited directly into
the Social Security trust fund rather than used for other government programs, such as defense.

Today the reserves in the trust fund are building up at a rate
of $40 billion or more a year. Though the figures change con-
stantly, estimates of the kitty on reserve for the Baby Boom
generation place the figure at $2.5 trillion early in the next
century. By 2030, when the crest of the retirement wave will hit,
the surplus will have reached $12 trillion, according to the
Morgan Guarantee Trust Company.

Debate today swirls less around the fundamental solvency
of the system than on how to avoid profligacy in the face of the
enormous size of the fund that Social Security will have available
for loans to other federal government departments. Warnings are
sounded lest anyone tamper with the system. By law, the taxes
paid into the system can only be paid out to beneficiaries, and
surpluses must be invested in federal government treasury securities. The Social Security trust fund buys these securities from the
U.S. Treasury, and the money becomes available to support the
general federal budget. By 2004, the trust fund could absorb the
federal debt—so says Morgan Guarantee. Given the growing
reserves in the fund, some fear a wild Congressional spending
spree. Others fear that politicians will take the politically popular
step of cutting Social Security taxes.

Schulz, Morgan Guarantee, and many others oppose any
such tampering or profligacy and hope that the crisis in Social
Security during the 70s and early 80s has taught us a lesson. The
reserves, which fell to about 3 months during that period, should
never again be allowed to decline to such a disastrously low level.
They say that unexpected bad times alone may well burn up the
surplus, and the next crisis of confidence may lead to chaos.

Some critics have raised another issue: Will the rate of return
on a person's payments into Social Security offer a reasonable
financial benefit? Will the amount paid out even equal the amount

taken in from paychecks and employers? Or would the individual be better off by making a safe investment with a private money manager? Morgan Guarantee has even proposed that 2% of the tax should be funneled into individual investment accounts rather than into the Social Security trust fund.

Analysts disagree about whether Social Security is a good deal, according to Schulz, but several factors ensure its promise of fairness to future generations. One is that present law requires upward adjustment of benefits payments to offset inflation, a feature that would be hard to match through private savings or investment. Another is that Congress will continue to modify the program as circumstances require.

The essential fact, though, is this: Social Security belongs to the American people, and Congress responds to the will of the American public. The promise of Social Security rests with the American people, young as well as old. Future generations can have as much faith in the system as they have in their own good judgment and will to sacrifice present income for a future pension.

DOES RETIREMENT MAKE A CONTRIBUTION TO THE GENERAL ECONOMY?

Withdrawal from the work force at retirement age may suggest that we terminate the useful period of our lives when we no longer make a positive contribution to the national economy. Professor Robert Atchley of the Scripps Foundation Gerontology Center at Miami University in Ohio (that's right, this Miami University is in Ohio, not Florida) thinks otherwise. He believes that retirement makes a major contribution to our economic well-being.

One argument in favor of Atchley's thinking is that retirement opens up jobs for younger workers. Although reducing unemployment was one of the goals of national policy behind the passage of Social Security, the program went further and actually helped to overturn businesses' previous thinking about the reason for offering pensions to employees. Prior to passage of the

Social Security Act, businesses wanted to hold onto their experienced personnel and to limit high rates of staff turnover. Passage
of the Social Security Act helped to reverse this type of thinking.
Business learned from government that retirement of senior
employees isn't bad if it opens up positions for new younger
ones. Today's practice of offering incentives to retirement reflects
this change in thinking.

One can roughly estimate the impact on unemployment if
Social Security and other pensions had not become available to
make retirement affordable for mature employees. In 1950, over
45% of male workers remained in the labor force past age 65. If
this ratio were the same today, 5 million more people would be
in the work force.

Add this to the 30% who now retire *before* 65, and you'd
boost the work force by about another 10 million. Even though
these estimates are approximations, they indicate that we might
need about 15 million additional jobs to have full employment.
This could at least double our rate of joblessness, bringing it to an
unacceptably high level of 10% even with our present near-
record employment rate. Our national pension system, along
with private pensions, obviously makes a crucial contribution to
the working of our economy.

But that's not all. Professor Atchley also cites the effect of
pension savings on economic growth. The Social Security trust
fund itself probably contributes to economic activity and business expansion because it becomes available for loans to government departments, and some of these funds are used to contract
with private companies for services and industrial production.
Private pensions, however, have a more immediate effect on the
economy.

Pension savings don't just stand idle, as if tucked away in a
sock. They earn interest because fund managers invest them in
business operations of various kinds. Among these are new plant
construction, purchase of equipment, mortgages, and the like.
These investments help to expand the nation's economy.

Some economists have argued against Atchley's view. They
say that pension savings don't make much of a contribution

because nations save as much as they need for business expansion with or without pensions.

The Morgan Guarantee Trust Company, however, sees things in the same way that Atchley does. A subsidiary of J. P. Morgan & Co., a major investor in the nation's businesses, Morgan Guarantee has proposed that we divert part of the Social Security trust fund surplus into business investments because this could increase the amount of U.S. capital available for economic expansion by as much as four times. According to Morgan Guarantee, this would do more than add to America's capital for business investment. It would help to eliminate our trade deficits and our present reliance on foreign investment for business expansion.

It's hard to dismiss the logic behind the idea that pension savings contribute to our economy. Whether or not Social Security has any direct effect, private pension savings do become available for loans to businesses. They also go into the purchase of bonds, stocks, mortgages, and money market instruments, all of which tend to contribute to the financial stream necessary for economic expansion. The national stream of pension savings inevitably flows into business as well as to the benefit of pensioners themselves. By making funds available for business growth, pensions help to create jobs and more products for everyone.

SHOULD BUSINESS INTENSIFY MARKETING TO OLDER CONSUMERS?

In recent years, some major corporations have looked at the growing numbers of older persons and have begun to adapt products and marketing strategies to the senior population. Among the leaders in this effort is that mellow veteran of mass sales, the Sears, Roebuck and Company, which has started a "Mature Outlook" club to promote the sale of Sears products to older shoppers. Other companies that have targeted products and marketing for the 50+ age group are Levi Strauss (specially designed slacks), and McDonald's (discounts during certain hours of the day). Industries that have joined the parade include airlines, hotel chains, retirement communities, beauty product and sporting goods manufacturers, magazine publishers, and the health care industry.

Why does the older population justify this kind of attention? What sort of spending power do older consumers have?

Figures presented earlier showed that the 65+ population has a lower gross income level than the rest of the population, but the story doesn't end there. If we take the population from age 50 years up, we find a market that represents one quarter of the population, 40% of our households, 60 million people, and more than $450 billion in purchasing power per year. In the next 30 years, the 50+ generation will grow to more than 100 million, and will make up one third of the population and an estimated 50% of all households. The purchasing power of this block will be enormous—probably worth more than $1 trillion, and possibly as much as $2 trillion.

But not even these figures tell the entire story. If we break the U.S. population into segments, we learn that three age groups from 45 and up actually lead the younger groups in purchasing power. The 55- to 64-year-olds, frequently called the "young old," turn out to be number one in income in the United States.

Second place in income standing goes to the 45- to 54-year-olds, a category that includes the fifth decade of life, which we've used in this book to mark the beginning of old age. Besides that, this bracket has in it people of ages 50–54, who are likely to have a level of income close to that of their immediate seniors.

The 65+ age group ranks third. While its income isn't as high as that of the two other mature groups, it ranks ahead of every other age category up to age 44. That's better than one would expect considering the low income levels of some of the oldest Americans.

But, the tale still doesn't end there. As noted before, researchers have found that the older age groups have higher discretionary incomes than the young. This means that they have greater freedom to decide how to spend their funds. They can splurge on luxuries if they like, because they've already acquired such necessities as a home; furniture, including household appliances (e.g., refrigerator); and a car. According to David Wolfe, founder of the National Association of Senior Living Industries, this means that older people are in a better position than younger ones to spend for a wide range of products that fulfill the higher order needs of life—the sense of belonging, esteem, and self-actualization—identified by psychologist Abraham Maslow. Older consumers represent an attractive market now and will become an even more attractive one in the future.

WHAT TYPES OF PRODUCTS AND SERVICES DO OLDER CONSUMERS PREFER?

Do older consumers make an easy target for marketing? The answer rests with the kinds of products and services they want, but only in part. Older consumers can be wooed with the right products and sales strategies—along with a very large caveat: Advertisers must avoid marketing messages like those the AARP's *Modern Maturity* magazine has labeled as "esthetic downers." We'll learn more about these in the next section, but first let's see what products older consumers favor.

Senior buyers purchase certain types of products and services more often than other market segments do. Seniors buy 48% of the annual new stock of large luxury cars, and they generally leave the sporty two-seaters to the young crowd. They account for a startlingly high proportion of the annual recreational vehicle (known as "RVs") trips—72%. They buy 34% of all package tours, 32% of all hotel and motel nights, and 30% of all air trips. Besides this, when they travel, they go farther, stay longer, and seek out entertainment and shopping tours more often than anyone else.

As was shown in Chapter 5, the GSS shows that older people are more likely to be readers than are other age groups. Consequently, age-specialized mass-circulation magazines, such as *New Choices* (formerly *50 plus*) are beginning to catch hold. Older persons also buy 37% of all facials, slenderizing treatments, and health spa memberships. One of every four golfers is over 55, so sporting goods manufacturers have begun to develop special products for senior swingers.

Women over 55 pay out $1 of every $4 spent on cosmetic

and bath products. Consumers over age 55 consume nearly 50% of all decaffeinated coffee and 30% of all instant coffee. They're the main buyers of vitamins, prescription drugs, and health services. And the massive retirement community industry is theirs alone.

ARE BUSINESSES RESPONDING EFFECTIVELY TO THE OLDER MARKET?

They're beginning to, but advertisers have not yet analyzed how to motivate older consumers to buy their products and services. The elderly are good bank customers because they save their dollars, but this also means that we know little about how to appeal to them to buy products.

Interestingly, some progress in marketing to older consumers has come through mistakes. One of the errors was committed by the H. J. Heinz Company when it decided to develop "Senior Foods" for older shoppers because its sales personnel learned that they sometimes bought baby foods for their own consumption. The product fizzled out because it tore aside the curtain of anonymity—older shoppers had formerly hidden their embarrassment at buying baby food under the guise of making purchases for their grandchildren. In another case, *Modern Maturity* magazine dropped advertising for "Attends," a disposable incontinence pad brought out by Proctor & Gamble. The magazine coined the description "esthetic downer" for such products, and a decline in sales of "Attends" followed. Later, the editors of *Modern Maturity* apparently changed their minds because they joined *New Choices* and other magazines in accepting advertising for "Depend," featuring the attractive one-time American film sweetheart, June Allyson. Both products compensate for urinary incontinence, which is most frequently suffered by women, as a result of muscular weakness caused by childbearing.

The term *esthetic downer* raises an interesting question regarding products that compensate for disabilities. Today, these hardly have much design appeal, yet Dr. Eric Midwinter, director of the British Centre for Policy on Aging in London, suggests that such products could have more appeal than they now do. Business has done little to make these stylish, fashionable, or pleasing. Today, such products carry the image of incapacity. They're unpleasant reminders of the hospital sick room.

One hundred years ago, beautifully designed canes and parasols were a standard of elegance for the well dressed. Today, Americans shun these, and older people use these only at the risk of losing face. Most devices to overcome disability look plain ugly. Even the functionally constructed, electrically propelled wheelchairs could exhibit a sleeker, more colorful appearance. With better design and marketing, these and other products could win greater acceptance and perhaps become as fashionable as eyeglasses and the once-disdained blue jeans and sneakers.

But we've begun to overcome mistakes and find ways to deal with problem products. Marketers are making better appeals to the older generation. Older men and women appear as models more frequently in television commercials and magazines advertisements. The attractive, gray-haired Kaylan Pickford is one of the front-runners. *Smithsonian* magazine, which itself has a large number of older subscribers, has carried highly appealing advertisements for the Chevrolet "Caprice," featuring six older men and women. The ad is ageless because it projects an affirmative and definitely upbeat image.

Penetration of the older market has begun. As marketer David Wolfe has said, business must realize that *cognitive age* (the age that people feel) is well below *chronological age* (actual age in years). Older consumers don't like to be designated as "golden agers," "senior citizens," and other patronizing terms.

Elaine Sherman, a professor of marketing at Hofstra University on Long Island, sees a strong potential in the older market. She observes that, "interests of seniors are more varied than [those of] nonseniors. Their energy levels in pursuit of these interests can be every bit as intense as those expended by young people."

The mature market, coming on 100 million strong in the next century, promises a great future for enterprising businesspeople.

With economic situations securely based on a combination of public and private pensions and personal savings, the old are assured the latitude of choice. Many of the elderly may not be rich, but they are and will continue to be comfortable.

Intangibles, which grow in importance over life, are of most value to older consumers. Their economic status means more than ample riches—it means autonomy, a guarantee of independence, and the opportunity for continued growth and development. It's the quality of life, not mere survival, that counts most at any age. And, the surest guarantee of intergenerational equity lies in sustaining this same quality for young people as they age.

8

Women and Men

I n 1983 the American Sociological Association proposed to devote its annual meeting to the eternally engaging subject of gender—the characteristics of women and men. But, Alice Rossi, president of the association during that year, insisted that the theme of the meeting needed to be "gender *and age,*" not the sexes alone. Members of the association pressed her on the reason for including the topic of age, as if the subject of the sexes would be quite enough by itself. Professor Rossi promptly replied that you can't understand the sexes without bringing age into the picture.

Let's turn this idea around: You can't understand age without bringing in the sexes. In fact, precisely because gender does influence the way that we experience aging, the sexes need to capture us as much in age as they have captured mythology, poetry, ballets, operas, novels, and daily soap operas at other times of life.

To bring the sexes into the picture adds another vital dimension to our vision of seniority. Even if there were no other reason to include it, we'd have to observe that the average woman outlives the average man by about 7 years, and that this gap is expected to remain and grow into the next century even as the average length of life advances for both sexes. (The word *gender* has become the preferred term for designating the sexes in the social sciences, probably because the flow of everyday language has linked the word *sex* with biological intercourse. However, in this chapter, we use the word *sex* more often, as it's a more familiar term, unless ambiguity might result from its use.)

DO WOMEN AND MEN GROW MORE ALIKE AS THEY AGE?

Some think so. The word for similarity between men and women is *androgyny*, from the ancient Greek words for man (*andros*) and woman (*gyne*—as in *gynecologist*). The hormones that determine our male–female sex-linked characteristics (bodily hairiness, beards, voice pitch, breast forms, reproductive organs, bone structure, muscle tone, and proportion of bodily fat) may decline in potency during old age. This decline may cause some of these distinctive sexual characteristics to recede. Such features as facial hair become more common in women, while men's muscle tone declines as life goes on. Although the list of biological sexual characteristics is long, we do not address those here, as they are not relevant for our discussion. Rather, attitudes, behavior, roles, and statuses are most important when it comes to gender.

For instance, the GSS tells us that men and women do indeed share many attitudes. But they're not alike; they remain separate and distinct throughout life. The French troubadour Maurice Chevalier says it best: "Vive la différence!"

The GSS shows a persistent pattern of similarities and differences between women and men over the lifespan. This can be illustrated by reference to a great many of the GSS topics, but one of the more interesting ones concerns feelings about premarital sexual relations. Sexual attitudes are explored more fully later in this chapter, but here we use this particular subject to show the pattern of common yet different outlooks of the two sexes.

The question here reads as follows: "There's been a lot of discussion about the way morals and attitudes about sex are changing in this country. If a man and woman have sex relations before marriage, do you think it is always wrong, almost always wrong, wrong only sometimes, or not wrong at all?" The combined proportions of each female and male age group who answered "always wrong" or "almost always wrong" appears in Figure 8.1.

Do the women answer differently than the men? They certainly do—we see that the sexes, when asked if premarital sex is always wrong or almost always wrong, remain apart throughout life (excepting 85+, when the sexes converge because almost 9% of the women respondents "don't know" or give no answer). The gap begins at about 6% at ages 18–24 and persists, becoming wider at some points, over the entire lifespan.

At the same time, we shouldn't overestimate the differences. When 54% of the men and 45% of the women at ages 18–24 agree that premarital sex is *not wrong at all*, and 55% of the men and 62% of the women past 85 say it's *always wrong*, then the two sexes in the same age categories obviously share fairly similar views. Clearly children of their times, the graph shows that younger men have more in common with women of their own age than they do with older men. And older women have more in common with men in their age brackets than they do with the younger women—a perfect example of a cohort difference as well as of similarity between the sexes.

How can we respond to the question of androgyny then? When one looks through the GSS, the dominant impression is

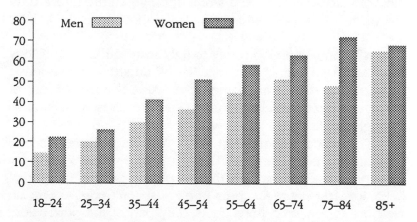

Figure 8.1. Is premarital sex wrong? (Data from the GSS.) How men and women respond to this question.

one of substantial agreement between the sexes. Likeness is the predominant pattern at all stages of life. Besides that, research shows that many men and women converge in the roles they perform as they age—men take part more in household work, while women assume more responsibility for family financial management.

The sexes remain separate, but when contrasts and differences appear, they're subtle. They seem to create that slight variation, or counterpoint, that makes the relationship between the sexes so interesting, and so aptly described as filled with an exquisite mystery—mystique.

DO SEXUAL RELATIONS CONTINUE IN LATER LIFE?

One of the most persistent myths about aging, more often held by the young than by the old, is that sexual interest and activity disappear with the years. The butt of numerous jokes today, written records of senior sexlessness goes back at least to the tales of Boccaccio and Chaucer in the 1300s. Both related stories of older men who had married younger wives and were objects of ridicule because they'd become cuckolds, victimized by more lusty, sexually powerful younger men. Yet, with typical human contrariness, older men who express libido often get labeled dirty old men (D.O.M.), and women, though more rarely, dirty old women (D.O.W.). What is the truth about sexuality in later life?

A beginning notion comes to light in a headline, "Still Sexy After All These Years," that once led off an article published in *Modern Maturity*, the magazine of the AARP. The article is one of the many sources which reports that sexual interest remains alive throughout life.

The difficulty, though, is to get solid, nationally representative data on the subject of sex during the later years. For reasons given in Chapter 5, surveys that accurately portray the sexual behavior of the entire American public just don't exist. As a result, we have to rely on reports about only part of the population, mainly from those who took the trouble to volunteer for a particular survey.

It's surprising, then, to find that we have in aging one of the more extensive pieces of research on sexuality. This is a study carried out by Consumers Union and published under the title *Love, Sex, and Aging*, under the authorship of Edward Brecher and the editors of the Consumers Union magazine. Although this survey can't be said to be any more representative than the Hite report, it did net responses from 4246 *Consumer Reports* subscribers over age 60. As such, it represents the largest body of data available on sex and the older population, and it definitely offers some interesting insights.

The Consumers Union study begins by showing that most of the respondents were aware of the mythology about the death of sexuality in later life—the first question asked in the survey is whether "society thinks of older people as non-sexual." Three thousand (70%) of the age 60+ survey group agreed with this statement, only 500 (12%) disagreed, and the rest (18%) had no opinion.

However, did the survey prove that the mythology was true? Hardly. Over half of these 60- to 90-year-old respondents, including considerable numbers past age 70, said that they continued to be sexually active. Besides this, *Consumer Reports* noted that frequency of sexual intercourse seemed to have some relationship to marital happiness. The comparison was between married persons who reported sexual activity more than once a week and those who engaged in it less often. Though the difference in percentages of happiness was not great, it seemed worth noting to the authors because it did correspond to the level of sexual activity. Of those who engaged in sexual intercourse more than once a week, 94% reported having happy marriages, whereas 89% of those who engaged in sexual activity once a week or less said their marriages were happy.

Frequent sexual activity, however, was not always essential to happiness in married life. Those who were classified by the authors as having Victorian sexual views reported less frequent sexual activity and lower enjoyment of sex, but they matched the others in the proportion with happy marriages. So, no one in later life needs to feel anxious because he or she doesn't have an active sex life.

What about declining sexual activity over the years? The Consumers Union study did indicate a fall as age progresses, a finding that came as no surprise considering the usual opinion about sex in age. Quite unexpected, though, was the high level of continued participation in sexual activity. During their 50s, 98% of the men reported being active, as did 91% of those in their 60s and 79% of those 70 years or over. For women, the rates during this same set of years were 93%, 81%, and 65%.

Evidently, the factor of having a partner available was important in promoting activity because married persons of both sexes remained more active than the unmarried. Further, even well after age 80 (when comparatively few women are married because there are not enough men to go around), half of the men and one third of the women remained sexually active.

DO SEXUAL ACTIVITIES REMAIN PLEASANT?

The *Consumer Report* survey respondents answered with a definite yes.

There is some decline over time, though. During their 50s, 90% of the men who reported being sexually active rated their experience as one of "high enjoyment of sex." After that, the proportion fell to 86% during the 60s and 75% at 70+. Sexually active women experienced a high level of enjoyment less often than men. During the 50s, this stood at 71%, but from then on, it didn't drop as much as it did for men. During their 60s, 65% of the sexually active women said they experienced "high enjoyment of sex," while 60% did so at 70 or above. Clearly, large proportions of those who remain sexually active enjoy the experience, and the proportion of women who do so converges with the proportion of men as the years go by.

Consumer Reports considered whether age, health condition, or lack of a partner most affected continuing sexual activity. Health, we should note, can dramatically affect sexual activity, not only because heart conditions and high blood pressure constrain participation, but also because afflictions such as arthritis may make sexual contacts and postures painful. Analysis of the survey responses did show that health does affect the level of activity, but that age and lack of a partner enter the picture, too.

The study also showed that the elderly are quite relaxed and individualistic in their sexual practices. The range and kind of sexual activity described was large and varied. Many of the respondents seemed untroubled by radical departures from social norms of appropriate sexual behavior. They revealed modes of performance that may be more common than one would think, but that have not previously been disclosed as occurring during the later years of life.

A group of respondents affirmed that their sexual desires remained alive even though they no longer engaged in sexual activities. They may well provide the best clue to understanding sexuality in later life. The simple truth is that human beings share in common with all animal life the quality of responding to stimulating, pleasant, and comforting physical sensations. In infancy, these start with being held, rocked, stroked, and cherished. Later, in youth and adulthood there's pleasure in being hugged, kissed, caressed, having sexual intercourse, and in giving as well as receiving sexual satisfaction. Older people don't suddenly become insensate or lose their sense of feeling. Older people also respond to closeness, touches, caresses, kisses, and tenderness, whether or not these activities involve direct sexual intercourse.

Humans are physical creatures who enjoy pleasant bodily sensations throughout life. *Consumer Reports* documents the proposition that the permanent bond of marriage appears to provide the greatest opportunity for satisfaction through sexual relations. Still, whatever the marital status, desire and the general capacity to respond remain alive always.

DO OLDER MEN AND WOMEN DIFFER IN THEIR SEXUAL ATTITUDES?

They do, but the differences aren't always dramatic. Conservatism in attitudes about sex appears more often among women than among men, but the two groups often share quite similar views.

The GSS shows that the lowest degree of conservatism for both sexes late in life pertains to the question of premarital sexual relations (as was shown in Figure 8.1). By ages 65–74, when attitudes on this subject become quite restrained, we see that 43% of the men still consider such activity "not wrong at all" or only "sometimes wrong." In contrast, only 30% of the 65- to 74-year-old women share the same view as the men.

The disparity between the sexes persists at 75–84, when 30% of the men and 20% of the women approve of premarital sexual relations. The difference nearly disappears at 85+—now only 21% of the men and 18% of the women approve—showing unexpectedly that some long-surviving men in the GSS have attitudes more like those of older women than those of younger men.

Attitudes toward teen sexual activity (between ages 14 and 16) generally show the sexes quite far apart before 65 but closer together after 65. Women during the early phases of late life remain considerably more opposed to teen sex than do men, but then there's a turn about. At age 65–74, when 76% of the males and 82% of the females say that such relations are "always wrong," only 6 percentage points separate the sexes. After that, the men become more conservative than the women, with 89% of the males and 88% of the females choosing "always wrong" at 75–84. After age 85, generalizations about the male population responding to this particular question are probably inaccurate because only one man appeared in the sample. He answered "always wrong," representing a 100% masculine opposition, compared to 87% for the women!

The sexes show more similarity in regard to extramarital sex—about 90% of the men and 95% of the women disapprove. In only one instance—regarding homosexual relations—does the disparity between men and women completely disappear during the advanced years. Eighty-six percent of both women and men disapprove.

The best characterization of late-life differences between women and men regarding sexual attitudes and relations may well be found in the aforementioned *Modern Maturity* story, "Still Sexy After All These Years." The study covered 164 men and women between ages 55 and 90 who had participated in interviews with Beverly Johnson of the University of Vermont.

Johnson, a registered nurse as well as a Ph.D., found that the women were more interested in, satisfied with, and apt to participate in such activities as sitting next to someone and talking, improving their own appearance, and saying and hearing verbal endearments. Men, on the other hand, favored reading or looking at erotic materials, caressing someone's body, or having sexual intercourse.

Whatever the differences, Johnson observed that the common stereotypes about the disappearance of sexual activity and sexual interest in age are wrong. Older people, she generalized, maintain their interest in sexual matters. They remain desirable, and they remain capable. She concluded that although interest and activity may taper off to some degree, the majority of women and men remain sexually satisfied in later life.

HOW DOES THE MARITAL STATUS OF OLDER MEN AND WOMEN COMPARE?

Women may have an advantage over men in length of life, but men have an advantage over women in marital status during the later years. The GSS parallels the census in showing that 76% of the men are married at age 65–74, compared to 41% of the women—a 35% advantage for men. At ages 75–84, when 64% of the men and 19% of the women are married, the advantage climbs to 45%. At ages 85+, it drops back to 34%, but only because both are more likely to be single: 40% of the men and only 6% of the women are now married.

Correspondingly, many more women than men experience widowhood. At ages 65–74, only 13% of the men in the GSS have become widowers, compared to 44% widowhood among women. At ages 75–84, a little over one quarter of the men say they've become widowers, while the figure for women has reached almost three quarters. At age 85 or more, about 53% of the men identify themselves as widowers, while the figure for women has now climbed to 86%.

If the data on widowhood and marriage for the 85+ age group doesn't seem to add up (6% of the women married, plus

86% widows, adds to only 92%), it's because not all unmarried women are widows. Around 5 or 6% of women (and men too) have remained single all their lives; some are divorced; and a few didn't answer the question about marital status.

Men marry or remarry in later life far more often than women. Grooms over age 65 outnumber brides two to one. When a woman over 65 marries, the average age of her new husband is 67 ½. When a man over 65 marries, the average age of his spouse is 57 ½. If marriage is bliss, then men have the better of it in old age because a higher percentage of them get married.

WHO ENJOYS LIFE MORE IN THE LATER YEARS— MEN OR WOMEN?

Despite popular opinion to the contrary, more women than men do *not* find married life to be a very happy experience. In early life, married men pretty well match married women in marital happiness—about 65% of each group aver having a "very happy marriage." In late life, however, men outstrip women in marital happiness, and the advantage grows with the years. At ages 65–74, 73% of the married men claim "very happy marriages" compared to 64% of the married women. At 75–84, it's 78% for the married men and 69% for the married women. And, at 85+ it's 65% for the married men and 57% for the married women—perhaps the lower percentages at this age reflect the respondents' poorer personal health or having a spouse who's in poor health.

HOW DO THE WORKING LIVES OF THE TWO SEXES COMPARE?

Women have always been workers, but today the home is no longer the center of work for all women. The employment patterns of younger women bear more similarity to men's than they used to. This means that the work history of the sexes in the older generation differs from that of the younger generation today.

The GSS points out that early in life (age 18–24), more women than men hold jobs outside the home. By late life, (age 65 and after), however, men report a higher level of lifetime work activity than do women. During these later years, nearly 100% of the men indicate having had full-time employment in the past, compared to 80% of the women.

The recent changes in employment of women outside the home shows up most clearly by comparing the 85+ generation with the 55- to 64-year-olds, who represent the first mature age category to show the changing lifetime work pattern of modern women. Only 69% of the 85+ women say they were ever employed outside the home compared to 85% of those aged 55–64.

Controversy about equal job opportunities for women since the 1960s has highlighted issues concerning the levels and types of jobs held by the two sexes. Generally speaking, more older men than women have held jobs with higher prestige (*job prestige* is rated by the U.S. government for all occupations)—about 4% of the men have held the jobs with highest prestige, compared to only 1% of the women. But, this isn't true for everyone over 65— more men have held jobs in blue-collar industries while more women have worked in white-collar retail and office occupations.

Too, among those over age 75, some women actually exceed men in job prestige because certain higher prestige occupations have traditionally been female. Women more often than men have held positions in the teaching and nursing professions—both of which rank high in occupational prestige. About 15% of the women over 75 report this level of prestige, compared to only 6% of the men.

What proportion of the older population continues to earn income from work outside the home? At ages 65–74, only about 12% of the men in the GSS work full-time, while another 8% work part-time. Nearly 77% say they're retired. Only 5% of the women at this age say they hold full-time jobs, while about 7% of the women work part-time. Far fewer women say they're retired— only 30%—while 55% report keeping house.

After age 75, involvement in work tapers off for both sexes. But, at age 85+, about 7% of the men still say they work outside the home, 4% of them full-time and 3% part-time. Less than 1% of the women at this age claim to hold jobs, while 49% still say they keep house. Only 44% of women at this age claim retirement compared to 85% of the men. It seems that work is never done for many women; if they retire, then they retire to housework.

DO LIVING ARRANGEMENTS DIFFER FOR THE SEXES?

We've already learned from the Harris Poll that 60% of the American public believes that loneliness is a very serious problem for older people. Only 12% of the older population itself agreed with this. What lies behind this difference? Maybe facts about the living arrangements, social activities, and daily habits of older men and women throw light on the problem.

First, a very large proportion (from 75 to 85%) of the older population doesn't favor the idea of sharing a home with its children. This suggests that older persons prefer independent living in their own quarters even if they must live alone. This seems to fit with the Harris poll findings on loneliness reported earlier—apparently solo living arrangements don't promote loneliness as much as we may think.

Actual living arrangements bear out the independent attitude of the older generation. Because many are still married at ages 65–74, the rate of solo living is at its lowest then, but it's still substantial for women, and it increases for both sexes thereafter. For men, it's 19% at this age, while for women it's 45%. By ages 75–84, it's climbed to 68% for women and 32% for men. At 85+, nearly 70% of women live alone, compared to 46% of the men. Whether male or female, being widowed is the main reason for living alone.

When older persons do live with someone other than their spouses, it's almost always with a relative—97% of women past 65 who reside in households with others live with relatives. So do 98% of the men. These joint residences rarely involve more than two persons and almost never more than four.

What about multigenerational residence with minors (17 years or younger)? The figures show that older people rarely share a home with families that have any children. At ages 65–74, only about 6% of the population live in a residence with a minor present, and the figure declines after that for both men and women.

Home ownership, as we saw before, is common for the elderly—over 70% at 65+ years. In the earlier stages of old age, though, it's more common for men than for women. At ages 65–74, almost 80% of the men in the GSS own their own homes, while only 70% of the women say they live in a family-owned home. At this age, too, 26% of the women rent their residences compared to 18% of the men.

By ages 75–84, women match men in home ownership— about 69% of women and men own their homes, while 23% of the men and 28% of the women rent. By 85+, the balance of home ownership shifts toward women—80% now own their homes, compared to 70% of the men. At this stage, 30% of the men and 16% of the women rent a residence.

HOW DOES THE INCOME OF THE SEXES COMPARE IN LATER LIFE?

Older women are definitely financially less well off than older men. According to recent census figures, men receive an average income of about $17,850 at ages 60–65, whereas women of this age receive an average of $6,850. At 65–69, when most men are retired, their average income drops to $12,580, but women receive only $6,525. At age 70 and over, men have an average income of $10,025 while women stand at $6,225, so the gap narrows slightly as age advances.

For the 85+ age group, we have no more recent figures than those collected in the 1980 census. Using these as a base for estimating the present incomes of persons at 85+, we would give a figure of $8,000 for men and $4,500 for women—rough approximations to be sure, but probably not far from the target. In general, then, men experience a considerable drop in income from the preretirement years, but women's incomes start at a lower level and remain there.

But, how do the two sexes feel about their incomes? Do women feel deprived and men satisfied? The GSS includes three questions that tell us how people feel about their incomes. One asks respondents how they think their income compares with the incomes of other persons ("far below average," "below average," "average," "above average," or "far above average"). Another asks how satisfied the respondents feel with their income ("pretty well satisfied," "more or less satisfied," or "not at all satisfied"). The last inquires whether incomes have improved, have become worse, or have stayed the same over the last few years.

In spite of their lower income levels, older women are more likely than men to say that their incomes are average, at least in the early years of late life. At age 65–74, 54% of the women say their incomes are average, compared to 51% of the men. At 75–84, 58% of the women give the average rating, compared to 52% of the men. At 85+, about 58% of both groups choose average.

Income differences between men and women seem to influence the way the sexes compare themselves to others in only one respect: More men than women rate their incomes as "above average" or "far above average." From ages 65–84, about 13% of the men feel they're in these upper brackets, while only 8% of the women think so. When it comes to the below-average ratings, the sexes tie at about 35% at ages 65–74 and at 31% at ages 71–84. At 85+, however, a slightly greater proportion of men than women selects the below-average category (28% of the men compared to 25% of the women).

Too, in spite of real differences between the two groups, women in two of the three older age groups express as much or more satisfaction with their incomes as men do. At ages 65–74, about equal proportions (around 82%) of each group express themselves either as "pretty well satisfied" or "more or less satisfied." At ages 75–84, this proportion for both groups increases to 87%. By 85+, there's a change: A slightly higher proportion of men than women selects the "pretty well satisfied" category—men 57% to women 48%, perhaps suggesting that more women at this age really begin to feel a financial pinch.

The last question relevant to income in the GSS asks

whether respondents feel that their financial situation has been getting better, staying the same, or getting worse. The results show that women and men in the senior years differ little, and, more important, evaluate improvements in their financial situations *less* favorably than the younger age groups do. From age 65 and up, not more than 20% of the population cites an improving financial situation. For those under 65, the proportions who cite an improving income range from a low of 31% at 55–64 to a high of 49% at 25–34.

Further, between 55 and 60% of those over age 65 feel that their financial situation has stayed the same over the last few years. This compares to 35 to 40% of those under 65 who say so. However helpful the improvements in Social Security have been, they have not made many older persons feel that they are better off.

WHAT ABOUT WATCHING TV, DRINKING, AND SMOKING?

The GSS provides information on a few of the preferences of women and men. The relevant areas are time spent watching TV, listening to the radio, newspaper reading, smoking, and drinking.

During the later years, women show slightly more disposition to watch TV than do men. The majority of both age groups watch 2 to 4 hours per day, but about 20% of the women compared to 15% of the men watch 5 to 6 hours daily.

Women also listen to the radio more than men do. From ages 65–84, women average 2 hours of radio listening per day, whereas men only average 1 hour. At 85+, this difference disappears—both sexes average an hour.

Although the margin isn't great, a slightly higher proportion of men read the newspaper daily (maybe just the sports page and comics?). The GSS shows that over 75% of the men at ages 65–74 and 75–84 read the paper daily, compared to less than 70% of the women. At 85+, the daily reading rate for men drops to 54%, but that's still ahead of the women, who've fallen to 47%.

Moderation is the key word to describe the elderly when it comes to drinking alcohol and smoking, and women are even more moderate than men—more of them abstain completely. Comparison with the younger age group tells this tale clearly. When we take all age groups together, the peak ages for drinking for the two sexes are 25–34, when 87% of the men and 78% of the women say they use alcohol. After 65, the peak age for drinking is 65–74, when 66% of the men and 50% of the women say they drink.

By ages 75–84, drinking has dropped to 58% for men and 38% for women. At 85+, nearly half of the men still drink compared to only one quarter of the women.

These figures, of course, may not actually show withdrawal from drinking as age advances. They may relate to socially approved patterns of abstinence that date back to the Prohibition era or to the antisaloon movements at the turn of the century. Women especially may reflect the nearly forgotten times when young girls joined the Prohibition movement as "Little Temperance Leaguers."

When asked, "Do you sometimes drink more than you think you should?", about three times as many men as women at 65+ admit to the weakness (about 25% men to 8% women). None of the women over 85 confess this failing. The young show far less moderation than the old in this respect—at 18–24, 60% of the men and 42% of the women disclose that they sometimes drink too much.

Older women smoke far more rarely than men do, and those men and women who survive to old age smoke far more rarely than the young. At 65–74, 36% of the men say that they smoke compared to only 20% of the women. By 75–84, the ratios for the sexes are down to 32% and 7%. At 85+, none of the women report being smokers, and the rate for the men is down to 17%.

For comparison with the younger age groups, the peak smoking age for men is 45–54, when the rate is 53%. For women, it's the youngest age group that most often smokes—almost 40% do so. No one has yet produced indisputable proof that smoking causes cancer, but it's certain that smoking is less common among those who survive the longest.

HOW DOES THE HEALTH OF OLDER MEN AND WOMEN COMPARE?

In terms of health, we've already seen that men tend to have different kinds of diseases than women do—more coronary heart disease, lung problems, and hearing impairments, for example. Women more often experience hypertension, arthritis, and bone and joint problems. Men tend more toward deadly diseases, whereas women experience disability rather than deadly illness.

It's important to emphasize once again, though, that seriously ill health is *not* normal among older persons. Most older persons do indeed suffer from one or more chronic problems (which include poor eyesight and mild arthritis), but they can generally manage them satisfactorily. The GSS includes two indicators that demonstrate the generally good health of older men and women. One of these is experience with hospitalization.

At ages 65–74, less than half of the men or women in the GSS had experienced hospitalization during the preceding 5 years. Even though persons over 75 experience more frequent hospitalization than individuals under 75, such an event is by no means universal or frequent for everyone in their seniority. For persons over 75, about 30% of the men and 45% of the women had experienced *no* hospitalizations whatever in the preceding 5 years.

The GSS also gives an indication of *seriousness* of illness by comparing hospitalization figures for the preceding year with the figures for the 4 years before that. Looking at these two periods shows that repeated hospitalization is unusual even in the most advanced ages. At ages 65–74, only 16% of the men and women had been hospitalized during both of these periods, and the rate never gets above 25% even for those past age 85.

Self-described health shows that the majority of both sexes

have positive feelings about their health throughout their lives. At age 65–74, 55% of the men and 51% of the women describe their health as good to excellent, and there's little change after this. At no age does more than 20% of the older population in the GSS describe its health as "poor."

The GSS doesn't stand alone in reporting that older men and women both give quite favorable assessments of their health. Its findings are consistent with surveys made by the federal government's National Center for Health Statistics (at the NIH—National Institutes of Health). These show that about 70% of all persons aged 65 or more rate themselves as in good to excellent health, while only 30% say they're in fair to poor health. Physician examinations carried out in the course of the NIH studies support the favorable self-ratings of health made by the elderly.

Most older men and women in the GSS also express considerable *satisfaction* with the condition of their health. From age 65 and up, the majority express contentment with their health—specifically, 39% state that they experience a great deal of satisfaction and 33% a fair amount. Less than 20% of men and women say they're dissatisfied.

WHICH GENDER IS MORE SOCIABLE AND HAS MORE FUN IN LATER LIFE?

Earlier, we observed several things when we looked at the GSS question about how often respondents spend a social evening with someone. For one thing, the question sets a tough standard for older persons because they're more likely to socialize in the daytime than in the evening. Second, the 65+ generation shows different patterns of social activity—they visit primarily with brothers, sisters, other relatives, and neighbors, while people at earlier stages of life more often visit with friends. (Also, socializing doesn't necessarily correspond with happiness—the youngest age groups (18–34) do more socializing but display lower levels of happiness than the older age groups.)

Keeping these facts in mind, we learn that women appear more sociable than men, at least in the earlier stages of late life. At 65–74, 54% of the women say that they spend a social evening with neighbors at least once a month, compared to 49% of the men. This difference holds true until 85+, when there's a turn-around—59% of the males now claim monthly socializing, compared to 35% of the females. The explanation for this change may be that the women have become frail and, being widowed, lack the help or the incentive of companionship for getting about.

Too, until age 85+, higher percentages of women than men socialize with relatives—about 66% of the women report at least monthly visits, compared to about 63% of the men. After age 85, the balance shifts toward the men, 55% of whom record such visits, compared to 47% for the women. The shift at this age may be caused by the widowhood status of women; the vast majority of women at this age live alone, whereas many men are still married. The two sexes, however, stand about equal when it comes to visiting with friends—46% socialize at least once a month at ages 65–74, and then drop to 35% or less from age 75 on.

Membership in organizations offers another kind of social involvement. The GSS includes questions about membership in church-affiliated groups, hobby clubs, professional societies, social clubs, fraternal organizations, service clubs, unions, and business associations, among others—a very wide range. Men in the early years of late life hold an advantage over women, but this may be due to their former experience in business or their continuation of union membership after retirement. At ages 65–74, close to 75% of the men hold one or more organizational memberships, as compared to 66% of the women. By ages 75–84, participation in one or more organizations increases to 76% for the men and 70% for the women, suggesting that this age bracket may have more time for organizational activity than do younger groups. A surprisingly high percentage of both sexes maintain memberships past 85—over 60% do so. It appears, however, that these types of memberships don't prompt men to be more socially active than women.

But, does this comparatively active social life for women introduce more excitement into their lives? It seems not—two out of the three older age groups of men report more excitement in life than do their feminine counterparts. The reason may be that more men are married, but, whatever the explanation, 43% of the men at ages 65–74 find life exciting and 49% find it routine, compared to only 35% of the women who say "exciting" and 54% "routine." At ages 75–84, the two sexes match each other—34% exciting and about 51% routine. At 85+, the men again take the lead—44% exciting and 38% routine, compared to 28% exciting and 58% routine for the women. It's rare for either men or women in the advanced years to find life dull—only 11% or less as a rule. After 85, however, more men than women find it dull—16% to 11%.

IS EITHER GENDER MORE CONSERVATIVE THAN THE OTHER?

Two of the subjects of religion and politics discussed in Chapter 5 offer us a good basis for judging whether one sex may be more conservative than the other. Let's start with religion because research shows that strong religious convictions tend to go along with a conservative outlook in life. Is either gender more religious than the other?

Strength of religious commitment shows up in the GSS question that asks, "Would you call yourself a strong or not very strong . . . [Protestant, Catholic, Jew, etc.]?" Women outdo men over the lifespan, and the gap increases, even though both sexes show a rising level of commitment in later years. At ages 65–74, 59% of the women, compared to 42% of the men, express strong dedication. By ages 75–84, 62% of the women profess a strong attachment, while the proportion of zealous males holds at 44%. At 85+, the men leap 15 points, to 59% strong commitment—but the women still lead them with 70%.

Attendance at a church or a synagogue offers another test, this time measuring whether people actually behave in accord with their religious convictions. Again, women outstrip men by a large margin, especially so in the earlier years of later life. At ages 65–74, 60% of the women attend religious services weekly or more often, compared to 46% of the men. By ages 75–84, 61% of the women attend at least weekly, but the men, now at 49%, catch up a bit. After age 85+, the men take the lead, with 50% attending once a week or better, compared to 45% for the women. This last difference may be due to the greater difficulties that women may have in getting to services; more men are married, and they may have help from their spouses.

Using belief in life after death as yet another criterion, we find that women lead men until age 85. At ages 65–74, 75% of the women are believers, compared to 64% of the men. In the next decade, women still hold a substantial lead because 74% of them are believers compared to 65% of the men, but at age 85+, the men suddenly overtake the women—77% of them believe in life after death, compared to 68% of the women.

When we use religion as a standard, then, it seems as if women may be more conservative than men. But does this apparent greater conservatism hold up when it comes to politics?

WHAT ABOUT DIFFERENCES IN POLITICAL OUTLOOK?

At 65+, the largest proportion of both sexes consider themselves moderates—neither as conservatives nor as liberals—41% for the women and 38% for the men. The men, however, edge the women out in labeling themselves as "conservatives"—roughly 38% to 33%.

The two sexes differ little in political party affiliation in later life. About 54% of each say they're Democrats, compared to 36% Republicans. Most of the rest claim status as Independents (unaffiliated with any party).

In presidential voting, both sexes have helped the winning candidate, whether Republican or Democrat, about equally. Older women, however, were less enthusiastic about Ronald Reagan than were older men. Younger women were also less enthusiastic than were younger men. This was especially true in the 1984 Reagan–Mondale election contest, when about 54% of the women over 65 in the GSS said they voted for Reagan compared to about 60% of the men. The difference between the sexes in the younger age groups was even greater than this— about 53% of the women voted for Reagan compared to 66% of the men.

Too, older men showed greater conservatism than women

in one of the early elections recorded by the GSS. This was in 1968, when about 10% of the 65- to 84-year-old males, but only 6% of the females, voted for Governor George Wallace of Alabama. Interestingly, none of the GSS respondents over 85+ said they voted for Wallace.

Over the years, older men may have influenced the elections more than older women. Generally, men have held a 10% lead in the proportion who say they've registered and voted in presidential elections. Presidential elections have often been won by very narrow margins, sometimes by less than 1%, so the higher male voting activity could have had considerable influence on national policy. This may change in the future—male influence may wane because oncoming generations of women have nearly caught up to men in political participation. If the trend persists, older women, who outnumber men more than 2 to 1, could well prevail in politics because of their greater numbers.

Attitudes on specific political issues also reveal the comparative conservatism of the sexes, and they may, quite incidentally, give some clues to the direction of policy if older women become more politically active in the future. The GSS data suggests that older women hold somewhat more humanitarian, if not liberal, attitudes than men. They're more willing to say that too little money is spent on welfare, social security, education, and improvement of the living conditions of black people. Though a majority favor both capital punishment and harsher treatment for criminals, the proportions among women are not as great as they are among men.

Men express more support for government spending on space exploration, and they endorse an active role for the U.S. in world affairs more affirmatively than do women. More men than women approve military spending, and fewer express uncertainty about the issue. Likewise, men are more willing to commit themselves to the proposition that income taxes are too high.

On the whole, it seems that older men tend toward greater conservatism than women when it comes to political matters. The difference is not drastic, though, and it depends somewhat on the particular issue. Even in politics, we find a common ground between women and men, along with subtle differences. This may be one of the similarities balanced by differences that creates the mystique drawing the sexes together.

IS THERE A DOUBLE STANDARD OF AGING FOR MEN AND WOMEN?

Although no one has made a national survey specifically dedicated to the way that the sexes feel about aging, a number of gerontologists believe that a double standard exists for the two. They argue that the cultural values of our nation, which emphasize youth and beauty in women more so than in men, impose old age earlier on women and make it more burdensome for them. As beauty fades and wrinkles take over, they say that women experience a greater loss than men do. For evidence, they cite data showing that men label women as "old" at an earlier age than women apply the term to themselves.

But can we truly attribute differences in the way women and men experience age to a double standard that appears to favor men? The situation is probably too complicated to draw such a conclusion. For instance, the American gerontologist Bernice Neugarten and Norwegian Gunhild Hagestad agree that gender is the main cause of variations in life-course patterns. They add, however, that women experience different transitions in life (e.g., motherhood, menopause) than men do. Even with the shift toward greater employment of women outside the home, these two researchers observe that women remain more bound to their immediate social environment—the family. The perspective of these two researchers suggests that the idea of a double standard of aging for men and women is not accurate.

A study by Robert Kahn and Toni Antonucci of the University of Michigan has produced other findings countering the idea of a double standard of aging. These two researchers made a national survey to find out about the help that older persons exchange with others. Women were found both to provide more support to others than men were, and to be considerably more satisfied with their friends. They turned out to have wider social networks than men, and the wider these networks were, the greater the satisfaction the women had in their marriages.

Other researchers hold that women have greater interpersonal skills and are better than men at social relations. Late in life, these skills help in maintaining a social support system, they say. Similarly, older women rely more than men on trusted friends and have them in greater numbers. In contrast, men rely principally on their wives for intimacy, including emotional and social support.

According to the anthropological research carried out by Jennie Keith of Swarthmore College, women actually age with less difficulty than men. The reason? Women's lives attain greater continuity through family attachments. She agrees with another observation made by Neugarten and Hagestad: The family remains central for women even when they work outside the home. Men, on the other hand, must make a sharp break with the past when they retire.

Retirement, says Keith, represents a more severe transition for men than for women. Working women have an advantage when they retire because they have had more experience in adjusting to transitions: Their lives in general require more transitions than men's do. They go through more physical changes, take on childbearing, and commit themselves more totally to the modifications in life-style required by child rearing. Because they're more accustomed to change, they're better equipped to cope with alterations brought on by a departure from the work force.

All this would seem to balance out the experience of the two sexes as they age. Any disadvantages women might suffer from our nation's emphasis on feminine beauty would be counterbalanced by their superior sociability, their social skills, and their adaptability.

But if a double standard does exist, it may have nothing to do with the fading of beauty. It may rest with the different rates of sexual and social maturation between the two sexes; women mature earlier than men in both respects. These in turn underlie our marriage customs; men usually marry women who are their juniors. This, together with the shorter life expectancy of men, destines most married women to widowhood, and this status, frequently accompanied by a considerably reduced income, tells us more than any idea of a double standard regarding beauty.

The GSS shows us important differences in the late-life happiness of the sexes, which may well reflect these other considerations. Throughout life until age 65, more women than men report feeling very happy. At age 65–74, coincident with retirement, men suddenly take the lead in happiness by a full 6 percentage points—42% of the men are very happy compared to only 36% of the women—while during the previous decade (ages 55 to 64), women had led men 36% to 35%. From age 75 on, the men in the GSS continue to hold the lead in happiness, though by a slimmer margin—38% very happy men to 37% women at 75–84, and 35% very happy men to 33% women at 85+. Being out of the work force seems to have a strong positive effect on men's happiness.

Does the double standard regarding feminine beauty account for this sudden change in the relative positions of the two sexes? Probably not. There's no great decline in the proportion of women who report being very happy, as one might expect if they experienced a severe problem with their personal self-image. From age group 45–54 (the peak category for women's happiness) on up, close to 36% of the women report being very happy until age 85+, when there's a drop to 33%.

The increase in happiness for men may relate more to the pleasures of a leisurely retirement, while the slight decline for women could result from widowhood, poor health, lower income, or other factors. The best explanation may very well rest with the ultimate double standard between the two sexes—men usually die younger and leave widows.

WHAT CONSEQUENCES GROW OUT OF SEX DIFFERENCES IN LATER LIFE?

What conclusions can we draw from this survey of similarities and differences between women and men in later life? First, the sexes continue to enjoy their unique and special characteristics as they age. The biological and social forces that make us what we are, that create our variety and endow us with sexual identities as males or females, remain active in late life. We retain those special skills and sensitivities that belong to us as members of a particular sex while we share profound similarities with our opposites.

We retain, too, the capability of relating creatively to the sex antipodal to our own, a capability that can make life supremely delicious. We can share reciprocally with each other, engaging in those delicate exchanges and the gracious manners that normally characterize male-to-female and female-to-male relationships as they defer to one another's special qualities.

We continue to hold the power to complement one another, to create new wholes out of those things that make us different. Because of our distinctiveness, we are interdependent. Age remains a time when we can celebrate and enjoy our identities as members of opposite sexes. Opposites attract; there seems to be a unity in opposites.

9

Leisure and Last Things

What's the link between the subjects of leisure and the last things of life (including death) that makes them fit companions for the penultimate chapter of a book that aims to increase the enjoyment of age? Simply that they share the quality of being unmentionable—leisure somewhat so, and last things, or death, very much so.

Take leisure first. Until modern times, most persons had to have an excuse to retire, not to mention to indulge in relaxation. Work was considered the only worthwhile activity of life. Leisure was useless, a pursuit of matters of no consequence. Only a life filled with the daily round of toil and productivity could satisfy the prevailing public outlook. Time after work was "spare time," presumably frittered away in worthless loafing.

Today there's a lingering negativism toward leisure which undoubtedly reflects the longstanding American work ethic. No one ever expressed this hostility better than Thorstein Veblen, who descended from austere Norwegian Lutheran Minnesota. Veblen made a lifetime career of bashing the "leisure class" (meaning the rich) of the nation. A professor of economics successively at the University of Chicago, Stanford University, and the New School of Social Research in New York City, Veblen condemned the "theory of the leisure class." He proclaimed this theory to consist in a showy display of wealth and idleness, an occupation that he scathingly denounced as "conspicuous consumption."

The sentiment of the country was with Veblen, for he wrote at the turn of the century when harsh opinion about idleness was stronger than it is today. But even now, an odor of indecency still clings to the idea of nonwork. It helps to animate the hostility of the public toward our national welfare system—in the GSS, nearly half of the respondents think we're spending too much for the welfare program.

Regarding retired older people, our doubts about nonwork make us think it impossible for them to spend their leisure time in honorable pursuits. The Harris poll showed that the public believes the number one activity of the old is idly watching television. "Sitting and thinking" ranks second in their minds. But self-reports recorded in the Harris poll suggest otherwise. When asked to rank the frequency of various activities, TV watching fell behind socializing and gardening. Our evaluation of the use of leisure by older people seems colored by the suspicion that no one can use free time constructively.

Even researchers in gerontology during the early days after the 1951 White House Conference on Aging shared the public skepticism about the way elders used their leisure. Influenced by the low public esteem for spare time, their first research findings documented the notion of its misuse by the old. They were haunted, too, by the idea that the elderly felt lonely and bored. Today, gerontologists know better, but it's little wonder that they began as skeptics. Even science sometimes begins with everyday observations and common sense.

If it's true that leisure still remains a questionable activity in the public mind, how do we feel about death, that most unmentionable of unmentionable subjects? Death used to have a more powerful presence than it does today. It could, and did, come at any time in life. Many persons died during infancy, youth, and midlife, as well as old age, because we lacked the medical expertise and public health systems to combat illness the way that we do now. Death was a normal event, an ever-present reality for everyone. Besides, the event of death usually took place at home, so that most people had witnessed it directly and close at hand.

Today, death comes late in life for the vast majority—about

11 people per 1000 die by age 14, compared to 23 per thousand at 55–64, and 442 after 65. Few die at home. Rather, we die in the aseptic and impersonal environment of hospitals and nursing homes, away from family members and friends. Because of these circumstances, we have limited exposure to death compared to our predecessors.

The customs of our times suppress discussions of death, treat them as cheerless, and sequester them to the hushed surroundings of funeral parlors. We view frankness about death as deviant. The subject is definitely not one for social conversation, and to try to make it otherwise would be an unimaginable gaucherie.

In this book, the experience of death is referred to as "last things," but not to escape an unmentionable subject by clothing it in ornamental language. Death is not an unexpected, single terminal event of life for older individuals. Rather, it is part of a series of last experiences, which may include affectionate support from and relationships with loved ones, planning for disposition of property, selecting a resting place, performing final charitable acts, producing last works, and the like. For the majority of people, death becomes one of the conscious realities at the conclusion of life. Many, if not most, older people acknowledge it and deal with it openly. The old do not retreat from death; it is simply one of the final events, or last things of life.

Because a questionable aura surrounds the subjects of leisure and last things, we present analytical discussions supporting the view that both are vital, potentially creative aspects of later life. Though we offer analysis, solid facts are few. Though researchers have studied these subjects, the studies are generally limited to small samples of persons who do not represent the entire nation. Even the GSS doesn't help much because it touches rather briefly on the relevant topics.

We primarily draw on the work of scholars who've summarized the numerous individual research studies on leisure and last things. Because we're departing from our usual extensive reliance on the GSS, we identify the researchers we'll rely on. The first is Russell Ward of the State University of New York at Albany,

who has written lucidly on both leisure and last things in his book
The Aging Experience.

We call also on the work of Richard Kalish, formerly Clinical
Professor of Psychiatry at the University of New Mexico, in his
comprehensive review of the research on thanatology (the study
of death) published in *The Handbook of Aging and the Social
Sciences.* A major national authority on death, Kalish's studies
take on special poignancy because he himself was an untimely
victim of cancer.

Finally, we refer to the survey of research in late-life leisure
prepared by Lei Lane Burrus-Bammel and Gene Bammel of West
Virginia University, published in *The Handbook of the Psychology
of Aging.* With these and other supplementary sources, we continue to pursue the objective of this book—to help readers to
achieve an enlightened view of old age.

WHY IS LEISURE SOMETHING NEW IN
HUMAN HISTORY?

The reason is that life used to be so short and the workweek so
long that only the well-to-do had much time for leisure. As late as
1900, the average person didn't live beyond age 47, so retirement
was practically unknown. Persons frequently started full-time
work in their early teens and spent 60 hours a week at labor (6
days a week, 10 hours a day) throughout life. As Veblen observed, leisure belonged to the idle few.

Times have changed. With an increased lifespan and the
establishment of retirement as an institution in our society, leisure
in late life has almost become a national birthright. We generally
enjoy far more leisure than our ancestors, and it's a special
blessing of old age.

One can get an idea of the significance of leisure in later life
by putting the GSS and the Harris poll together. The GSS shows
that the last years of life are the happiest. The Harris poll showed
that most of the persons who claimed the last years of life as the
best gave "more leisure" as the reason. Taken together, these
suggest that leisure during the late years of life accounts in part for
the greater happiness of the older generation.

Besides this, the psychological function of leisure changes

over the life course. It becomes particularly important during periods of transition. Old age represents one such period, and leisure offers the elderly time in which to make the adjustments necessary for personal fulfillment. It helps individuals to maintain a lively state of arousal and to build the integrity of their inner selves. As Gene and Lei Bammel have written, "In leisure occur the most important events of one's life: insights, personal relationships, choice of careers, and delights in ourselves, our friends, and the natural world."

IS LEISURE AN ACTIVITY?

We usually think of leisure as inactivity, the opposite from work. Philosophers and contemporary researchers studying leisure think otherwise. They call it an activity. Some have even labeled leisure as the career of later life.

It was Aristotle, the Greek philosopher of 350 B.C. (we cited his uncomplimentary views on old age earlier), who said that leisure is the goal of all activity. "For we are busy that we may have leisure," he wrote over 2000 years ago. He added an important idea for our present topic—leisure is only for those who pursue it passionately. He meant that we must employ leisure well, and treat it just as we do any other serious pursuit. Interestingly, modern research evidence shows that people who understand the seriousness of leisure and pursue it accordingly enjoy it more.

Under these circumstances, what makes us think of leisure as nonwork and idleness? Aside from our traditional commitment to hard work, the most likely reason is that leisure is an activity we undertake without obligation. We can do what we want with our leisure time. No one directs us in it. We're in charge and accountable only to ourselves.

Besides this, leisure has what psychologists call an "expressive" quality. It's emotionally tinged and can engage us deeply. It's satisfying and pleasant. We take part in leisure activity for a different reason than we perform work. Work has a cash payoff. Leisure activity has none. Work is instrumental for achieving the goal of survival. We pursue leisure for its own sake, simply because we enjoy it.

In his 1967 book, *Toward a Society of Leisure*, Joffre

Dumazedier described leisure as an activity to which people turn by their own free choice for relaxation, diversion, or broadening of knowledge. Often carried out in the company of others, leisure activity may tap our capacities for creativity more so than ordinary work.

In addition to relaxation, the functions of leisure include diversion, entertainment, and sometimes escape. A number of leisure activities, such as education, travel, and artistic pursuits contribute to personal growth. Volunteer services also fit into the picture. Some activities, such as competitive sports and sexual intercourse involve an intense, peak experience, which researchers have termed "sensual transcendence." This suggests that leisure provides fulfillment because it takes us outside of ourselves.

Russell Ward speaks of leisure as a crucial issue in the lives of the old. At retirement age, people need to find new goals and to direct their energies into new channels. They pass beyond the period of work and major family responsibility and enter a new stage of life. Whether their new endeavors involve reading, exercise, volunteer activities, hobbies, socializing with friends, or other engagements, people need to use such activities to develop a different sense of identity, a new center for their "selves." Thoughtful use of freedom in leisure can become an avenue to renewed personal meaning. To hark back to Erik Erikson, finding new meaning is a special challenge of age. Life without meaning is emptiness, so leisure plays a crucial role in meeting the challenge of age.

WHAT DO OLDER PEOPLE ACTUALLY DO WITH THEIR TIME?

Because of the importance of leisure in later life, gerontologists have made inventories of the activities older people engage in. Among these, TV watching has captured much of the attention because of the allegation that old people spend too much time in front of their TV sets.

Just what is the story on TV watching by older people? How

many hours a day do they really spend watching TV? We've seen from the Harris poll that the public thinks that the elderly spend many hours in front of their sets. Fortunately, the GSS provides us with information on actual hours of TV watching time.

We can use these data to compare the habits of the old to those of other age groups. This may not help us to answer anyone who charges that Americans in general spend too much time watching TV, but it does give us a way to look at the behavior of the old in relation to the normal pattern for our population, and thus to judge the accuracy of public opinion.

It may come as a surprise, then, to learn that the vast majority of the older population spends about the same amount of time watching TV as everyone else does. About 60% of the GSS respondents report that they watch TV 2 to 4 hours a day, and the elderly are no exception. Persons over 85 actually watch less— only 51% of them specify 2 to 4 hours of watching time.

Where the elderly do edge the others out a bit is in the proportion who watch 5 hours or more. Of the persons age 65+, 24% fit into this higher category. But, this doesn't differentiate them too much from the rest—17% of those under 65 watch 5 hours or more per day. Even here, the proportion of 18- to 24-year-olds who watch 5 hours a day matches that of the 65+. Once more, the young and the old show they have more in common with one another than they do with the rest of the population.

If the old show little difference from the rest of the population when it comes to TV watching, what about listening to radio? In this case, younger Americans overmatch them—one third of the 18- to 24-year-olds and a quarter of the 25–34 group listen 5 or more hours per day, whereas only 19% of those over 65 listen this much. Listening time for people from 35 on up is quite uniform—41% listen just an hour a day, and 36% from 2 to 4 hours—and the old are no exception.

If reading the newspaper is a better use of time than watching TV or listening to the radio, then the older age groups fairly well run away with the prize. At ages 18–24, only about a third say that they read a paper daily. This increases to almost half by ages 25–34 and to 61% by ages 35–44. At 45–54, the ratio of daily readers hits 70%, and it climbs slightly above that for the next three age groups. At 85+, half the population still reads the paper daily—a far higher proportion than those under 35.

We can get a better idea of the meaning of these figures if we consider studies that compare the content of TV programs watched by young and old. Scholars have found that older viewers spend more time with shows that broadcast serious informational material, such as news, documentaries, and travel programs. No one can tell whether this transfers to more serious reading of newspapers, but it does suggest that the old may do more than simply read the comics, sports, and social pages. It's likely that the old spend their leisure time with the media in more serious, less lighthearted and frivolous ways than the young.

WHAT ABOUT OTHER ACTIVITIES?

Time spent with TV and the other media in no way exhausts the inventory of activities carried on by the older generation. Perhaps the most impressive of their other activities is volunteer work. Many consider this one of the great prerogatives and contributions of age. An interesting comparison is with the honorific status formerly assigned to old people in the Polynesian islands of the Pacific. It was they who had the job of weaving the cloth, baskets, and mats used in marriages and community ceremonies.

Research has shown that volunteers among the old have greater life satisfaction and a greater will to live than their age-mates. We can't resort to this to recommend that everyone rush into volunteer work, though, because it brings up a chicken-and-egg problem quite common in social science research. Which comes first? Does volunteering lead to greater life satisfaction and a will to live, or do persons who have a stronger will to live and enjoy higher life satisfaction become the one's most likely to volunteer? Or does a third factor, such as good health, explain all three? Our guess would be that volunteering, like most activities for most people, does make a positive contribution to the enjoyment of life and the will to live.

In any case, the federal government has enough conviction about the value of volunteer work in late life to have adopted special programs to support it. These include Foster Grandparents, Retired Senior Volunteers Program (RSVP), and the Service Corps of Retired Executives (SCORE). Church activities are also known to attract regular senior participation.

The Harris poll reported that one quarter of the population over 65 now takes part in some type of volunteer activity and that another 10% would be willing to do so—providing a potential of almost 10 million volunteers now and more in the future. This poll also showed that the elderly typically donate services to hospitals and mental health clinics, transportation for the handicapped, civic activities such as voter registration and lobbying for legislation, psychological and social support services (telephone reassurances and visiting of shut-ins), foster and day care for children and youth, and staffing of thrift shops and emergency food services.

Other studies have disclosed that the repertoire of leisure activities appears to change over the lifespan. Relaxation is one element of the repertoire that changes—it increases. However, drinking, dancing, sports and exercise, gun sports, outdoor activities, frequent short-distance travel, reading, and production of cultural works all tend to decline. And TV viewing, talking with others, watching sports events, entertaining, participating in clubs and organizations, and home improvement activities remain about the same.

Changes in the leisure repertoire, of course, don't apply uniformly to every individual. The aforementioned activities represent general patterns, so not everyone conforms to them. There are differences by age, and an activity that declines for most may actually increase for some. Such is the case for dancing. It may become a late-life hobby for some people simply because they have more time for it.

WHAT ABOUT EXERCISE?

Studies have shown that most older people are in unnecessarily poor physical condition. This is true in spite of the growing body of evidence demonstrating that exercise not only makes life more enjoyable but also actually prolongs it. For years, researchers suspected that there was a connection between good health, sound mental function, life satisfaction, longevity, and exercise, but it was only with the publication of a study of 17,000 Harvard graduates in the *New England Journal of Medicine* in March 1986 that an indisputable link was established. This research disclosed the startling truth that death rates were 25 to 33% lower for those who had engaged in moderate exercise (walking, stair climbing, and other physical activities) than for those who were least active. Subsequent research suggests that exercise not only retards the effects of aging but also can actually reverse them.

Today, physiologists are investigating in detail the effect of moderate exercise activities on well-being. Among exercises suitable for older persons are walking, certain gently performed yoga-style movements and postures, swimming, and mild stretching. Physiologists want to know more about how these improve the way individuals experience life, but enough is known already to say that older persons should make sure to include enjoyable physical activities in their leisure regimes.

WHAT ABOUT GAMBLING?

Studies of gambling provide an unexpected source of information about the value of participating in leisure activities. Bingo certainly has a great appeal to the older generation, and seniors often join tours organized by travel groups and descend on Atlantic City and other gambling meccas in masses for a fling at the one-armed bandits and gaming tables. Casino magnate Donald Trump undoubtedly owes part of his fortune to patronage of his Atlantic City establishments by these luck-hunting elders.

Does gambling offer more to older persons than a big payoff for the rare few who win? Ken Stone and Richard Kalish threw light on the question when they studied older poker players in a legal private club. According to their findings, gambling provided excitement, an opportunity to socialize, and stimulated enthusiasm over victory. Even when the participants didn't really expect to win, they still enjoyed having a shot at a big payoff. They found it entertaining, and liked pitting their skills against those of others. One might suppose, then, that such experiences motivate the typical older gambler. Most persons like to test their luck from time to time, and the fun of taking a chance or seeking a thrill seems to have lifelong appeal.

ANYTHING ELSE?

Lest the reference to gambling gives one the impression that the elderly fritter away their time in trifling pursuits, we should recall that "free time" in late life isn't necessarily free. More so than the young, the old devote their time to shopping, housework, and personal care. Some of their free time activities involve working, helping their children, and caring for grandchildren.

It's not uncommon, in fact, for older people to find that they're busier than ever with a wider variety of activities and associations than at any time during their earlier years. For many, there simply is not enough time to get everything done. Leisure in late life is a legitimate pursuit. The challenge is, as Aristotle said, to pursue it with a passion, so that it becomes a source of enrichment and a doorway to a full life.

ARE OLDER PEOPLE MORE LIKELY THAN THE YOUNG TO BELIEVE THAT THERE'S A LIFE AFTER DEATH?

Turning to that other unmentionable subject of later life, do older persons try to overcome death by adopting a belief in life in the hereafter more often than young do? The GSS tells us that the answer is essentially "no," but not because the old have any less conviction than the young. The simple truth is that the great majority of all Americans believe in a life after death. Recall that 70% or more of us from age 24 and up answer "yes" when asked if we are believers. Even 67% of those under 24 share in the general viewpoint.

What's especially interesting is that there may be a decline in disbelief in the most advanced years. This could be due to the characteristics of the persons who remain alive for interviews late in life—more women, better educated, higher incomes—whatever the reason, a drop in "no" answers occurs after age 75. Until then, about 20% of the population assert that they don't believe in life after death, and that proportion stays almost constant for every age group from 18 to 75. Slightly higher proportions of men than women give a "no" answer.

At ages 75 to 84, the proportion who say "no" drops to 18%—not a very great change but a change nevertheless. At 85+, the proportion who say "no" falls to 11%, with men and women about equal.

But, this doesn't mean that there's any increase in the proportion who say "yes" when asked if they believe in life after death at these ages. Instead, there's a rise in the ratio of those who say they don't know or give no answer. About 10% of every age from 18 to 75 either respond "don't know" or don't answer. At 75–84, however, there's a slight increase to 11%, which is followed by a sharp climb to 19% at 85+.

While we can't say for sure what causes these changes, it may be that there's a decline in rock-ribbed skepticism after age 75. People who've never believed in an afterlife may become insecure about their past convictions. Strong disbelief in life after death may give way to uncertainty as the event approaches.

IS THERE ANY SCIENTIFIC EVIDENCE TO SUPPORT OUR WIDESPREAD BELIEF IN LIFE AFTER DEATH?

Some observers believe so, resorting to the growing number of reports of near-death experiences to offer confirmation for their beliefs in a postlife. According to these reports, people who've revived after being declared clinically dead generally have pleasant recollections of their death. Many say they pass through a long tunnel at the end of which they see a warm light radiating from a godlike figure. They sense a loving reception by relatives. In some cases they report an out-of-body experience in which they see themselves, their rooms, persons around their hospital bed, and so forth.

What do these reports prove? Not much, according to a study carried out by George Gallup, the founder of the well-known Gallup poll. He surveyed a large group of physicians (chosen by a standard statistical method to represent U.S. physicians), and found hardly any support for a positive interpretation of verge-of-death experiences.

Personally religious himself, Gallup had carried out many surveys over the years that confirmed America's conviction concerning a life after death. In this case, however, he was obliged to report that most physicians simply dismissed the credibility of verge-of-death experiences or described them as a type of hallucination. Some compared them to the mental states of drug users. With the present level of knowledge, no scientific evidence upholds the near-ubiquitous American belief in a hereafter. The issue of life after death remains one of the great unknowns, a matter of faith rather than scientific certainty.

WHAT ABOUT FEAR OF DEATH?

Older persons fear death less than any other age group. Vern Bengtson, Director of the Gerontology Research Institute at the University of Southern California and a prolific scholar, was one of the first to produce data showing that our population has little fear of death and that the vast majority of elderly persons fear it even less. The peak of fear, he learned, comes at 45–54, the time when full realization of the prospect of oncoming death seems to emerge, but most people feel they still have a lot left to accomplish. For the old, fear does not even increase as the time of death approaches.

Does religious conviction make any difference in fear of death? Strangely, the answer is both yes and no. Richard Kalish learned that it's those with *uncertain* religious convictions, not those with *no* convictions, who are most appalled at the thought of death. Those with strong religious beliefs fear it little, but those without religious conviction also express little fear. Strength of religious belief, as well as strong disbelief seem to yield the greatest fortitude in facing death.

HOW DO YOUNG AND OLD COMPARE ON OTHER ATTITUDES TOWARD DEATH?

Besides being somewhat more fearful of death than the old, younger people exhibit different attitudes toward death in a number of ways. One of these relates to the idea of euthanasia, or mercy killing, where the GSS reveals a wide difference of opinion between the generations. GSS interviewers have asked, "When a person has a disease that cannot be cured, do you think doctors should be allowed to end the patient's life by some painless means if the patient and his family request it?"

At ages 18–24, 71% of the group answered "yes" while 26% were opposed. At 85+, however, only 39% agreed and 53% were opposed, demonstrating one of the greatest differences between the very young and the very old in the entire survey. The ages between the very young and the very old tended steadily toward the percentages at 85+ (for instance, at 45–54, 56% "yes" and 40% "no"), but they didn't match the persons at the two extremes. It's possible that young persons don't visualize the possibility of mercy killing very keenly, whereas old people think of it as applying to themselves. This may suggest that our longest surviving oldsters keep a tenacious hold on life. It certainly shows that the old have no desire to leap into the arms of death even though they fear it less than others.

Young and old differ in other respects regarding death. Studies show that the young don't perceive their lives as having any end. To the young, time is infinite. The old, however, clearly perceive an end to their lives. To them, time is finite. The young measure time into the future. The old measure the time that's left to them.

When asked if they would prefer a sudden death to a slow death, young people opt for a sudden death. The old, on the other hand, favor a slow death, apparently because it would allow them more time for reminiscing, arranging their affairs, and bidding family and friends farewell.

Elders are more contemplative about death, according to Kalish and his associate David Reynolds. The old react differently to the prospects of their own death than the young do. When asked what changes they'd make in their lives if informed that they had but a short time to live, the old speak less often of completing projects or of altering their life-styles. They express less anxiety about death, and they are more willing to talk about it even though they're not obsessed with the subject. They think more about death, make preparations (such as funeral arrangements) for it, face death better, and accept it more peacefully.

The young very frequently react negatively when confronted by the open attitude of the old toward death. Unaware that elderly openness on the subject is a way of placing death into a proper psychological perspective, they consider the views of the old to be morbid. Anthropologist Jennie Keith of Swarthmore College has studied death in developing countries of Asia and Africa, as well as America and modern European nations. She characterizes the typical reaction of younger Americans toward their elders' frankness about death with the statements, "Oh mother, don't talk about that!"

The candor of the old by no means represents a morbid preoccupation with death, according to Kalish and others. It reflects instead the proximity of the actual fact and a personal, or subjective, awareness. Good counsel would suggest that younger people who care about older family members or friends will do well to accept their openness. This should help the old persons to work out their own attitudes and develop a positive approach to the reality before them. Rather than shunning the subject as a vulgarity, the great taboo of modern times, the young should simply accept it if the old bring it up.

IS EXPERIENCING DEATH UNPLEASANT?

Apparently not for most persons. The scenes of torment so often portrayed or implied in operas, literature, drama, films, and the media don't accurately represent the quiet passage that most of us experience. This was first attested to early in this century by Sir William Osler, a world-famous Canadian physician, who kept a notebook of observations regarding the dying moments of some 500 patients. He reported that the great majority quit this world as they had entered it, without knowledge or fear. About two-thirds, he said, passed on during sleep. Many of the rest died in an unconscious or semiconscious state, and pain or psychological trauma rarely occurred. Modern studies support these findings.

Also, there's usually no protracted period of lingering on the way toward death. For most, the process takes less than 3 months and often not more than a few days. The portrait of the dying Prince Andrew in Leo Tolstoy's *War and Peace*, who steadily turned away from the surrounding world of friends and family, appears to be an accurate description of how many persons experience death. Relatives and friends may feel greater distress at this time than the dying individual. Remarkably, though, people sometimes actually seem to determine the time of their own death, postponing it to participate in family festivities or advancing it to avoid conflict with a celebration. American history offers an intriguing example: Thomas Jefferson was the primary author of the Declaration of Independence; John Adams had been one of the four other members of the committee assigned to prepare the declaration. Both former U.S. Presidents were very old and had been quite ill, but they both clung to life until July 4, 1826—the golden anniversary of the signing.

Although most persons say they would prefer to die at home, the event of death usually occurs in a hospital or nursing home. In this respect, the rise of the hospice movement, designed principally for cancer patients, offers an interesting model for smoothing the way to a tranquil death. Originating in 1967 at St. Christopher's Hospital in London, England, under the inspiration of Cicely Saunders, the hospice idea quickly caught hold in the U.S. Today, there are over 200 hospices, plus many home-support hospice programs in operation here.

Committed to the belief that persons can die in dignity and repose, the approach of the hospice is personal. The aim is to help individuals maintain control over their own death experiences. Among the kinds of services offered are companionship, spiritual help, comfort, social contact, personal care and hygiene, and medical care to the extent necessary for comfort. Studies at St. Christopher's demonstrate the underlying idea and success of the model—78% of the patrons compare the experience to being in a family.

The word *hospice* derives from the great tradition of hospitality that has animated agreeable and bountiful catering to people's needs in many types of settings over human history. Its application to the experience of death is one of the distinctly forward steps in human service during our modern age.

ARE THERE STAGES TO DEATH IN LATER LIFE?

Probably one of the best-known authorities on death is Elisabeth Kübler-Ross, a psychiatrist who identified a series of psychological stages experienced by dying cancer patients whom she attended at the University of Chicago hospital during the 1960s. Kübler-Ross observed that her patients met with five stages in their experience: denial, anger, bargaining, depression, and acceptance.

Although her work was an important breakthrough, subsequent research has not supported the proposition that these stages occur as an unalterable sequence for everyone, and that acceptance of the oncoming reality is the most common attitude of dying people. Gerontologist Russell Ward has observed that these stages are best thought of as an inventory of moods that may, but do not necessarily, accompany death.

Kübler-Ross developed her idea of stages during therapeutic sessions with cancer patients of all ages. For many, death was an unexpected, unwanted, and frustrating event–provoking reactions that generally do not occur to most persons in advanced years of life. Older persons have had time to prepare for death, are openly aware of its onset, and usually accept it. The special value of Kübler-Ross's work is that it has taken the discussion of death out of the closet, where it's been hidden away as the unmentionable grim reaper for years. She has described death as "the last stage of growth" and brought it into the open where everyone has a chance to face it.

HOW DO OLDER PEOPLE COME TO TERMS WITH DEATH?

Why do older people rarely fear death? What accounts for such equanimity regarding the final event of life? Is it merely a passive attitude, like simple resignation, or is it something more positive?

Awareness of death as a real future event seems first to arise during middle age. This realization, however, does not simply degenerate into despair and resignation. It sets into motion a process that leads to perception of the boundary of life, its finitude. While we know from early childhood that death exists, our own future death does not become a psychological reality for us until our middle years or later.

One of the features of this development is that older people appear to undergo a changed sense of time. Instead of seeing time ahead as perpetual and infinite as the young appear to, they shift to thinking about how much time they have left and the preparations they need to make within that frame.

As people age, the prospect of death generally becomes less stressful for them. Besides that, they seem to share the common public view that a late-life death is less tragic than an early one. Russell Ward cites a study in which older persons were asked if they wanted to live to be 100. Most answered "no," and even those who did want to reach the century mark set conditions, such as good health and mental alertness, for achieving the goal.

Recognition of the prospect of death appears to touch off an effort to put one's past life into perspective. Some years ago, Robert Butler formally introduced this process into the medical lexicon, labeling it "reminiscence," and recommended it as a valuable psychological therapy.

It seems that many persons do engage in a review with an underlying aim of putting things in order. Some go so far as to write a biography, not only recounting interesting events and personal history for their families, but also seeking to account for their lives. Long ago, the Italian poet Dante Allighieri used the term *apology* when he sought to justify his life, but today we'd probably use the word *explanation*. An enterprising teacher in Puyallup, Washington, Leone Noble Western, has even written a how-to guide for writing a life-review biography entitled, *The Gold Key to Writing Your Life History.*

A successful life review helps individuals to come to terms with age and oncoming death. It's a positive activity that carries the seeker toward a sense of wholeness. It accords with Erik Erikson's idea that the central task of the last stage of life is to achieve ego integrity.

DO OLDER PEOPLE MANAGE TO TRANSCEND THE DEATH EXPERIENCE?

There's evidence that many actually do, but personality appears to be a factor. Research shows that those who've coped well with life, have experienced greater life satisfaction and a sense of fulfillment, and have had good marriages, appear to confront death most successfully.

These individuals take specific steps to achieve their victory. Planning for death is one of them. A survey carried out by the National Opinion Research Center (the same organization that conducts the GSS) and reported by John Riley for the Russell Sage Foundation showed that 80% of the public thinks it's better to make plans for death than to deny or disregard it. Few had carried through on this conviction—only 25% had made funeral arrangements and drawn up a will. Still, 50% had discussed death with others, and 70% had bought life insurance.

Talking about death is another way that older people master the experience. Such conversation is normal and provides a means for addressing the reality. Unaware of the therapeutic benefits of the process, younger people generally greet a conversation about death negatively and quickly dismiss it, but open talk about death represents a kind of rehearsal for the events to come. With due regard for reasonable boundaries, it can be helpful to older individuals if one simply listens to their reflections and plans for death.

The concept of dying an "appropriate death," in accord with personal values, preferences, and beliefs offers another avenue that helps individuals to rise above the experience. A key element here is to manage the event. Individuals achieve this sort of control by planning their own funerals. Sometimes they set up living wills that direct their physicians and families to avoid heroic life-saving measures if they become terminally ill. Whatever the means employed, the idea is to remain in charge of the last event of life. Autonomy at that time is as important as it is at any other time of life.

Sometimes it's possible to arrange to die at home, a plan that helps to maintain interaction with others and the stimulating presence of family and friends. Richard Kalish pointed out that this can be burdensome for the family, but that it can work well under specific conditions. Success is most likely when the dying person is alert, requires limited treatment and care, is close enough to death to make it appropriate to be continually in the presence of loved ones, and a specific value is involved, such as being in the presence of family members rather than in an empty apartment. Under these terms, the home environment offers an excellent locale for death.

Individuals who have definite religious convictions about life after death have a unique means for transcending the final event. For them, death is a beginning, not an end. Life continues, and this offers a clear means for mastering death. A patriarch of the Judeo-Christian tradition, St. Paul, joyfully declared, "Death, where is thy sting? Grave, where is thy victory?"

While the GSS can neither confirm nor deny the validity of such convictions, it does reveal a rich variety of thoughts about an afterlife. The majority of respondents see life after death as like life on earth, only better. A majority also think that they will live a spiritual life, involving the mind but not the body.

Most do not expect that postlife will take place in a paradise of delights. Rather, they see it as a peaceful and tranquil time, free of intense action. Nearly three quarters expect complete physical and spiritual fulfillment. They eschew the vision of the pale shadowy experience, "hardly life at all," held by the ancient Greeks. Large majorities anticipate a loving intellectual communion, reunion with loved ones, and union with God. Altogether, Americans hold a powerfully hopeful vision of the life hereafter.

GSS questions on parapsychological experiences provide

data that some people feel give intimations of immortality. An astonishingly large proportion of the GSS respondents report having had one or more parapsychological experiences. For example, about two thirds say they've thought they've experienced *déjà vu*, the sense of having been in certain surroundings before, but then realizing that these particular surroundings are new. Approximately the same proportion say they've felt that they were in touch with someone who was far away.

Most don't claim clairvoyance, but a few state that they've seen events very far away at the time that they happened. Somewhat less than half have felt that they were really in touch with someone who had died. Almost half have sensed themselves very close to a powerful spiritual force that seemed to lift them out of themselves. Well over 80% feel either very close or somewhat close to God most of the time.

Consciousness of the rituals that surround death can provide another means for transcending mortality. Rituals work for society at large as well as for the individual. Funerals are among the most ancient and distinctively human of all ritual traditions; archeologists have found likely evidence for a funeral ceremony that dates back 40,000 to 50,000 years. In the grave of a young Neanderthal man, a heavy mixture of flower pollen was dispersed around the skeleton. Evidently, the family had covered the young man with wild flowers when they laid him in his shallow resting place in their cave, leaving to us a touching vision of tenderness and love at the dawn of our species.

Visiting hours (sometimes called "wakes") and funeral services serve as a rite of passage for a dead person much as a wedding or a baptism does earlier in life. Participants offer support to surviving family and friends. It's thought that funeral rites have a therapeutic effect because they allow for the expression of grief and for an opportunity to say farewell. In her intensive study of widowhood, Helen Znaniecki Lopata concluded that the rituals helped the widow to reach beyond the event of death to achieve a transcendent meaning for herself and for her loved one.

Customs surrounding death serve to sanctify the life of the

individual who has died. Eulogies (even those for arrant scoun-
drels) help to give continuity to the human community because
they provide a formal means for relating to the dead. In ancient
times, and even now in Africa and some Pacific islands, ancestor
worship accomplished the same goal. It lent an aura of holiness
to those who had passed on, and it created a symbolic link with
the past of the social group. The dead became spirits to whom
one might pray for good things, or call upon for power to control
daily events.

Knowledge of the rituals provides us with a concept of what
will happen at our own passing. This, too, can create a sense of
continuity and control, a mastery over future events. Individuals
appear to gain a sense of satisfaction when they arrange for their
funerals, their burial, and an appropriate headstone. They sometimes even provide for the refreshment and entertainment of their
family and the guests at these events.

Whether an individual believes in life after death, as most
people do, holds strong religious convictions, or shares in the
secular outlook widely held in these times, there's no doubt that
recognition of one's own mortality is one of the critical adjustments of later life. Those who take a positive approach to this task
based on a realistic understanding of our typical experiences
have the greatest chance of achieving success in old age.

IS IT POSSIBLE TO DIE A FELICITOUS DEATH?

Gerontological experts on thanatology who use the term *appropriate death* seem reluctant to go one step further to speak of the
possibility of a *felicitous death*. The reason may be that they
realize that most of us do not look kindly on death even when we
openly accept it. Under these circumstances, associating a favorable word with the idea of death seems patently absurd. A
conservative approach appears most appropriate when adopting
scientific terminology regarding human mortality.

But, what if we do consider the possibility of a felicitous
death? What does the research carried out so far tell us about the
conditions under which death might be a felicitous event? *Felici-*

tous goes beyond "happy" to include a variety of important meanings, such as "timely," "opportune," "successful," and "joyous." "Apropos" is another meaning, as when one thinks of something as apt, fitting, or suitable. *Felicitousness* also refers to a state of supreme happiness, perfect contentment, and bliss. Although no one in gerontology has gone so far as to speak of death in these terms, studies done so far make them seem quite appropriate.

Research tells us fairly clearly how a death might be felicitous. Such a death would follow a completed life review, where we would have come to terms with the events of our lives and have achieved a sense of wholeness, or ego integrity, even if we were not entirely pleased with every incident. We would have accepted death, and we would be ready to die, even if preferring to wait for death rather than to seek it out. We would have made a will and other provisions for appropriate disposition of property and care of loved ones. We would have completed plans for death, including arrangements for funeral services and burial. Family and friends would be nearby as death approached. Death itself would be tranquil. And, should we have the good fortune to hold religious convictions, we would have a reasoned faith in the attainment of a future life.

Can the majority of us achieve these conditions? According to the research done so far, many already do. There's no reason why the rest of us shouldn't expect to do so too.

10

The Good News

More than 2000 years ago, the Greek philosopher Plato opened his most famous dialogue, *The Republic*, with a conversation between Socrates and Cephalos, a man probably in his 80s. Socrates asked the old gentleman what it's like to experience advanced years. Cephalos quickly answered that in age "we are freed from the grasp not of one mad master only, but of many," a colorful way of saying that we put aside the wild passions and the heavy obligations of youth.

Besides that, Cephalos had little patience with persons who complain and express regrets about their late maturity. This sort of attitude, he said, does not accurately convey the way that all persons experience age, but rather the "characters and tempers" of certain types of individuals. Then he added, "For he who is of a calm and happy nature will hardly feel the pressure of age, but to him who is of an opposite disposition youth and age are equally a burden."

Does this have a familiar ring? It should, because Cicero said the same thing, and so have the modern psychologists Paul Costa and Robert McCrae. Still, Plato didn't go far enough. His concern in *The Republic* was to discuss justice and examine what kind of a utopian society would bring it about. He did not go on to explore, as we have done in this book, what persons need to know to achieve the good life in old age regardless of their personal dispositions. Even though he implied it here and elsewhere, Plato never revealed the startling truth about old age—it's the best time of life.

Our journey through old age, with hard facts from the GSS as our principal guide, discloses that late life is generally the time of greatest self-esteem, confidence, and happiness. Someone has said that today's elderly are the healthiest, wealthiest, and longest-lived generation of older people in history. Yet, we're still just at the brink of the Aging Boom. In the next century, when the children of the post–World War II Baby Boom reach their full maturity, we'll have arrived at a new time for the old—a time when doubts about the values and pleasure of age will have vanished into the dim past.

The present generation of older people is one of pioneers. Led by organizations like the AARP, the National Council of Senior Citizens, Aging, and Ken Dychtwald's Age Wave, older Americans have been breaking new ground ever since the passage of the Social Security Act in 1935. But it's only now that we're beginning to build the structures—the retirement villages, the pensions and savings plans, the stronger base for good family relations, the organizations and clubs, the media messages—and all the other things needed to assure an enjoyable and worthwhile old age for everyone. By the next century, these structures will be well in place. The new elderly of the Baby Boom generation won't have to break the soil. They'll be able to develop the refinements that make old age bring forth its richest fruit.

Although we're building the structures now, attitudes still need to change. Plenty of evidence shows that older people enjoy life, but many still think we have little to rejoice about in advanced maturity. Never mind the proof that the old are more relaxed and count more happy people among them than the young, or that the most difficult time of life is probably from the teens to the mid-30s—many of us still think it's no fun to be old.

We predict that even these negative attitudes will change. Persons will begin to understand the full potential of age. A hint of an upturn has already appeared. In a recent poll by the Roper organization, an unexpectedly high percentage (31%) of the older population said that old age is the best time of life, and more than half of those over 60 said the years from 40 on were the best.

A few closing propositions suggest that this kind of thinking will grow even more in the future.

Today, more than half of all the persons in the world who ever reached age 65 are alive—that's how much better things are now than in the past. The trend in the growth of the older population will persist well into the next century. Meanwhile, life will continue to lengthen for the average person.

Most surprising, men may start to catch up with women in longevity. Contrary to what many gerontologists have said (and what this book has said as well) a new report by the U.S. Bureau of the Census predicts that longevity for men will increase even faster than longevity for women. This doesn't mean that there will be fewer years for women. It just means that men will begin to match the pace of women as both sexes race to reach the full potential of the human lifespan—115 to 120 years.

With this growth in years, we can anticipate the development of a new stage in life. The advent of this new stage will be like the arrival of adolescence near the turn of the century. Adolescence became a distinctive stage for the first time in history when children and teenagers were exempted from work and allowed to postpone entry into adulthood. The status of full maturity will become as clear and as well defined in everyone's mind as this earlier stage of life is now. We may find ourselves borrowing from the word *adolescence* itself to call this new stage something life *gerontescence*, or maybe *geronthood*, instead of relying on G. Stanley Hall's failed word, *senescence*.

During this new stage of life, our family, kin, and age peers will be with us in greater numbers because more persons will have longer life expectancies. Women can expect to live longer with their husbands, and grandchildren will enjoy grandparents longer than in the past. The incomes of the old will be better than present incomes of older persons because pension savings will flow more copiously out of growing company benefit plans and personal savings.

The status of old people in society will become more firmly recognized than before. People will consciously plan for their late maturity. Business will join government and health services in acknowledging the old. Companies and salespeople will direct their product development and marketing strategies more strongly toward the senior population. We can anticipate more intense marketing drives beamed at the older consumer, supported by restyling of existing products and development of new ones emphasizing attractiveness. Mature tastes in clothing, hairstyles, and appearance will once more become fashionable. They may even become pacesetters, as they were before the rowdy frenzy of youth styling broke out and conquered the fashion world in the 1960s.

The educational level of the coming older generation will be higher than ever before, not that we disparage the lower educational levels of past times, which gave us the extensive educational system we have now. The advantage of wider education bestowed on the Baby Boomers by past generations is that education opens the mind to a greater range of possibilities, increases awareness of personal potential, and offers insights into ways to achieve a full life. The coming generations of older people will have a wider vision that will show them the way to get the most out of their long lives.

Most of all, though, the psychological state of age will become more fully and firmly established. The experience of aging will be robust, rich, and full of vitality. The quality and style of life will expand. Self-actualization and self-realization through effective use of leisure time will become more common. We'll hear more often the ringing cry of the octogenarian who heralded old age as, "a place of fierce energy, of wild life—a place I had no idea existed until I had arrived there!"

The boom times of old age are upon us. This means good news for America!

Sources of Information

Readers who wish to consult the sources used for this book will find the following list covers most of the basic information. For individual authors, such as Simone de Beauvoir, the original source cited in the specific chapters of this book serve as the reference.

1. The General Social Survey (GSS)

Many of the statistics from this source appeared in a book of tables, *The General Social Survey, 1972–1986: The State of the American People*, compiled for researchers by the author of the present volume and his wife, Inger Megaard-Russell, who was also associated with the present work.

Persons who wish to find out more about the GSS or who would like to draw on it for their own studies may contact The Roper Center for Public Opinion Research, P.O. Box 440, University of Connecticut, Storrs, CT 06268. Phone: (203) 486-4440.

2. The Harris Polls

These polls were commissioned by the National Council on the Aging, a Washington-based confederation of social welfare agencies, which has played a substantial role in promoting legislation on behalf of the elderly.

- Louis Harris and Associates, *The Myth and Reality of Aging*. Washington, DC: The National Council on the Aging. 1975.

- Louis Harris and Associates, *Aging in the Eighties: America in Transition.* Washington, DC: The National Council on the Aging. 1981.

3. Handbooks on Aging

In spite of the use of the word *handbook* in the titles of each of the three volumes in this set, the collection represents an encyclopedic survey of current research on aging totaling more than 3000 pages. Among the authors and editors are the foremost authorities in the fields of gerontology and geriatrics. Comprehension of most articles requires specialized background, but some are quite accessible to the dedicated general reader, and any effort spent on them is definitely worthwhile.

- Robert H. Binstock and Ethel Shanas (Editors), *Handbook of Aging and the Social Sciences* (Second edition). New York: Van Nostrand Reinhold Co. 1985.
- Caleb E. Finch and Edward L. Schneider (Editors), *Handbook of the Biology of Aging* (Second edition). New York: Van Nostrand Reinhold Co. 1985.
- James K. Birren and K. Warner Schaie (Editors), *Handbook of the Psychology of Aging* (Second edition). New York: Van Nostrand Reinhold Co. 1985.

4. Census statistics

The first census source listed here is an exhaustive reproduction of data about the older population taken from government and other publications. Types of topics included are basic census statistics and projections, social characteristics of older people (education, marital status, etc.), health, employment, income and economic well-being, public and private expenditures for the elderly, and the like. The second is the standard annual U.S. Bureau of the Census book on the nation and our population, and the third is the census bureau's up-to-date publication in the international picture of aging.

- Frank L. Schick (Editor), *Statistical Handbook on Aging Americans.* Phoenix, AZ: The Oryx Press. 1986.

- Bureau of the Census, *Statistical Abstract of the United States* (annual editions and title). Washington, DC: U.S. Government Printing Office. Annual. 1987.

- Bureau of the Census, *An Aging World*. International Population Report Series P 95, No. 78. Washington, DC: U.S. Government Printing Office.

5. Comprehensive books on aging

Both of the following were written by recognized leaders in the field of gerontology as textbooks for use in college courses on the sociology of aging. They offer a comprehensive survey of aging and include sections on the biological and mental development of older persons.

- Robert C. Atchley, *Social Forces and Aging* (Fifth edition). Belmont, CA: Wadsworth Publishing Co. 1988.

- Russell A. Ward, *The Aging Experience* (Second edition). New York: Harper and Row, Publishers. 1984.

6. Specialized aspects of aging

The first of the following books was written by the major U.S. authority on the economics of later life and was used extensively in composing Chapter 7 of the present volume. The next three make definitive reviews in their special areas, the first including a summary of the biological causes of aging. I am indebted to Linda Breytspraak's book for the material on William Butler Yeats. The last, although not based on a scientific sampling, is the only substantial survey of sexuality among the elderly.

- James H. Schulz, *The Economics of Aging* (Fourth edition). Dover, MA: Auburn House Publishing Company. 1988.

- Linda M. Breytspraak, *The Development of Self in Later Life*, Boston: Little, Brown and Company. 1984.

- Cary S. Kart, Eileen K. Metress, and Seamus Metress, *Aging, Health, and Society*. Boston: Jones and Bartlett Publishers. 1988.

- Jack Botwinick, *Aging and Behavior: A Comprehensive Integration of Research Findings* (Third edition). New York: Springer Publishing Co. 1984.
- Edward M. Brecher and the Editors of Consumer Report Books, *Love, Sex and Aging.* Boston: Little, Brown & Co. 1984.

7. Scholarly journals

Three scholarly journals serve as the principal outlets for new research in aging. The first of the following regularly contains four major parts, each publishing recent findings in these specific areas: social sciences, medical sciences, psychological sciences, and biological sciences. The second is designed for practitioners and providers of services in aging, as well as for researchers in aging. Many of its articles are quite readable and require no specialized background. The last, like the first, is designed for researchers and specialists.

- *The Journal of Gerontology.* Washington, DC: The Gerontological Society of America.
- *The Gerontologist.* Washington, DC: The Gerontological Society of America.
- *Psychology and Aging.* Arlington, VA: American Psychological Association.

8. American Association of Retired Persons (AARP)

In addition to publishing the magazine *Modern Maturity* and a host of excellent books, such as *Retirement Edens* by Peter Dickinson, the AARP publishes useful information packets, called "Info-Paks," on various special topics, such as "Money Matters" and "Healthy Questions." Some of the information in the Chapter 7 section on older persons as workers and consumers came from these sources. The AARP also manages "Age-Line," an on-line computerized database, listing and summarizing articles on aging in numerous important publications. Individuals may conduct searches through this service at a reasonable cost.